Richard Michael Levey

Annals of the Theatre Royal, Dublin

From its Opening in 1821 to its Destruction by Fire, February, 1880

Richard Michael Levey

Annals of the Theatre Royal, Dublin
From its Opening in 1821 to its Destruction by Fire, February, 1880

ISBN/EAN: 9783337155995

Printed in Europe, USA, Canada, Australia, Japan

Cover: Foto ©ninafisch / pixelio.de

More available books at **www.hansebooks.com**

ANNALS

OF THE

THEATRE ROYAL, DUBLIN,

From its Opening in 1821 to its Destruction by Fire, February, 1880;

WITH

OCCASIONAL NOTES AND OBSERVATIONS.

BY

R. M. LEVEY AND J. O'RORKE.

𝔇𝔲𝔟𝔩𝔦𝔫:
JOSEPH DOLLARD, PRINTER, DAME-STREET.

1880.

INTRODUCTION.

In the following pages I purpose to give, not a history of the Theatre Royal, but a chronicle of the most important theatrical events which have occurred therein, from the time it was first opened to the public to the date of its most sad and unfortunate destruction. The data which I have collected will be found useful to the historian of the future—and such I cannot doubt will be found at no distant period—who will weave the salient facts into a consecutive and complete narrative. This has not been my object. I have sought merely to put together, as far as possible, in chronological order, the notable events which have taken place since the Theatre was opened, of the vast majority of which I myself have been an eye-witness.

My original intention was of narrower scope, as I purposed dealing merely with the annals of Italian Opera, which of themselves could not fail to be highly interesting to music lovers and play-goers, not only in Dublin, but throughout Ireland, and to many friends within and without the operatic profession beyond the "silver streak." The advice of friends, whose opinions are in the highest degree worthy of respect with regard to all matters connected with the Dublin stage, induced me to enlarge the plan of the work, so as to include the entire period of the theatrical existence of the Royal, and to embrace its dramatic history as well as that which relates to the lyric stage.

I have therefore noticed, in chronological order, the principal events which took place in the Royal during the whole period of its existence as a Theatre, the appearances of renowned actors, actresses and vocalists, the productions of famous plays and operas, together with other incidents and events which I thought likely to interest my readers.

The casts of the Italian Operas will, I confidently expect, be found exact and complete in every essential, and the record of the successive appearances in Dublin of the most brilliant stars of the operatic firmament, will, no doubt, have a special interest for Irish amateurs.

In the compilation of the Annals of the " Old House" in Hawkins-street, I have availed myself of all sources of information at my disposal—newspaper files, collections of play-bills, books and programmes, private memoranda and diaries, and my own notes, which go over a period of fifty-four years, during which I have had the honour of being associated with the National Theatre.

The work has been to me a labour of love; and no one will be more pleased if the chronicle that I have set down in the following pages should form the basis of a more extended and elaborate history of the Theatre Royal.

It is a gratification to me that I have been enabled to collect in proper sequence, to give form and shape to the record of events, especially some which are preserved only by tradition, or are hid away in places not easily accessible. I am fully aware of many defects in my work; but I trust to the good-nature of my readers to overlook what is defective for the sake of whatever of interest they may discover.

ANNALS

OF THE

THEATRE ROYAL, DUBLIN;

From Opening, 1821, to Destruction by Fire, 1880.

PART I.

1821.

THE new Theatre Royal, Hawkins-street, opened on Thursday, January 18th, 1821, with Shakspeare's "Comedy of Errors," with the following cast: Antipholis of Ephesus, Mr. Humby; Antipholis of Syracuse, Mr. Farren; Dromio of Ephesus, Mr. Williams; Dromio of Syracuse, Mr. Johnson; Adriana, Miss Byrne; Luciana, Mrs. Humby. The bill also bore the following announcement: " Previous to the Play, an Address, written for the occasion by George Coleman the Younger, will be recited by Mr. Farren. To conclude with the Farce of the 'Sleep Walker;' Somno, Mr. J. Russell. Entrances to the Theatre:—To the Boxes, through Townsend-street portico of the new Arcade; Pit, ditto; Galleries, Poolbeg-street. Carriages and Chairs (Sedan) to enter from

Townsend-street and drive out at Hawkins-street; extra door for egress from the Pit in Poolbeg-street. Box Office at Willis's Music Saloon, Westmoreland-street. Mr. Lowther, Box-keeper. Prices:—Boxes, 5s. 5d.; Pit, 3s. 3d.; Middle Gallery, 2s. 2d.; Upper Gallery, 1s. 1d. The dimensions of the Theatre exceed that of Crow-street by six feet in depth, and an aggregate of seven in breadth; its form that of a deep oval."

This will determine the question so often disputed of the relative dimensions of Crow-street and Hawkins-street. It is curious that the Box Office, after so many years, should have returned to No. 7 Westmoreland-street (now No. 4, 1880).

With reference to the above interesting cast of the "Comedy of Errors," it may be remarked that the two Dromios continued for many years to be represented by Johnson and Williams. The likeness between the two was most striking, in consequence of the care with which Johnson "made up" to resemble Williams, adding a little to the nose by artificial means, as nature had been more bountiful to the other in that important feature. Williams did not exactly see the fun of Johnson's exact imitation, following closely every look and peculiar turn of his, and all the more remarkable because of his being so full of mannerisms. He therefore tried all means of baffling Johnson by change of dress, or "touching" of face, &c.; but Dromio of Syracuse watched too closely, and ever appeared the exact prototype of the other, no matter how altered. At last Williams good-humouredly gave in.

On January 19th was performed "Romeo and Juliet."

Juliet, by Miss Kelly (her first appearance in this kingdom).

On the 23rd, "Guy Mannering." Henry Bertram, Mr. Pearman; Julia Mannering, Miss Byrne. (Miss Byrne, an excellent actress and vocalist, was familiarly known as "Miss Byrne of Cabinteely," having belonged to a most respectable family resident in that locality).

On the 27th was given the Opera of "The Marriage of Figaro." Count Almaviva, Mr. Farren; Figaro, Mr. Russell; Fiorello, Mr. M'Keon; Cherubino, Mrs. Humby; Susanna, Miss Byrne. This was Bishop's meagre English version of Mozart's work. Mrs. Humby was a most fascinating actress, and an immense favourite. Her husband also belonged to the Company, and soon afterwards established himself in Dame-street as a dentist, to which profession he had served his time.

At this period flourished Pat M'Keon, who had been a painter, and, like a great many of that calling, possessed a very sweet tenor voice, and "came on" the stage with success. He was a nice ballad-singer, and a great favourite with the gallery boys, who familiarly called him by his Christian name. A very favourite song of M'Keon was an old ballad called "Your melting Sighs reach my Heart." On one occasion, when he arrived at the words, "Your melting Sighs," one of his friends in the upper gallery called out, " Ah ! now, Pat, sure you had enough of *meltin' size* when you were a painter."

Mrs. Haydn Corri made her first appearance on the 31st January as Rosina. Mrs. Corri continued for many years a Dublin favourite. Her husband became organist of the

Roman Catholic Cathedral, which post he filled with credit for upwards of a quarter of a century. Mr. Henry Corri, the eminent English Opera vocalist, is their son.

February 8th. Mr. Chippendale played Vortex in "A Cure for the Heart-ache." This was the father of the present well-known and favourite actor.

February 12th was the date of the first appearance of the great Charles Young in "Hamlet."

· On March 15th, first appearance in Dublin of William Farren, as Sir Peter Teazle.

On July 9th, Miss Stephens made her first appearance in Polly, "Beggar's Opera."

Bochsa, the great harpist, played on the 3rd August.

August 15th. Charles Kemble's first appearance. "Hamlet."

August 22nd. George the Fourth was present. Sheridan's "Duenna," and the Farce of "St. Patrick's Day," were performed.

An Installation of the Knights of St. Patrick took place on Thursday, 30th, the King being present.

1822.

Charles Horn and Alexander Lee appeared in English Operas.

Charles Horn was one of the sweetest of English composers, and one of the first of English musicians, author of "Cherry Ripe," "I've been Roaming," &c., &c. Alexander Lee was also a much-admired ballad-writer, and was afterwards musical director to the Theatre Royal.

April 8th. First night of "Tom and Jerry ; or, Life in

London," "New Classic-Comic-Didactic-Moralistic-Aristophanic-Localic-Analytic-Terpsichoric-Panoramic-Camarac-Obscuric Extravaganza, or Melange, in Twenty New Scenes." This piece had an enormous "run," and was made doubly attractive by the nightly "set-to" of many celebrated professional and amateur members of the then popular art of "self-defence."

July 15th. Edmund Kean made his first appearance in Richard III. On his benefit night, August 12th, he played "The Roman Actor; or, the Drama's Vindication," Octavian in "The Mountaineers," and Tom Tug in "The Waterman" (with all the original songs). On a former occasion, in England, he played Harlequin after Richard III.

November 25th. Liston's first appearance—Tony Lumpkin. Liston was not duly appreciated in Dublin.

On Saturday, December 14th, the celebrated "Bottle Row" took place. The following is extracted from the *Theatrical Observer* of Monday, December 16th, 1822:—

"His Excellency the Lord Lieutenant (the Marquis of Wellesley) honoured the Theatre with his presence on Saturday evening. All the rank and fashion of the metropolis crowded to receive him. On his arrival he was cheered with the most ardent and enthusiastic plaudits, which continued without interruption for several minutes; but soon a serpent's hiss, poisoning the atmosphere of the house, became a signal to some sanguinary confederation of satanic monsters and rebellious cowards to mar the harmony of the evening, and kindle within the Theatre the torch of political discord and religious fanaticism, &c., &c. The play proceeded amidst the most tumultuous uproar. The close of every act redoubled their vociferations, and the interposition of the noble Marquis was totally insufficient to abate them. But soon we were confirmed in our belief that a confederation of rebels and cut-throats was organized in the galleries. The play ended, the curtain fell, the stage-lights were withdrawn. At that moment, in the midst of the darkness, some sanguinary and diabolical wretch threw a large bottle at his Excellency. It passed over Mr. Barton's head in the orchestra and providentially missed inflicting a deadly wound. The stage-lights were instantly raised, and Mr. Barton held up the bottle for public inspection."

After some further remarks, the account proceeds :—

"A large watchman's rattle was also thrown from the gallery. It struck the front of the box in which were Lady Anne Gregory, Mrs. Goulbourn, Lady Rossmore, &c., &c., and passing violently to the adjacent box, in which his Excellency sat, rebounded from the cushion on which his hands were resting and fell upon the stage. The noble Marquis immediately arose, and, with the most undaunted heroism, presented himself in full front to the ruffianly monsters in the galleries."

The Marquis of Wellesley had given much offence by causing the annual dressing of the statue of King William to be discontinued.

In Nolan's *Theatrical Observer* of Tuesday, December 27th, 1822, it is announced :—

"We are happy to state that the rioters have been discovered. The following are the names of the persons apprehended for creating the disturbances on Saturday evening :—

James Petford, servant to an officer of the 5th Dragoon Guards.
Bernard Tuite, a journeyman baker.
Matthew Handwich, a carpenter.
Henry Handwich, brother to the above.
George Graham, a shoemaker.
James Forbes : who was bailed on the same night by Mr. Charles Slater, of Brunswick-street.
Mr. Lodge, of Kennedy's-lane.
James Birmingham—liberated.

1823.

January 5th. Mr. Horn and Miss Stephens—twelve nights, English Operas.

February 26th. Mr. John Philip Kemble died at Lausanne.

April 15th. Clara Fisher's first appearance in the "Spoiled Child."

June 4th. The name of Mr. O'Rorke first appears in the bills in the play of "Kenilworth." Mr. O'Rorke, who formerly played the violoncello in Crow-street, remained for many years with the Company; a good and most useful character-actor, who could "make much of little." One part in particular (very little in itself) he was particularly identified with, viz., the Cook in "Love in a Village." His admirable "make-up" as the fat female cook caused great fun, and his singing "The Roast Beef of Old England" always called forth an *encore*. He was the father of Mr. John O'Rorke, who has given such valuable aid in this compilation.

June 16th. Mr. Braham's first appearance—"The Devil's Bridge." This work is Braham's own composition, except the pretty duet, "Rest, Weary Traveller," which is by Horn. The "Devil's Bridge" is replete with pure melody, such as "Behold in her soft expressive Face," "Tho' love is warm awhile," &c., &c.; then the Picture Song, "Behold a poor desolate Maid." With modernized dialogue, grand scenery, dresses, decorations, &c., &c., and with first-rate vocalists, this work might be profitably revived.

July 7th. Miss M. Tree's first appearance in "The Haunted Tower," with Braham. This lady was sister of Ellen Tree (afterwards Mrs. Charles Kean). She somewhat later made quite a sensation by her performance of Clari, in a very interesting domestic drama of the same name (music by Bishop). The ever-popular song, "Home, Sweet Home," was sung by Miss M. Tree in this piece.

August 7th. Madame Catalani's first appearance. The performance commenced with "A Day after the Wedding," after which "A Grand Musical Festival." Catalani sang "Regno piu grati," "Rode's Air with variations," "Non piu Andrai," and "God save the King." On her fifth appearance she sang the airs, "Comfort ye my people" and "Every Valley," also "Rule, Britannia." Catalani certainly gave a varied programme, infringing on the domains of tenor, bass, and soprano.

September 3rd. The new Olympic Circus, Great Brunswick-street, near the College, was opened by permission of the Lord Mayor.

October 2nd. Mr. Mathews (at home) made his first appearance in the youthful days of Mathews (father of the lamented Charles).

Nov. 12th. "Blue Beard" was introduced, with the addition of Mr. Cooke's magnificent stud of Arabian and Hanoverian horses; also "The Cataract of the Ganges," with, for the first time, a cataract of real water. Master Smith, the American Roscius, made his appearance during the same month in Richard III.

1824.

January 13th. Macready's first appearance—"Virginius."

August. Edmund Kean fulfilled another engagement.

October 5th. Mr. Abbot, the new lessee, was now in office.

October. First appearance of Mdme. Vestris as Lilla in "The Siege of Belgrade." The most versatile and accomplished actress and vocalist of her day, afterwards Mrs. Charles Mathews.

November 22nd. Mr. Liston's appearance as Tony Lumpkin.

December 27th. Mr. Calcraft's name appears for the first time in Varney, "Kenilworth."

December 29th. Mons. Ducrow and his Equestrian Company in the interesting spectacle, "The Battle of Waterloo." Ducrow was indeed the Napoleon of Equestrians.

1825.

Mr. T. Philips and Miss Dillon Harvey appeared in "The Barber of Seville." Tom Philips, called "Gentleman Tom," from his aristocratic person and bearing, was a very finished actor and vocalist, retaining for years a hold on public favour. He unfortunately met with an accident on the Liverpool Railway, about the year 1838 or 1839, from the effects of which he died. Miss Harvey was charming in person and a most "insinuating" actress and vocalist. As Mrs. Browne, she remained on the stage for some time after her marriage, having contracted a happy union with Captain Browne, member of a Galway family.

January 3rd. Ducrow opened the Olympic Amphitheatre, Bachelor's Walk (now a large furniture wareroom).

Thursday, February 7th. "Der Freischutz" performed for the first time. Miss Forde, Agnes; Miss Harvey, Anne; T. Philips, Rodolph; Mr. Calcraft, Casper. The performance was a great success.

Mr. (afterwards Doctor) Smith's Oratorio of "The Revelation" was given for the first time this year at the Rotundo.

April 11th. Mr. Vandenhoff's first appearance in Rollo (" Pizzaro ").

April 22nd. A new Opera, written by a lady of this city. Overture and music by Sir John Stevenson (first time), entitled "The Cavern; or, the Outlaws." It is surmised that Lady Morgan was the authoress.

May 28th. Edmund Kean's engagement previous to his departure from Europe.

July 7th. Miss Foote (afterwards Lady Harrington) made her first appearance in "The Belle's Stratagem."

August 23rd. Mr. Sapio (tenor) re-opened the Theatre as Orlando in "The Cabinet."

October 27th. Braham played Rodolph in "Der Freischutz."

November 7th. Miss Stephens joined the Company.

1826.

November. Mrs. Waylett's first appearance. She was an actress and vocalist of the style of Vestris.

Mr. Levey entered the Theatre Royal Orchestra.

1827.

Mr. Booth appeared as "Richard the Third."

Miss Paton made her first appearance in "Der Freischutz." "Oberon" was performed for the first time. The soprano music of "Oberon" was composed expressly for Miss Paton by Weber, and his estimation of her powers may be judged by his giving her such a scena as "Ocean, thou Mighty Monster," her singing of which has been equalled only by Titiens.

In October, Mr. Alfred Bunn became Lessee, and the Theatre having been newly decorated, was announced to open on Nov. 3rd, with the following Company :—Signor Begrez, Messrs. Bennett, Melrose, Guibiler, Balls, Charles Ross, Roe, F. Cooke, Daly; Madame Cornega, Miss Graddon, Mrs. S. Booth, Miss Kenneth, Miss Hamilton, and Miss Aston. Stage Manager, Mr. Calcraft. Prompter, Mr. Collier. Ballet Master, Signor Nenafra. Leader of the Band, Mr. James Barton. (The opening was delayed until December 11th, when O'Keefe's "Castle of Andalusia" was played.)

In this month "The Brothers Hermann" appeared in the Rotundo, introducing, it may be said for the first time, the classical instrumental quartets of Beethoven, Mozart, Haydn, &c., &c.; also the vocal quartets of the

Orpheus Collection, &c., &c. The brothers had but very limited voices, but managed, by extreme united practice and severe attention to the marks of expression, to produce an effect in part-singing until then unheard in Dublin. Mr. W. S. Conran (father of Elena Conrani) presided at the pianoforte.

1828.

February. J. B. Cramer appeared at the Rotundo.

March 1st. The Marquis of Anglesea entered Dublin in state.

March 22nd. The Ladies Paget attended the Theatre. "The Duenna" was performed by desire.

April 2nd. A Concert was given by command of his Excellency for the benefit of the Irish Musical Fund Society, at which Mr. Alday, Mr. J. Barton, Mr. Pigot, Mr. Weidner (flute), Mr. Duncan (pianoforte), and Mr. Haydn Corri (Conductor) assisted.

April 10th. Weber's "Abon Hassan" was produced.

April 21st. First appearance of Mr. Charles Kean as Young Norval. Mr. Kean acted during the engagement in "Romeo and Juliet," "Venice Preserved," "Barbarossa," "Lovers' Vows" (Frederick), Lothair in "Tragedy of Adalgetha," &c., &c.

April 26th. Mr. Logier gave a Grand Concert in the Rotundo in commemoration of the arrival of the Marquis of Anglesea.

June 17th. Mr. Luke Plunkett made his first appearance as "Richard III." Mr. Plunkett was a most respectable and intelligent gentleman, only eccentric on one point—he thought himself the greatest Richard III. in existence; he was in consequence called "Mad Plunkett." He acted Richard once every year for a considerable time in the cause of charity, and filled the house, the performance creating the reverse of a tragic effect, shouts of laughter occasionally concluding each scene. He usually rode into Bosworth Field on a donkey, in which position he fought the combat with Richmond, dismounting only when he received the fatal stab. On the last occasion, when Richard died, a universal *encore* was the result, when Mr. Plunkett raised himself from the ground, came forward to receive the plaudits of the audience, and then cooly returned and died a second time.

June 19th. Bradbury, the great clown, appeared in "Harlequin Poor Robin."

July 15th. Madame Vestris appeared as Phœbe in "Paul Pry," singing Balfe's song, "The Lover's Mistake," (one of his earliest compositions).

July 29th. Mr. Sinclair (a very popular tenor) appeared in English Opera.

August 25th. Ducrow commenced an engagement with a melodramatic spectacle, called, "The Massacre of the Greeks; or, the Siege of Missolonghi." On this occasion Ducrow was obliged to retain some of the Stock Company, amongst whom was the favourite Brough, who was cast for a part, but did not attend punctually at rehearsals. On the late arrival of Brough one morning, Ducrow exclaimed—"Prompter, fine that gentleman!" Brough, annoyed at the sarcastic tone, said, "Sir, I have a name." "Well," replied the great equestrian,

"I said, 'that *gentleman.*' I beg pardon if I made a mistake."

September 27th. The Theatre Royal was advertised to be sold by public auction on November 6th, by Mr. George Robins, in a most elaborate announcement, quite up to his style. No sale took place. On the 13th November following an advertisement appeared from George Robins: "In consequence of a very eligible offer having been made for the purchase of the property, which will probably terminate by a sale by private contract, the auction will be postponed to the 10th December."

November 26th. The Theatre re-opened with the play of "The Hypocrite." Mawworm, Mr. Dowton. Stage Manager, Mr. Calcraft; Acting Manager, Mr. Elrington (father of S. N. Elrington, Esq.). Mr. Elrington was highly respected—a manager of much experience, an excellent actor, with fine stage presence, and a courteous gentleman in office.

December 1st. Mrs. Humby's first appearance on her return from London.

December 2nd. Miss Coveney's (only 11 years of age) first appearance as Mandane in "Artaxerxes."

December 13th. Mrs. Waylett joined the Company.

December 27th. Engagement of Miss Paton. "Love in a Village," &c.

1829.

Jan. 4th. Miss Paton played Desdemona to Bennett's Othello, and sang the original Shaksperian song, "My

Mother had a Maid called Barbara." Miss Paton's Desdemona was pronounced a great success.

January 26th. Engagement of Miss Foote.

March 14th. Catalani commenced a farewell engagement, after which she proceeded to the provinces, taking Mr. Levey as Violinist.

March 20th. Edmund Kean being prevented by illness from fulfilling his engagement, Charles Kean came in his stead. Miss Huddart also played.

March 28th. Madame Caradori Allen appeared, singing between the pieces.

May 18th. Appearance of Edmund and Charles Kean together. Edmund Kean having recovered, appeared in " A New Way to Pay Old Debts," as Sir Giles. Charles Kean played Welborn.

May 21st. "Othello." Othello, Edmund Kean ; Iago, Charles Kean.

May 23rd. " Brutus." Both appearing.

June 6th. Catalani re-engaged for five nights.

June 18th. First appearance of Mr. Tyrone Power, as Sir Lucius O'Trigger in the " Rivals." Madame Vestris also appearing. Concluding with the Farce of "The Irish Tutor." Doctor O'Toole by Power. Some nights after Power appeared in " The Irishman in London," the following criticism appeared in the *Freeman's Journal:*—

" The new piece, 'Home, Sweet Home,' on its second performance last evening, went off so so. It is a trifle, in which the principal redeeming feature is Madame Germance (Madame Vestris) and her songs. The principal feature in the evening's entertainment was the importation of an Irishman, as some of our contemporaries designated him, 'second only to Jack Johnstone.' We feel every respect for the efforts of Mr. Power, but he would require a *power* of brogue, in addition to what he possesses, to make us for a moment institute a comparison. We have seen Mr. Barry play Corporal O'Slash; and the remark is not dictated by invidiousness, but the rich and racy pronunciation of his Munster tongue we missed. Mr. Barry has his defects, and Mr. Power has his own perfections; yet whenever he performs before a Dublin, nay, an Irish audience, he should lay aside the 'Irishman in London,' and feel himself breathing that air which, as St. Patrick says in the song, 'banished all the vermin.' It is more than ridiculous to see a Cockney twang mixed up with an Irish brogue; it is like Heathen Greek with Christian English. These remarks may seem severe, but they should not be used did we not know Mr. Power to possess qualifications of a high order. The house was tolerably well attended."

W. Dillon, well known as "Billy Dillon," a most talented and popular writer for *Saunders*, died this month. He was married to a sister of Gaudry, composer of many celebrated glees, amongst which, "Descend Celestial Queen of Song," stills holds ground. Gaudry was also composer of the charming song, "Art Thou, too, gone?" Gaudry was Mr. John O'Rorke's uncle.

July 11th. Mr. Charles Young appeared in "Rienzi," Power acting in the afterpiece.

Charles Kemble was also engaged, playing Charles Surface; Joseph Surface, Mr. Young; Sir Benjamin Backbite, Mr. Power (what a trio!) Power was a very good light comedian, and had he never taken to the Irish characters, must have made his mark in almost any walk of the drama. Leaving first impressions aside, and all cant about the good old times, really no idea can be formed of the Kembles, the Youngs, Edmund Kean, &c.—they were indeed giants. Young's voice was like musical thunder, but capable of the most varied and exquisite modulation. Zanga, in the "Revenge," he made his own, none even of his great contemporaries attempting the character. If any very elderly playgoer can (with the writer of these lines) remember the climax of the speech where Zanga incites Alonzo to the murder of Carlos and Leonora, concluding with the words, "Thus tread upon the Greek and Roman glory," the sound must still ring in his ears. Young talked, even in private, in measured terms, slowly and ponderously, and with a very slight lisp. He lodged at Burnside's, in Hawkins-street, in the house now occupied by Mr. Farrelly, saddler; he slept in the front drawingroom, and was disturbed one morning at four o'clock by a tremendously loud knocking at the hall-door. Young arose from bed, opened the window, and appeared in a long white night-cap, and beheld a "rale ould" Irish donkey and cart, the ragged proprietor of which still continued the dreadful knocking. Young called out in his thundering and blank verse style—"In the name of G—d, sirrah, what is the meaning of this unseemly clamour, disturbing sleepers from their natural rest? Desist, man, desist!" The culprit looked up, and beholding the tragic face and white night-cap, replied in a rather guilty tone, but with a lovely brogue, "We're come to empty out the dust-pit." Young related this in his dressing-room with great unction. Perhaps the elderly gentleman above alluded to may remember Charles Kemble's Charles Surface, or his Mercutio; also

Edmund Kean's Sir Giles Overreach, or Sir Edward Mortimer: if so, he has some compensation for his old age.

November 11th. Mr. Braham and Miss Byfield appeared in "The Devil's Bridge."

December 2nd. "Massaniello" produced for the first time in Dublin. Fenella, by Miss Huddart; the Prince, by Mr. Newcombe, who sang his music most sweetly and effectually. Mr. Newcombe married Miss Garbois, the principal *danseuse* of the Theatre Royal, and still the first mistress of her art in Dublin.

1830.

January 23rd. The new Adelphi Theatre was opened, now "The Queen's."

February 22nd. Macready appeared as Virginius; Miss Smithson, Virginia; ending with "Black-eyed Susan," in which T. P. Cooke played William (his first appearance).

May 10th. The Theatre opened with the "Colossal Elephant." Mdlle. Djeck, in the "Elephant of Siam."

May 19th. First appearance of Mr. Yates (father of Edmund Yates). Mr. Yates in Sylvester Daggerwood. Mrs. Yates also appeared.

The imitations of the great actors by Yates have never been equalled.

June 19th. Miss Paton and Mr. Wood appeared in "Love in a Village." Mr. Joseph Wood, a former pupil of Tom Philips, had appeared in London with success as tenor. He afterwards married Lady Lennox (*née* Paton) on her divorce from Lord William Lennox. They continued for years to visit Dublin, always drawing great houses.

June 23rd. Power appeared in "The Irish Tutor," after Bishop's Opera of "The Slave."

June 25th. Theatre closed for night rehearsal of "The Maid of Judah," a work by Rophino Lacy. The story taken from Sir Walter Scott's "Ivanhoe;" the music culled from Rossini's Operas.

June 27th. Theatre closed in consequence of the death of George IV.

June 30th. "Maid of Judah." First time.

July 12th. Miss Fanny Kemble performed Juliet; Mr. Charles Kemble (her father) Mercutio (and such a Mercutio!); Mr. Abbott, Romeo.

July 16th. Sanspareil Theatre, Fishamble-street, advertised.

October 5th. Mr. Bunn issued an address announcing the opening of Fishamble-street Theatre, under His Majesty's patent. Mademoiselles Celeste and Constance, *danseuses*, were the stars. "The French Revolution" was produced, in which Dick Barry acted an Irish part (Terry Regan) with immense effect.

November 20th. The Theatre opened under the management of Mr. John William Calcraft. "Speed the Plough" was performed. Sir Abel Handy by David Rees (his first appearance).

1831.

February 19th. Farewell engagement of Mr. Charles Young, previous to his retiring from the stage.

April 13th. Production of the English version of Mozart's "Cosi fan tutti"—"Tit for Tat."

August. Miss Inverarity, a soprano of Scottish birth, played a short and successful engagement.

August 29th. The Dublin Musical Festival commenced with a Full Dress Ball at the Rotundo.

August 30th. The first musical performance at the Royal Theatre. A Miscellaneous Concert.

August 31st. Afternoon performance. "The triumph of Faith," by Ferdinand Ries.

September 1st. "The Messiah."

Paganini, then the wonder of the world, appeared during this Festival. The concerts at which he played were well attended; but the sacred performances were comparative failures. The name of the great violinist appeared in the bills on the last day, and a strange novelty presented, viz. :—Paganini, mounted on a platform, performing his wonderful solos between the parts of "The Messiah." This event considerably increased the receipts. Messrs. Litolf and Adams' French Band performed at the Balls.

November. Theatre opened for the Dramatic Season with "The School for Scandal." Sir Peter Teazle, Mr. David Rees; Lady Teazle, Miss Huddart (afterwards Mrs. Warner).

November 26th. "The Warden of Galway," produced. A successful Tragedy by the Rev. Edward Groves.

1832.

The principal event of this year was the production of "Robert the Devil," an English version of Meyerbeer's "Robert le Diable;" with Mr. and Mrs. Wood.

1833.

First appearance of Madame Taglioni (the greatest *danseuse* then in existence). She received £100 per night. Mons. Silvain accompanied her, a great *Maitre de danse*. Silvain, changed from Sullivan, was a Cork "boy," who, displaying an early predilection for the Terpsichorean art, was sent to France to study, where he attained great eminence in his profession. It has been stated (without proof) that he was a brother of Barry Sullivan.

1834.

October. Henri Herz, the great Pianist, played in the Theatre Royal. Mr. and Mrs. Wood appeared after their return from America.

December 3rd. The drama of " Eily O'Connor," from Griffin's "Collegians," performed.

1835.

May. Barnett's Opera of "The Mountain Sylph" produced. A masterly work, founded on Scottish melodies, and scored with the pen of a sound and sensitive musician. This Opera is destined to meet with a welcome when revived.

1836.

January 2nd. Tyrone Power.
January 11th. Mrs. Waylett.
April 5th. Mr. and Mrs. Yates. Production of "The Jewess."
May 4th. Production of "The Siege of Rochelle." Miss Betts, Mr. H. Bedford, Mr. Ranesford, Miss Adams.
May 23rd. Mr. C. Mathews and Madame Vestris.
July 4th. Mr. Kean.
October 8th. Mrs. Honey and Mr. Collins.
October 11th. Mr. Butler, Tragedian.
November 6th. Mr. and Mrs. Honey.

The chief event of this season was the disappointment of Malibran. (See Second Part.)

1837.

February. Sergeant Talford's play of "Ion" produced. (Macready.)

February. The Theatre in Abbey-street opened, under the title of "Theatre Royal, Irish Opera House, Lower Abbey-street, under the King's Patent, granted to Messrs. Jones, of the original Theatre Royal, Crow-street." Mr. A. Lee, part proprietor.

March 27th. Templeton and Miss Sheriff, a *prima-donna* of much fame, commenced an engagement.

May 4th. A grand fancy and full-dress Ball took place in the Theatre Royal. Pit boarded over. An amusing incident occurred relative to this entertainment. Mr. Mitchell, the well-known and much respected confectioner, of Grafton-street, had given an estimate for the provision of refreshments. Mr. Calcraft, in the hurry of business, having mislaid it, sent for Peter (the stage door-keeper and messenger), and told him to go, with his compliments, to Mr. Mitchell for a copy of the estimate. Peter, after a rather lengthened absence, returned with a large book under his arm. "What the —— is that?" said the manager. "The Testament, sir," replied Peter. "Mr. Mitchell says this is the only one he has in Grafton-street; the small one is at his private house." Mr. Calcraft's rage knew no bounds. He seized the poker, but Peter escaped down the stairs, the governor following, and calling out, "Go back for the Es-ti-mate, you scoundrel." Peter Connell was a Kerry boy, a real original, and possibly may have provided Sam Lover with the model for "Handy Andy." His mistakes were ludicrous, but he had a strong national touch of sarcastic humour. "Fiddlers," he did not admire as a class, and the Saxon "play-actors" were not favourites. It gave him great pleasure to hear that Edmund Kean and Macready were of Irish "distraction," as he called it. An actor called Sparrow, who during the winter months took advantage of the stage-door fire, was in the habit of abusing Ireland, and when leaving at the end of the season, he gave expression to his ideas. "How glad I am to get out of this dirty, filthy kentree," &c., &c. "Faith, an' Mr. Sparra," said Peter, "you're a very different bird from what you war when you kem to this dirty, filthy counthry. You war lean and moultherin', without a feather on you, and it's fat and fledged you're going away." After the Dublin

Musical Festival (1830), Paganini arranged with Mr. Calcraft for a series of concerts. The great violinist called at the stage-door and inquired for the manager. Peter ascended to Mr. Calcraft's room, and asked, "Are you within, sir, for the foreign fiddler; he's below at the doore?" Mr. C.: "It is Signor Paganini, you rascal. Let the gentleman up to me instantly." Peter retired muttering, "A fiddler a gentleman! O Lord, since when?" Poor Peter was an athlete, and had many fights at the upper gallery door, where he received the passes. He was on one occasion thrown over from the top banisters to the stone flooring, a fall of forty feet, from the effects of which he died.

Oct. 12th. Miss Julia Nicol (afterwards Mrs. J. Harris) first appeared, playing Bella Shandy in "My Uncle Toby."

1838.

January. Thalberg appeared at the Theatre this month. He received £50 a-night. After the third night the manager proposed a renewal of the engagement, offering half the gross receipts. Thalberg refused, keeping to his first arrangement. The houses for some time averaged about £180, by which he would have received £90 per night. He was, however, quite content, and rejoiced at the result.

February 6th. Power played an engagement ending on this date.

March 6th. Mrs. Fitzwilliam played Cherubino in "Le Nozze."

May 19th. Engagement of Mr. and Mrs. Wood. Mr

E. Horncastle, Miss M. Hamilton, and Mr. A. Giubilei were of the Company.

July 10th. Power commenced an engagement ending July 18th. He was advertised to sail in the "President" on the 21st (delayed).

November 10th. Mr. and Mrs. Wood commenced an English Opera engagement. Principal Baritone, M. W. Balfe. Rooke's Opera of "Amelie, or the Love Test," produced for the first time in Dublin. Balfe did not possess a powerful voice, but his vocalism was simply perfection. Bourdogni was his singing-master, and it was indeed a treat to hear the pupil sing the elaborate and difficult solfeggios composed by the master for him. The two lovely baritone songs in "Amelie," "What is the Spell?" and "My Boyhood's Home," received a fine interpretation. A revival of "Amelie," with some revisal, would be profitable.

During the engagement, "Der Freischutz" was performed. At one of the rehearsals of the Incantation Scene, during the casting of the magic bullets, Mr. Calcraft, who was Casper (also the caster of the balls), was much annoyed by the irregularity with which the echoes were given. The *performers* of the echoes were "supers," chosen from the Dublin Militia, then called the "dirty Dubs." The echoes should follow each other; as, when Caspar calls "one," the echo should be "one! one! one!" &c., but the "ones" all came together, and therefore the effect was lost; and Mr. Calcraft, who had been in the army, had all the "Dubs" summoned before him, and being placed in a line, he explained and told each man the order, saying, "You, Murphy, are first; you, Daly, are second; you, Callaghan, are third; and, mind you, give the echoes in this order." All returned to their places up in the wings; the casting recommenced, and Caspar called out "One!" "*One!*" said Murphy. "*Two!!*" roared Daly. The effect may be imagined. Mrs. Wood was convulsed with laughter; she had heard of the Killarney echo—now it was almost verified. Poor Daly said, "Sure, I was tould to be second."

1839.
May. Abbey-street Theatre burned.

1840.
October 14th and 15th. "O'Donohue of the Lakes" produced. Madame Balfe made her first appearance at Concerts in the Theatre Royal. Thalberg and Balfe performed. Hackett, the celebrated American actor, appeared.

October 24th. Balfe's "Maid of Artois" produced, with Balfe, Templeton, Miss Romer, and G. Horncastle in the cast.

November 7th. The "Siege of Rochelle" produced for first time.

Tyrone Power played his last engagement in June, 1840. He sailed shortly after for America, in the "President," which was wrecked on the return voyage. Not a soul was left to tell the tale, nor has a plank of the ill-fated vessel ever "turned up." The yearly loss to the treasury from his death was a great blow to the Calcraft government.

1841.

November 6th. Mr. and Mrs. Wood appeared after their return from America. "Norma" was given for the first time in English; also "The Postilion of Longumeau."

1842.

May 9th. Miss Adelaide Kemble commenced an engagement in English Opera, supported by Miss Rainsforth, Mr. Brough, Mr. Shrivall, Miss A. Hyland, Mr. Houghton. Conductor: Mr. J. L. Hatton; Leader: Mr. Levey. Opened with "Norma." Balfe joined the Company, and played Figaro in "The Marriage of Figaro." Mr. Weiss (pupil of Balfe) also joined, and played Oroveso. Adelaide Kemble inherited all the dramatic genius of the family, which also displayed itself remarkably in her musical powers. "Norma," even with the recollection of Grisi fresh in the public mind, produced quite a sensation; many considering Miss Kemble's rendering in some particulars even superior to that of the great Italian songstress. Adelaide Kemble was a musical Mrs. Siddons. This Company proceeded to Edinburgh and Glasgow, under the direction of Mr. Calcraft.

1843.

February 4th. Engagement of Mr. Glover, Madame Victor, C. Mathews, and W. Farren.

May 6th. English Opera Company. Mrs. Alfred Shaw, Miss Sabilla Novello, Miss Poole, Miss A. Hyland, Mr. Manvers, and Mr. Giubilei. They played "The

Secret Marriage," "Sonnambula," "Semiramide," "Cinderella," "Artaxerxes." Mr. T. Bishop and Mr. Chute were in the Company.

June 10th. Mr. D. Leonard was engaged for six nights.

June 19th. Engagement of Miss Helen Faucit and Mr. Anderson. Opened with "Romeo and Juliet;" also played "The Gamester," "Lady of Lyons," "Cymbeline." (End of the summer season.)

August 7th. The Theatre announced to open with the following artistes:—Sig. Camilio Swori, the unrivalled violinist, pupil and successor of Paganini; Miss Clara Novello, Mdlle. Albertazzi, Miss Howson, Mr. Balfe; with a Grand Concert and the English version of the Opera of "L'Elisire d'Amore," called "The Love Spell." In consequence of the severe illness of Mdlle. Albertazzi, the Opera was withdrawn, and they had Concerts only, in three parts.

It was announced that, in consequence of the great political agitation then existing, which so frightened the Italian Artistes they demanded so much additional terms, there would be no Italian Opera that season.

August 26th. Fanny Elsner appeared for four nights, assisted by Mons. Silvain and Mdme. Proche Giubilei.

The Theatre was then closed till October 28th, when it opened with Mr. Mackay in "Rob Roy."

November 4th. Engagement of Mr. and Mrs. Wood for eight nights. Their farewell engagement, previous to their final retirement from the stage, opened with "Sonnambula;" they also played "Norma," "Fra Diavolo," and "Maid of Judah."

On the 8th inst., during the above engagement, Professor Risley and his son (the wonder of the age) made their appearance, and continued in addition to the Opera engagement.

November 25th (Saturday). Engagement of Mr. and Mrs. Charles Kean. Bulwer's |play of "Money" was played for the first time.

1844.

May 14th. Madame E. Garcia (sister to the celebrated Malibran) appeared in "Sonnambula."

May 27th. The first of three Concerts, with Madame Dorus Gras, Signor Salvi, and Miss Poole.

June 24th. Miss Rainsforth, Mr. Stretton, and Mr. Harrison commenced an engagement. "The Bohemian Girl" was played for the first time.

November 25th. Braham's last appearance in Dublin, at Concerts, under the direction of Mr. John Mackintosh, in the Music Hall, Abbey-street; also Charles Braham and H. Braham. Revival of "The Tempest."

1845.

Monsieur Duprez and Madame Eugenie Garcia appeared in a Grand Concert. Duprez sang Balfe's song, "While I gaze on those dear Eyes," in English.

Duprez appeared in the last act of "Guillaume Tell" as Arnold (his original character).

July 7th. Miss Romer, Mr. Borrani and Mr. Harrison commenced an engagement. "The Bohemian Girl" was given, and with increased effect.

August 16th. Taglioni commenced an engagement of four nights.

October 18th. The following artistes commenced an English Operatic engagement:—Mr. and Mrs. Alban Croft, Mr. J. S. Reeves (his first appearance in Operas). The following works were given:—"Lucia," "Sonnambula," "Love in a Village," "Fra Diavolo," "Bohemian Girl," "Beggar's Opera," "Der Freischutz," "Guy Mannering." Mrs. Alban Croft came to Dublin, fortified by a London reputation. Her charming appearance, beautiful soprano voice, and high artistic attainments won all hearts at Covent Garden, and the Dublin public fully endorsed the London verdict. Mrs. Croft fully reciprocated Irish feeling towards her by soon giving up theatrical life and becoming a permanent resident of Dublin, where her talented husband still enjoys high patronage and favour, as amongst the first professors of his art. Mr. Reeves made his first appearance during this engagement, and all hearers immediately predicted a great future for him. To his wonderful voice he added a style refined and elevated to a degree that was marvellous for so young a vocalist; but he had evidently received a sound early musical education, which all through his great career has done him good service. He repaired to Italy, and soon made his appearance at the Covent Garden Concerts, under the direction of Jullien, who possessed an extraordinary aptitude for discovering great talent. The result is now patent. Sims Reeves is still in the enjoyment of his powers, and long may he continue to delight his countrymen, who are so justly proud of the greatest tenor they have as yet produced. (This engagement was a great success.)

1846.

July 18th. Carlotta Grisi appeared, also Mdlle. Louise, Mdlle. Adele, Mons. Adrien, Mons. Berthier, and Mons. Silvain. Carlotta obtained favour as a *premiere danseuse* only second to Taglioni. She commanded high terms, and drew large audiences. The appreciation of *la danse* has evidently declined in Dublin.

October 8th. Taglioni again engaged. This was the last appearance of the greatest of all *danseuses*. She was accompanied by her father, the *beau-ideal* of an old gentleman, remarkably handsome in appearance, and of the greatest refinement of manner. His daughter was his pupil—and such a pupil! On the night of her benefit, Mons. Taglioni danced a hornpipe with all the agility of youth. On being congratulated on the wondrous artistic powers of his daughter, he replied, "*Ah! Elle ne danse pas avec les pieds, elle danse avec la tête!*" The following is a "cutting" from a London journal of a recent date:—

"The famous *danseuse* (Marie Taglioni) for whom the *impresarii* of Europe once contended, and who still possesses many memorials of her triumphs, has preserved, even unto her seventieth year, her bright, hopeful glance, and a certain harmonious elegance not general in ladies who have nearly achieved their fourteenth lustre. Marie Taglioni is not only an artist to the tips of her toes, but a *femme du monde*, whose talk is full of charming simplicity and candour, and a fresh enthusiasm which exercises a curiously rejuvenating effect upon the listener. Neither passionless nor cold, the dancing of Taglioni, while eminently dramatic, was yet endowed with a peculiar airiness and diaphanous grace which deprived it of every trace of earthiness. The slender, elegant figure, waving like a lily on its stem, was beautiful without any trace of gross materialism, charming without appeal to the grosser senses. In the opinions of contemporary critics, the difference between Taglioni and her imitators was that her dancing was devoid of 'earthiness' or 'fleshly' attributes which disfigured their otherwise admirable performance."

November. Mr. Allen and his pupil, Miss Julia Harland, with Mr. H. Corri, performed in English Opera. Mr. Allen was from Cork, and obtained eminence in London as an excellent tenor vocalist and singing-master.

December. Helen Faucit appeared with G. V. Brooke —production of "Antigone."

1847.

February 9th. Madame Anna Bishop (first appearance), Mr. P. Corri, Mr. T. Bishop, Mr. H. Corri, appeared in Balfe's "Maid of Artois." (Madame became soon afterwards Lady Bishop, by the elevation of her husband, Sir Henry Bishop, to knighthood).

"The Light of other Days," from the Opera, was the song of the day. Mr. Levey had to visit Clonmel professionally at the end of this month, and at the request of a pupil (a captain of a company on the station), brought down a copy of "The Light of other Days." On a fine summer evening, after dinner at the captain's lodgings, the pupil requested the master to give an idea of how the song should be interpreted. The parlour-window was open and "gave" to the street. The professor repaired to the pianoforte and illustrated to the best of his ability

"The Light of other Days," according to the intention of the composer. The captain was quite delighted, lauding highly the vocal efforts of the professor, remarking, " I had no idea you could sing so well; really I never heard anything I liked better," &c., &c. And he was proceeding in this most flattering strain, when a fellow appeared at the open window, popped in his head, and exclaimed, " Well, Captain James, be gorra, you're aisily plaised !" This severe critic was a " boy " who did the captain's messages.

April 8th. Herr Pischek appeared at Jullien's Concerts, Music Hall, Abbey-street.

April 14th. Master William Levey played for his father's benefit for the first time. He is now (1880) Musical Director of the Adelphi Theatre, London, and Member of the Society of Artists and Musicians of Paris.

April 28th. Madame Anna Bishop played in " Linda di Chamouni," and in the last scene of " Tancredi," for Mr. Stapleton's benefit. Mr. Stapleton was Treasurer to the Theatre Royal from the opening to 1850 ; he was much respected, and his annual benefit filled the house.

1848.

January 29th. Miss Rainsforth, Mr. Travers, Mr. Stretton, and Mr. Henry Corri commenced an operatic engagement.

March. Mr. Allen and Miss Julia Harland re-engaged.

June 12th. Mr. Donald King and Miss Poole appeared in English Opera. One of the most remarkable successes in the annals of the " Royal " was obtained by

Miss Poole's singing of "Pray, Goody," in "Midas." She received encores nightly.

August 1st. Madame Wharton and troupe showed forth in an entertainment entitled "Poses Plastiques." Very classical, but not successful; as the paucity of drapery on the goddesses was strongly objected to.

August 2nd. Madame Persiani and Signor Bottesini appeared at Jullien's Concerts in the Rotundo. Persiani was one of the most perfect of Italian vocalists, and Signor Bottesini the Paganini of double-bass players.

1849.

October 20th. English Opera Company—Mr. Sims Reeves, Mr. Whitworth, Mr. Delevanti, Mr. H. Horncastle, Miss Lanza, and Miss Luscombe. Conductor, Mr. Lavenu; Leader, Mr. Levey. Operas: "Lucia," "Sonnambula," "Puritani," "Ernani" (first time). Miss Luscombe, a favourite soprano, became Mrs. Sims Reeves, and still remains the happy partner of his fame and fortune. Miss Lanza afterwards joined the Stock Company. Mr. H. Horncastle was a brother of George Horncastle, a great stock favourite, whose singing of the charming song (in "No Song, no Supper"), "I Locked up all my Treasure," was greatly admired. Mr. H. Horncastle published an excellent collection of Irish Melodies, now difficult to be obtained.

December 17th. An engagement with the same Company commenced.

1850.

January. Macready's farewell visit.

April 22nd. The French Opera Comique, under the management of Mr. Mitchell, commenced an engagement, with the following artistes—M. Chateaufort, M. Soyer, M. Lac, M. Buguet, Mdlle. Guichard, Mdlle. Danhausser, Mdlle. Mincini, Mdlle. Vigny, and Mdlle. Charton. Operas—" Le Domino Noir," " Les Diamans de la Couronne," " La Dame Blanche," "Fra Diavolo." Conductor: M. C. Hansenns; Leader, Mr. Levey. This was indeed a musical treat—the artistes individually excellent and the *ensemble* perfect. The very highest finish of the French school was displayed in the singing of Mdlle. Charton. It would be difficult to decide in which of the qualities of actor or vocalist M. Lac (tenor) excelled. As usual in the French school, all the small parts were performed by first-class artistes in their line, and the natural, satisfactory artistic effect followed, but—pecuniary failure! We have yet to learn to appreciate the efforts of French *entrepreneurs*. Mr. Mitchell proceeded to Belfast with this Company, with an unfavourable result. Some of the Dublin instrumentalists were engaged, amongst whom were Mr. Pigott, the eminent violoncellist, and Mr. Harrington, the principal contra-basso. These two stayed at the Temperance Hotel. Mr. Mitchell, who was very kind, and always looked after "his people," called at the hotel, entered the coffee-room, and rang the bell. After some delay, a waiter staggered in, maintaining his equilibrium with difficulty. Mr. Mitchell, astonished at seeing a drunken waiter, asked doubtingly : " Is this the Temperance Hotel?" "Oh, yesh, shir; but we had a temperance prochesshion to-day, and I took a little drop." Mr. Mitchell remembered and told this incident with great gusto.

June 11th. Miss Louisa Pyne, Mr. W. Harrison, Mr. and Mrs. Weiss, and Mr. H. Corri appeared in English Opera. This was Miss Pyne's *debut* in Dublin.

October 14th. Mrs. Wood appeared in the Rotundo (Concerts). Mrs. Wood had previously abandoned the profession and retired to a convent in Yorkshire, but tired of the seclusion, she left, and resumed her profession.

December 17th. Madame Anna Thillon appeared. Madame Thillon (a very beautiful and accomplished French vocalist) gave a most successful entertainment, in which she was assisted by Mr. Hudson, a former favourite actor in the Stock Company, who afterwards adopted Irish characters with success, but the recollection of Power lessened his chance. During his performance of "Rory O'More" (in which Power excelled), one evening a voice from the gallery called out "Very fair, Hudson, and more *Power* to you!"

1851-52.

June 4th. Mrs. Harris took her farewell benefit at the Queen's Theatre, Mr. Harris ceasing to be lessee. "All that Glitters is not Gold" was given for the first time in Dublin. Mrs. Harris appearing as Martha Gibbs.

June 14th. Mr. Harris's benefit at the Queen's, and last night of his Lesseeship. "Time Tries all," and the farce of "Apartments" were performed.

December. The Theatre Royal opened, under the proprietorship of Mr. John Harris, with "Love in a Maze," and the pantomime of "Bluff King Hal." Amongst the Company were Mr. T. C. King, Mrs. Hudson Kirby, Mr. John Webster, Mr. F. Robson, Mr. Granby, and many others, forming such a stock troupe as would now be difficult to collect together. The greater number became stars, and returned to Dublin as such. Robson's fame still lives throughout the dramatic profession. He left Dublin because he was refused a small increase (say of one pound), to his salary, and soon returned as a London "star," on sharing terms, receiving a large sum nightly. Whilst in the "team" he has played in Dublin to empty benches when acting in a farce after the first piece—the very same pitites crowding to see him when crowned with his London laurels. Unfortunately this is not new in Dublin, many similar cases could be quoted—Miss O'Neill, Richard Jones, Hudson, Davy Rees, Power, Catherine Hayes, and numerous others in the olden as well as in more recent times. When shall we judge for ourselves in dramatic matters? Up to the present we have waited for the London verdict. During the first few years of Mr. Harris's management he struggled hard against the starring system, and succeeded in keeping the Theatre open for upwards of three years without a night's interruption, by the production of Shaksperian revivals, amongst which were "The Midsummer's Night Dream," with Mendelssohn's music— "The Tempest." There were also some English Operas, in which Messrs. Haigh, Durand, Miss Lanza, the Misses Cruise (then all in the Stock Company), performed. The musical burlesques—"The Good Woman in the Wood," and "Once upon a time there were Two Kings"—were also successful. The struggle was a bold and hard one, and sustained with much energy; Mr. Harris receiving at the end of an unprecedented season of more than three years, a splendid testimonial publicly presented by the Company on the stage. However, the "houses" commenced to droop, and "pressure from without" forced the manager back, cruelly against his will, to the "starring system," to which he was compelled to cling up to the period of his lamented death.

1853.

July. The Misses Kate and Ellen Bateman made their first appearance in "The Young Couple," after which they danced the "Minuet de la Cour." These wonderful children did not follow the usual course of premature dramatic precocity, but by severe and careful study, continued to progress from year to year, and are now amongst the ornaments of their profession.

1854.

During this year were given Shaksperian revivals— "Hamlet," "Othello," "Tempest," "King Lear," with T. C. King as the principal actor. Dramas—"The Courier of Lyons," "Les Cœurs d'Or," "The Old Chateau;" also the Operas—"Bohemian Girl," "Love Spell," by the Operatic Stock Company, including Messrs. Haigh, Durand, E. Corri, Miss Lanza, Mrs. Bromley, the Misses Cruise, &c., &c.

1855.

April 9th. Engagement of Miss Helen Faucit (Juliet).

May 29th. Engagement of Mr. Phelps, who opened in "Macbeth." He also gave his wonderful impersonation of Sir Pertinax MacSycophant.

June 18th. First appearance of Miss Glyn. "Cleopatra."

1856.

March. First appearance of Miss Seamen (now Mrs. Chippendale), Miss Vandenhoff, Miss Rebecca Isaacs.

1857.

October 26th. Farewell engagement of Mr. and Mrs. Barney Williams.

1858.

April 5th. Opening of summer season. Theatre newly decorated, with new act drop by Telbin. Subject: "The Origin of the Drama," and "The Feast of the Vintage of Greece."

First appearance of Walter Montgomery in "Faust and Marguerite." Walter Montgomery, one of the most promising actors of the day, and an excellent Shaksperian reader, in the midst of a successful career, committed suicide in London, during a fit of temporary insanity, on the day of his marriage. Over-study was the supposed cause of the desperate act.

1859.

February 16th. Engagement of Miss Marriott, the eminent tragic actress.

Nov. 19th. Appearance of Mr. and Mrs. Charles Kean.

1860.

May 23rd. Production of "A Tale of Two Cities," with Madame Celeste's Company.

October 1st. Dramatic season commenced with "Hamlet." In the cast appears—Francisco (a Soldier), Mr. Irving, from the Strand Theatre, London. Henry Irving was therefore a humble member of the Stock Company—a strong proof that he has not had "greatness thrust upon him," but has "become great" from the result of intense and conscientious study in his art, by which means only could he have arrived at his present high position. Differences of opinion may and will exist as to some of his readings, &c. : this is always the penalty of greatness ; but the public, "the many-headed monster," have given their verdict, which verdict, in the long run, is always right.

October 8th. Appearance of "The Zouave Artistes," announced as "The original Founders of the Theatre at Inkermann, during the Crimean War, where, under the enemy's fire, they gained such renown, and have since performed in all the principal cities in Europe."

NOTE—"The military papers proving the authority of the Zouaves may be seen at the Box Office."

The Zouaves acted and sang capitally, the female parts being performed by men.

October 22nd. First appearance of John Drew in the "Irish Ambassador," and "Handy Andy," one of the best representatives of Irish character who ever performed in Dublin. "Handy Andy" was nature itself.

1861.

April 1st. Production of "Colleen Bawn," with Mr. and Mrs. Boucicault.

May 2nd. Alfred Mellon's Opera of "Victorine" presented or first time by the Pyne and Harrison Company.

Mr. Watkins Burrowes was boxkeeper at this period. He had been a theatrical manager of great repute, while in possession of the Belfast Theatre several years before. Alfred Mellon was his leader. A strong feeling of friendship naturally existed between the old manager and his former *chef*. At the conclusion of "Victorine" (which was a great success), Burrowes rushed round from the front to the manager's room (where, at that time, the principal artistes repaired after the opera for refreshments). Burrowes was very demonstrative, and proceeded in the most glowing terms to congratulate the composer on his work. "Yes, Alfred," said he, "that's the sort of music *I* like. That's the music to please the public, so like everything they have heard before." A roar of laughter of course followed, in which the composer heartily joined. Poor Burrowes "meant well."

October 7th. First appearance of G. V. Brooke since his return from Australia, after an absence of seven years.

October 26th. First appearance of Adelina Patti.

November 11th. Engagement of Mr. and Mrs. W. Florence. Mrs. Florence is sister to Mrs. Barney Williams. Two more popular favourites than "Billy" Florence and his nice wife, both in and outside their profession, do not exist.

1862.

February 17th. Engagement of Mr. and Mrs. Alfred Wigan—"A Scrap of Paper" and "First Night." The English stage has produced few artistes superior to Alfred Wigan. His performance of a Frenchman was matchless. He was a perfect master of the French language, and therefore gave his broken English correctly (so to speak); for to properly represent a native of any given country on the English stage a good knowledge of the language of such nation is absolutely necessary.

April 21st. Production of Benedict's "Lily of Killarney"—Pyne and Harrison Company. A great success, adding still to the already high reputation of the composer.

April 26th. First appearance of Mdlle. Guerabella as Mary Wolfe in Balfe's "Puritan's Daughter." Mdlle. Guerabella, then an excellent soprano, both on the Italian and English stage, is now known as Miss Genevieve Ward, the eminent actress.

November 6th. First appearance of Mr. and Mrs. Frank Mathews (with Charles Mathews).

November 19th. Mr. and Mrs. C. Kean.

November 22nd. "Courier of Lyons" produced.

1863.

April 22nd. Engagement of Mr. G. V. Brooke.

May 18th. First appearance of Lady Don in "Lady Audley's Secret."

August 29th. "Peep o' Day" first produced.

November 9th. First appearance of Mr. Sothern as Lord Dundreary."

1864.

May 6th. Operetta of "Fanchette," by W. C. Levey, produced by the Pyne and Harrison Company.

October 28th. First appearance of Miss Bateman in "Leah."

November 2nd. First production on any stage of "Arrah-na-pogue," with Mr. and Mrs. Boucicault.

1865.

April 17th. First appearance of Mr. John Collins, after eighteen years' absence in America (" Irish Ambassador" and "Rory O'More"). Mr. John Collins was son of a former proprietor of the Lucan Spa Hotel at one time a favourite resort of Dublin citizens. John's ambition was to grace the operatic stage as a tenor, and he made a fair success; but, like many others, he changed his mind, and "took to" the Irish characters, visiting all the cities in America and Great Britain, and realizing a sufficient fortune to retire.

August 28th. First visit of the Haymarket Company, under the direction of Mr. J. B. Buckstone—" School for Scandal."

Nov. 20th. Engagement of Mr. Toole.

1866.

First engagement of Mdlle. Beatrice—production of "Mary Stuart." In the scene between Queen Elizabeth and Mary Stuart, in which Mdlle. Beatrice so powerfully denounced the Virgin Queen, she was much encouraged by an enthusiastic pit-goer, who exclaimed at intervals—

"Ah, that's it! give it to her well! don't spare her!"—and when Beatrice gave expression to the name of Anne Boleyn, as Elizabeth's mother, he called out—"Ah, there you have her; a nice Virgin Queen, ha! ha! ha!" The enthusiast had to be silenced by a gentle remonstrance from a policeman.

March. Performance of "The Strollers," "Corsican Brothers," and "The Happy Man."

1867.

April. Mr. Felix Rogers and Miss Jenny Wilmore.

August 26th. Miss Herbert and Company, from St. James' Theatre.

1868.

March 23rd. T. C. King, with Miss Evelyn, for a short engagement.

March 31st. Amateur Italian Opera, "Il Trovatore." Leonora, Miss Annie Doyle; Azucena, Mrs. Shaw; Inez, Miss Levey; Count di Luna, Mr. J. J. Marlowe; Fernando, Mr. P. Hayes; Manrico, Mr. C. Cummins. Conductor, Mr. George Lee.

April 10th. Miss Amy Sedgwick and Mr. John Nelson. Engagement for twelve nights. Opened with "The Lady of Lyons."

. May 1st. Miss Catherine Rogers and Mr. J. F. Cathcart. Opened with "The Honeymoon." Twelve nights.

May 9th. Performance of "The Strollers," "Guy Mannering," and "Teddy the Tiler."

May 11th. Mr. Phelps, for six nights. "Man of the World."

May 18th. Mr. and Mrs. Herman Vezin commenced in a new drama, "The Man o' Airlie," by Wills. This engagement concluded the season.

Monday, August 24th. Theatre opened by Mr. J. L. Toole, assisted by Mr. Eldred.

August 31st. First night of "Dearer than Life," by Byron.

October 5th. Mdlle. Beatrice. "Mary Stuart."

October 19th. Mr. Sothern and Miss Ada Cavendish. "A Hero of Romance."

November 2nd. Mr. and Mrs. Boucicault. New version of "Arrah-na-pogue."

November 30th. Charles Mathews.

December 14th. Miss Neilson.

1869.

March 29th. Miss Bateman and Mr. Swinbourne. "Leah." Twelve nights.

April 12th. Mr. Bandmann and Miss Millie Palmer "Hamlet." Twelve nights.

April 26th. Lady Don. "Daughter of the Regiment."

May 10th. First performance of "The Grand Duchess" in Dublin. Miss Julia Mathews, Mdlle. Albertazzi, J. Stoyle, Aynsley Cook, Mr. Odell, W. H. Norton, W. H. Payne, Harvey Payne, Fred Payne, Mdlle. Esta, and Mr. Wilford Morgan. Conductor, Mr. Charles Hall.

Up to May 29th, closed season.

The very excellent interpretation given to the work on this occasion left a lasting impression in Dublin, and was preferred by many to the version of the Opera as performed by the French Company some time after, with Mdlle. Schneider as the star.

Monday, August 23rd. Season opened with "Dearer than Life." J. L. Toole.

Monday, October 11th. Beatrice.

October 25th. Mr. Creswick. "Macbeth."

Monday, November 8th. Mr. Fechter. "Hamlet." Ophelia, Miss Charlotte Le Clerg.

November 22nd. Mr. Sothern. "American Cousin." Twelve nights.

November 29th. Mr. T. C. King (up to Pantomime).

1870.

Monday, March 14th. French Company (twelve nights), under the direction of Mons. Raphael Felix. Three of Offenbach's Opera Bouffes—"La Grande Duchesse," "Barbe bleu," and "Orphée aux Enfers." Principal artiste, Mdlle. Schneider. (The manager, since deceased, was brother of the celebrated French tragedienne, Mdlle. Raphael.)

Monday, March 16th. Mr. Frederick Young's London Comedy Company commenced with "Caste" (first time in Dublin). Hon. George D'Alroy, W. F. Young; Esther, Miss Ada Dyas; Polly, Miss Brunton; Captain Hawtree, Mr. Craven Robertson; Eccles, Mr. J. W. Ray; Marquise de St. Maur, Miss Benyon; Sam Gerridge, Mr. Cannidge.

Monday, March 28th. Mr. Moreton Tavarez appeared for a short engagement. "Hamlet," "Stranger," "Richelieu," &c.

On the 6th of April, 1870, the first appearance of Barry Sullivan was announced as "the leading legitimate Actor of the British Stage."

The result fully justified the announcement; for it was true then, and remains so to the present time. Nearly eleven years have passed, and the great tragedian has appeared with increased success every season, except during the season of his wonderfully prosperous Australian engagement. Like all accomplished Shakesperian students, Mr. Sullivan seems never content to remain stationary in his art, for at each successive appearance every character is, if possible, more matured and highly finished. Circumstances will not admit in this limited work of the too extended notice which the subject prompts and would demand, more particularly as the great artist is still in his zenith, and we may hope, will yet live many years to visit the land of his birth, and delight his fellow-countrymen, who feel so proud that Ireland can boast of having produced "the leading legitimate Actor of the British Stage."

Saturday, April 9th. Amateur Italian Opera, "Faust."

Monday, April 18th. Barry Sullivan. "Hamlet."

Monday, May 2nd. Shiel Barry. Short engagement. "Handy Andy," "Barney the Baron," &c., &c.

Shiel Barry is still another artist whom the Dublin public left for a London audience to "find out."

Monday, August 22nd. Mr. J. L. Toole. "Oliver Twist."

Monday, October 3rd. Mr. Buckstone and Haymarket Company. "School for Scandal," &c., as before.

October 17th. Frederick Young's Company. "School."

November 7th. Mr. and Mrs. Wybert Rousby. "Romeo and Juliet." Twelve nights.

Nov. 21st. Miss Bateman, with Miss Isabel Frances and Mr. W. H. Vernon. "Leah" and "Mary Warner."

December 5th. Mr. Barry Sullivan. "Hamlet."

December 19th. Mr. Sothern and Miss Amy Roselle. "David Garrick," "Home," and "Birth."

1871.

March 11th. Amateur Italian Opera, "Marta" (for Mr. Levey's benefit). Mr. and Mrs. C. Cummins, Mrs. J. Doyle, Mr. P. Charles, &c.

Monday, March 13th. Mr. Compton. "Tony Lumpkin."

April 13th. Amateur Italian Opera. Second Act of "Il Trovatore;" concluding with "Don Giovanni."

Monday, May 3rd. Joseph Eldred, Miss Lizzie Wilmore. "Little Em'ly."

Monday, May 15th. "The Two Roses" (first time). Messrs. H. J. Montague, H. Irving, George Honey, W. H. Stephens, Miss Amy Fausitt, Miss Louise Claire, &c.

It is unnecessary here to recall the sensation created by the "Digby Grand" of Henry Irving, still fresh in the memory of Dublin playgoers, and never to be forgotten.

July 31st. Season opened with Mr. J. L. Toole. "Uncle Dick's Darling."

Monday, August 28th. Mr. Richard Young's Company for twelve nights. "M.P." (first time.)

Poor Fred Young having met an untimely death by a railway accident in England, his brother, Mr. Richard Young, became manager.

Monday, October 2nd. Re-engagement of the Young Company for six nights. Production of "Ours."

Monday, October 23rd. Barry Sullivan. "Hamlet."

November 6th. Mr. and Mrs. Boucicault, Shiel Barry. "Colleen Bawn."

Monday, November 20th. "Amy Robsart." Drurylane Company, under the direction of Mr. Chatterton. Miss Louisa Moore, Miss Annie Ness, Mr. G. F. Rowe, and Mr. S. Emery.

Monday, Dec. 11th. Joseph Eldred. "The Great City."

1872.

Saturday, March 2nd. "Maritana" (by the Strollers). Blanche Cole specially engaged.

March 23rd. Amateur Italian Opera—"Marta."

April 1st. Mr. and Mrs. Boucicault, Shiel Barry, &c. First production of "The Streets of London."

April 16th. Mr. Vining's Comedy Company. "The Woman in White." Miss Ada Dyas, Mrs. C. Viner, Mr. Reginald Moore, Mr. Peveril, &c., to end of season.

Monday, July 22nd. Mr. Buckstone and the Haymarket Company. Messrs. Chippendale, Howe, Kendal, Arnott, Gordon, Rogers, Buckstone, junior, Clark, Osborne, Braid, Weatherby, James, Everel ; Miss Robertson, Mrs. Chippendale, Miss Fanny Wright, Mrs. E. Fitzwilliam, &c., &c. Production of "Pigmalion and Galatea."

On Thursday, August 1st, "The Palace of Truth."

Monday, August 12th. Mdlle. Beatrice. "Nos Intimes."

Monday, August 26th. "Peep o' Day." Mr. Chatterton and Drury-lane Company.

Monday, September 9th. Barry Sullivan. "Richelieu."

Monday, October 21st. Miss Bateman. "Leah." "Medea" (on her benefit night).

Monday, November 4th. J. L. Toole. "Paul Pry." During this engagement Mr. Toole kindly gave an afternoon performance of "Paul Pry" at the Glencree Reformatory, to the great delight of the inmates.

Monday, November 25th. Mr. and Mrs. Bandmann.

Monday, December 9th. Mr. George Vining. Production of "Marlborough" (four Act Drama.)

1873.

March 3rd. Mr. T. C. King. "Ingomar."

March 22nd. Performance of "The Strollers," "The Brigand," and "Grimshaw, Bagshaw, and Bradshaw."

March 24th. Revival of "The Warden of Galway," first time for forty-two years. Walter Lynch, T. C. King.

Monday, March 31st. Amateur Italian Opera. Joint benefit of Mr. R. M. Levey and G. V. Lee. Two Acts of "Sonnambula" and "Lucrezia Borgia" (compressed). The Amina was Miss Lucy Shaw; Count Rodolpho, J. J. Marlowe, Esq.; and Elvino, R. W. MacDonnell, Esq. The three principal parts were very successfully performed.

April 4th. Amateur Italian Opera. "Il Trovatore."

April 7th. Charles Mathews. Twelve nights. "Married for Money," and "Mr. Gatherwood; or, Out of Sight out of Mind."

Monday, April 28th. Mr. and Mrs. Barney Williams, for a limited number of nights. "Fairy Circle" and "Yankee Help."

August 18th. Season opened with Haymarket Company. "Blue Devils," "The Wicked World," "Uncle Foozle."

September 8th. Mr. Craven Robertson's "Caste" Company.

October 6th. Mr. Barry Sullivan. "Hamlet."

November 3rd. Mr. Toole's farewell engagement,

previous to his departure for America. "The Weavers," "Off the Line," and "Oliver Twist."

November 17th. Miss Genevieve Ward. "Lucrezia Borgia." (Drama, English version.)

December 1st. Carl Rosa's Opera Company. Miss Blanche Cole, Miss Lucy Franklin, Mrs. Aynsley Cook, Miss Rose Hersee, Mr. Campbell, &c. Opened with "Maritana."

1874.

March 28th. "Guy Mannering," by lady and gentlemen amateurs, with a varied programme of musical selections, for Mr. Levey's benefit.

April 6th. The Theatre Royal opened under the direction of Messrs. John and Michael Gunn, for the first time guided by native proprietors. It is almost superfluous here to notice the ability displayed by those enterprising brothers and partners. The "Gaiety" proving a great success, they had the boldness to purchase the "Old Royal," and whatever difference of opinion may exist (for what manager can please all?), it must be admitted that the Theatre Royal has been governed with all the energy, tact, and capacity necessary for the conduct of a great establishment. All eminent artistes available, dramatic and musical, have successively and successfully appeared, and what might be termed "a failure" cannot with justice be recorded. The premature and much regretted death of Mr. John Gunn was a sad episode. Endowed with intellect which seemed to grasp all subjects, John

Gunn was a remarkable man. Only those who were in close and intimate relationship with him could appreciate his capabilities. A good practical musician, he could well judge of everything relative to that art. Of scene-painting he seemed to possess a naturally acute knowledge and appreciation. Indeed, he possessed all the attributes necessary for a theatrical manager. But in whatever position Mr. John Gunn may have been placed, he must have distinguished himself. All the weight and responsibility of the management of two theatres (a great task in any city—a fearful one in Dublin) have fallen on the younger brother, Mr. Michael Gunn, of whom circumstances will not here permit many words. It only remains to say, that the mantle has descended to one inheriting, in many respects in an increased degree, all the remarkable qualities of his brother John.

April 6th. (First engagement at the Royal under the management of the Messrs. Gunn.) Miss Charlotte Saunders, Mdlle. Annetta Scasi, Miss Blanche Sabine, Miss Edith Wilson, Miss Eugenie Valckenaire, Miss Page, Mr. J. Birchenough, Mr. Harding, Mr. Thurlow, and Mr. E. W. Royce. Revival of "The Good Woman in the Wood," preceded by Byron's drama, "The Lancashire Lass," in which Miss Louisa Wills appeared.

April 20th. Mrs. Dion Boucicault, Mr. George Belmore, Mr. Barry Aylmer, &c. "The Colleen Bawn."

May 4th. (Last week of season.) Miss Wallis, accompanied by Mr. and Mrs. J. B. Howard. "Romeo and Juliet."

May 8th. "The Strollers," "The Wonder," and

"Bulliondust's Bargain," written expressly for the occasion.

September 14th. Mr. Sothern, for six nights. "Area Belle" and "Our American Cousin."

October 12th. The American and Australian Actress, Miss Mary Gladstane, Mr. John Dewhurst, and a powerful Company, opened with "Marie Antoinette."

November 2nd. Miss Bateman, for six nights.

November 9th. Barry Sullivan. "Richard III." (Farewell engagement, previous to departure for America.)

1875.

March 8th. "Rob Roy." Mr. Levey's benefit, in which Miss Bessie Herbert, Miss Agnes Markham, Mr. Granby, &c., performed.

June 21st. A series of Promenade Concerts commenced, under the direction of Herr Karl Meyder. A complete orchestra of first-rate artistes. Pit boarded, and Theatre fitted up on the Covent Garden plan. In addition to the efficient band, instrumental soloists of European reputation performed nightly. First-rate vocalists also lent their aid. The works of the great masters were given faultlessly, as all who came admitted. Result—disastrous failure! Another instance which renders it difficult to deny the assertion of Karl Meyder, the late Alfred Mellon, and others who have essayed the like experiment, that Dublin is not a musical city in the true sense.

July 26th. Mons. Coulon's French Opera Company, Messrs. Fairvat, Herbert, Trillet, Barres, Preys, Martin,

Dauphin, Joinnesse, Pennequin; Madame Naddi, Mdlle. Cordier; Mdlle. Marie Albert, Madame Pennequin, &c. Chef d'Orchestra, Mons. Hasselmans. Orchestra and Chorus, seventy performers. Operas performed— "Les Mousquetaires de la Reine," "Zampa," "La Dame Blanche," "Lucia," "Les Diamans de la Couronne," "Guillaume Tell," "La Fille du Regiment." All admitted the perfection of *ensemble* with which all the performances of this Company were marked; but the usual result, when a great star is absent from the list, followed, viz., great pecuniary loss. A more accomplished conductor never wielded a baton than Mons. Hasselmans. He had made a marked impression in London among the English instrumentalists by the intelligence as well as decision of his beat. He had his forces in the most perfect command at all points, and it is much to be regretted that the receipts were not such as to encourage the *entrepreneurs* to risk a repetition of the engagement.

August 9th. Mr. Charles Dillon, for six nights, accompanied by Miss Bella Mortimer. Opened with "Virginius."

August 16th. Mr. Shiel Barry. Opened with Boucicault's new Comedy, "Daddy O'Dowd."

August 23rd. Mr. and Mrs. Bandmann. "Hamlet." Twelve nights.

September 6th. Mr. J. L. Toole. First appearance for two years. "Uncle Dick's Darling," "Wig and Gown," played for first time.

September 20th. Mr. Edward Saker and Company.

"Round the Globe in Eighty Days," one of Mr. Saker's numerous and successful Liverpool productions.

October 25th. Mr. Charles Calvert. "Sardanapalus," produced with great magnificence and perfection.

The death of Mr. Calvert has left a blank in the dramatic world, in which he was recognised as a conscientious student and successful organizer of what is familiarly termed the "Legitimate."

November 22nd. Mr. Sothern and J. B. Buckstone. "Our American Cousin," "Home," by Robertson.

December 6th. Carl Rosa's English Opera Company. Mdlle. Torranni, Miss Josephine Yorke (first appearance), Miss Laura Hyde, Mr. F. Packard, Mr. Ludwig, Mr. Santley. "Marriage of Figaro," "Maritana," "Siege of Rochelle," "Fra Diavolo" (Santley), "Bohemian Girl," "Zampa" (Santley), "Faust."

1876.

Monday, April 17th. Engagement of Signor Salvini, the great Italian tragedian. "Othello," in which the great artiste created a profound sensation.

Friday. "Macbeth."

Saturday. "Hamlet."

Thursday, 20th April. Benefit and presentation to Mr. Levey on the fiftieth anniversary of his connection with the "Royal."

Saturday, May 6th. First benefit of Mr. Michael Gunn, on which occasion was performed an original Comic Opera, entitled "Rhampsinitus," composed by Signor Cellini. Libretto by Edwin Hamilton.

August 28th. The Theatre opened with Mr. Charles Collette and Company, consisting of Mr. Alfred Maltby, Mr. Flocton, Miss Kate Harfleur, &c. New farcical Comedy, in three Acts, written by A. Maltby, entitled "Bounce," in which Mr. Collette assumed several characters. Concluding with Collette's patter Farce, "Cryptoconchoidsyphonostomata." Mr. Collette is one of the most rising young artists of the day, and should arrive at the foremost place in eccentric comedy.

Monday, September 4th. The celebrated Vokes Family, for twelve nights. "The Belles of the Kitchen."

Monday, September 18th. George Honey, for six nights (first appearance since his return from America). "Illustrious Stranger," "For Love of Money." The "genial George" has since gone to the majority. Who can forget his quaint turn of the head; his comic expression of eye; his "basso profundo?" It may be some time ere we "look upon his like again."

Monday, October 9th. Shaksperian revival. "The Winter's Tale," under the direction of Mr. Edward Saker, as produced by him in Liverpool. Mr. F. Clements, Mr. E. W. Lewis, Mr. E. Saker, Mrs. H. J. Loveday, Miss Rose Leclerg, &c. The music composed and arranged by Mr. H. J. Loveday.

Monday, October 23rd. Miss Bateman. Twelve nights. "Leah."

Monday, November 6th. Mr. Charles Calvert. Twelve nights. Opened with "Much Ado about Nothing." Mr. Calvert was seized with illness during the engagement; but on his recovery, performed Shylock, Louis XI., &c.

Monday, November 20th. Mr. Charles Mathews. Six nights. "My Awful Dad."

Monday, November 27th. Engagement of Mr. Henry Irving, accompanied by Miss Isabel Bateman and Mr. T. Swinbourne. "Hamlet," "The Bells," "Charles I."

The reports of Mr. Irving's wonderful success in "Hamlet" had, of course, reached Dublin. His bold innovations and original readings startled some, puzzled many, but set all a-thinking. Mr. Irving has passed through the ordeal of all great thinkers who are before their time, viz., not at first being understood by the many; but all now admire the courage which prompted him to lay out a new course for himself, independent of all old-fashioned conventionalism. He now has the satisfaction to feel that he has "educated up" his audience to his school. For the first time in the dramatic annals an actor has been forced to request his too numerous admirers to "aid him in bringing out new plays by staying away."

December 11th. Engagement of Miss Bella Pateman, the celebrated American actress, for six nights. "Romeo and Juliet," "Katherine and Petruchio," &c., and a new poetical Play by James Mortimer, entitled "Charlotte Corday."

1877.

Monday, March 12th. Dublin Operatic Society. Four performances. "Trovatore" (in Italian). Leonora, Madame Tonnelier (specially engaged); Azucena, Miss

Bessie Craig (first appearance in Opera); Manrico, Mr. R. Sydney; Ruiz, Mr. Ernest Alford; Ferrando, Mr. Vincent; Il Conte de Luna, Mr. Leslie Crotty. "Bohemian Girl" (in English). Arline, Miss Craig; Queen, Madame Tonnelier; Devilshoof, Mr. Richard Temple; Count Arnheim, Mr. Leslie Crotty. Each Opera repeated.

Monday, April 13th. Benefit of Mr. Levey. Second and third Acts of " Bohemian Girl," and " Trial by Jury;" the Plaintiff by Mrs. Michael Gunn.

Monday, April 16th. Shaughraun Company. Twelve nights, as before.

September 17th. Theatre opened for the season with Miss Heath, supported by Mr. Wilson Barrett's Company "Jane Shore."

Monday, October 22nd. Mr. and Mrs. Bandmann. Six nights. " Hamlet."

October 29th. Charles Mathews. Six nights. " My Awful Dad."

November 5th. Barry Sullivan. Twelve nights. Mr. W. Hallows, Mr. J. Amory, Miss Caroline Hope, Miss Adeline Stanhope. " Hamlet " (first night).

November 19th. Mr. Henry Irving and the Lyceum Company, for twelve nights. " Hamlet," " The Bells," " Richard III.," " Lyons Mail."

Monday, December 17th. Two special performances, being the last before Christmas. Robertson's Play of " David Garrick," the principal part by the well-known and talented amateur, Mr. Wright, whose performance was marked by all the repose and grace attending the school of Sothern and Charles Mathews. Ada Ingot by Miss Fanny Lee (sister of Mrs. Michael Gunn).

December 23rd. Mr. Phelps, for twelve nights. "Henry VIII.," "School for Scandal," "The Man of the World," &c., &c.

1878.

March 19th. Grand amateur performance for the benefit of the Drummond Institution, under the patronage of the Lord Lieutenant and the Duchess of Marlborough, &c., &c. "The Two Roses;" characters by R. Martin, Esq., Viscount Newry, Somerset Maxwell, Esq., Captain M'Calmont, A.D.C., Captain Farrar, A.D.C., W. Knox, Esq., Mrs. Michael Gunn, Miss Fanny Lee. Concluding with "The Happy Man."

Saturday, March 23rd. Original Comic Opera, in three Acts, entitled "The Rose and the Ring;" words by Miss Mary Heyne, music by Miss Elena Norton. Conducted by Sir Robert Stewart: benefit of Mr. Levey. The Dublin public have since to regret the early death of Miss Ellen O'Hea, composer of the above work, who gave much promise of future excellence in the art of which she was so enthusiastic a student. Her great musical abilities were accompanied with a manner and bearing so gentle and unpretending as to render her a special favourite in all circles.

Monday, 22nd April. Carl Rosa Opera Company, for three weeks. Miss Julia Gaylord, Miss Georgina Burns (first appearance), Miss Josephine Yorke, Mrs. Aynsley Cooke, Miss Blanche Cole, Mr. Joseph Maas (first ap-

E

pearance), Mr. C. Lyall, Mr. Ludwig, Mr. Leslie Crotty, Mr. Snazelle, Mr. W. H. Dodd, Mr. Aynsley Cooke, Mr. Fred. Packard. Conductor, Mr. Carl Rosa. Opened with "The Bohemian Girl." During the engagement, "The Flying Dutchman" (Wagner), "The Golden Cross" (Ignace Brull), and "The Merry Wives of Windsor" (Nicolai) were produced with success.

Monday, September 16th. Mr. J. L. Toole.

September 23rd. Mr. Henry Irving and Lyceum Company, commencing with "The Bells." Mr. Irving, during this engagement, performed "Richelieu" and "Louis XI." for the first time in Dublin.

Monday, October 7th. Mr. and Mrs. Sullivan, Mr. Thomas Nerney, &c. "Arrah na Pogue," "The Shaughraun," "The Colleen Bawn."

Monday, October 25th. Engagement of Mrs. Dion Boucicault, Mr. Edmund Falconer, Mr. Leonard Boyne, &c., &c. Production of Falconer's Irish Drama, "The O'Donoghue's Warning; or, the Banshee." Grace O'Malley, Mrs. Boucicault. Poor Falconer died not very long after this engagement. His real name was O'Rorke; he was a Dublin boy, and frequently boasted of having made a speech, as a youth, at the Corn Exchange, on the occasion of the presentation of an address to Daniel O'Connell from O'Rorke's fellow-pupils.

November 4th. Engagement of Mr. Barry Sullivan and Company. During this engagement, "The School for Scandal" was performed, in which Mr. J. F. Warden, of Belfast, played Sir Peter Teazle, and Mrs. M. Gunn, Lady

Teazle, with great success; Mr. Barry Sullivan sustaining his popular and unequalled representation of Charles Surface.

Monday, November 25th. Revival of Shakspere's "Tempest," with original music, by Arthur Sullivan (first time in Dublin). On this occasion Mrs. Michael Gunn gave another proof of her remarkable versatility as a dramatic artist and vocalist, by her admirable performance in one of Shakspere's most difficult characters—Ariel.

Monday, December 2nd. Mr. Sothern, for six nights,

Monday, December 9th. Jarrett and Palmer's great New York Combination Company, in "Uncle Tom's Cabin."

1879.

Saturday, February 22nd. Benefit of Mr. R. M. Levey, "Maritana."[1] Messrs. Vyvyan,[2] S. Vincent,[3] Fullar, Waters, Campbell, Byng; Madame Nina Castelli, Miss Kate Chard. Conductor, Sir Robert Stewart.

Monday, March 18th. Grand amateur performance for the Drummond Institution. Byron's Comedy, " Partners for Life," and the Burlesque of "Lord Lovell." Performers—Viscount Newry, Mr. R. Martin, Mr. Somerset Maxwell, Captain M'Calmont, Captain Litton, Mr. Gallatin, 23rd Fusiliers; Mr. Blyth, 23rd Fusiliers; Mr Schuyler, 77th Regiment; Mr. Banbury, 77th Regiment; Mr. Archdale, 12th Lancers; Miss Castleton and Miss Pearson.

Monday, May 12th. Mr. Sothern (farewell engagement), accompanied by Mr. E. Saker. " Our American Cousin " and " David Garrick."

[1] This was a most successful performance.
[2] Mr. Frank Smyth. [3] Mr. J. F. Jones.

On Monday, November 3rd, commenced the last season of the "Old Royal," with Mr. Charles Dillon, supported by Miss Bella Mortimer, in a new drama, written for Mr. Dillon by W. G. Wills, Esq., entitled "Bolivar; or, Life for Love."

Monday, November 17th. Miss Bateman, for twelve nights.

Monday, December 1st. Miss Genevieve Ward, for six nights. "Forget-me-Not" (first time in Dublin). The great success of Miss Ward in this drama is proved by the large audience still attracted in every important town in the United Kingdom.

Monday, December 8th. Engagement of Mr. John Coleman for twelve nights. The new dramatic Romance by Algernon Willoughby, "Valjean" (founded on Victor Hugo's work, "Les Miserables"), in which Mr. Coleman assumed four characters; Jean Valjean, M. Madeline, The Fugitive, and Urban Le Blanc. The rapid change of dress accomplished by Mr. Coleman, and his marked difference of appearance in this drama, made it difficult to believe that it could be the same individual who appeared in each separate part.

On December 26th was produced the last Pantomime, "Ali Baba" (see List).

1880.

On Monday, February 9th, the "Old Royal" was destroyed by Fire!

"Thus Ends it."

List of Pantomimes from 1820.

1820. October—Rotundo. Cinderella, with scenes from Gulliver.
 „   November 16th. Scenes from Mother Goose—Clown—Grimaldi.
1821. April 23rd—Hawkins-street. Harlequin and the Magic Pipe. Clown—Norman.
 „   October. Harlequin Friar Bacon. Clown—Grimaldi.
 „   December. Whittington and his Cat. Clown—Bradbury.
1822.⎫
1823.⎭ No Pantomime.
1824. February 17th. Harlequin and the Flying Chest. Clown—Paulo.
 „   April 19th. Harlequin Mother Goose. Clown—Bradbury.
1825.⎫
1826. ⎪
1827. ⎬ No Pantomime.
1828. ⎪
1829.⎭
1830. Harlequin Cock Robin (produced in March). Clown—Paulo.

1831. No Pantomime.
1832. Serious Pantomine—"Perouse, or the Desolate Island."
1833. Puss in Boots. Clown—Hogg.
1834. St. Patrick; or, Harlequin and the Sleeping Beauty. Clown—Usher.
1835.⎫
1836.⎭ No Pantomime.
1837. Harlequin and the Ocean Queen. Clown—Elsgood.
1838. The Goblin Dwarf. Clown—Elsgood.
1839. Harlequin Peeping Tom. Clown—Elsgood.
1840. O'Donohue of the Lakes. Boleno Family.
1841. Darby O'Donohue. Boleno Family.
1842. Harlequin and the Merry Devil of Edmonton; or, The Great Bed of Ware. Boleno Family.
1843. Baron Munchausen. Boleno Family.
1844. Harlequin Shaun a Lanthero; or, Fin M'Coul and the Fairies of Lough Neagh. Boleno Family.
1845. Harlequin Blunderbore; or, the Enchanted Fawn. Boleno Family.
1846. Harlequin and the Wizard of the Steel Castle. Boleno Family.
1847. Harlequin Sulpherino. Boleno Family.
1848. Harlequin Hurlo Thrumleo. Boleno Family.
1849. Harlequin Queen Tartanna. Boleno Family.
1850. Yellow Dwarf. Lauri Family—Herring.
1851. Bluff King Hal. Clown—Seymour.
1852. Gulliver. Clown—Seymour.
1853 Battledoor and Shuttlecock. Clown—Seymour.

1854. Whittington and his Cat. Clown—Seymour.
1855. Bluebeard. Clown—Stilt.
1856. Little Bopeep. Le Clerq Family.
1857. Babes in the Wood. Clown—Seymour.
1858. Sleeping Beauty. Clown—Deani.
1859. King of the Castle. Clown—Deani.
1860. Jack the Giant Killer. Clown—Buck.
1861. Aladdin. Clown—Buck.
1862. Cinderella. Clown—Buck.
1863. Puss in Boots. Clown—Hildyar.
1864. House that Jack Built. Clown—Morelli.
1865. Beauty and the Beast. Clown—Tanner.
1866. Sinbad the Sailor. Clown—C. Laurie.
1867. Ali Baba and the Forty Thieves. Clown—Huline.
1868. Red Riding Hood. Clown—Leopold.
1869. Robinson Crusoe. Clown—Huline.
1870. The White Cat. Clown—Hemming.
1871. Fee Faw Fum. Clown—Hemming.
1872. Bluebeard. Brothers Paulo.
1873. Valentine and Orson. Brothers Paulo.
1874. Yellow Dwarf. Clown—Robert Power.
1875. Whittington and his Cat. Clown—Laurie.
1876. Aladdin. Clown—Persiviani.
1877. Cinderella. Clown—Newham.
1878. Gulliver. Clown—Newham.
1879. Forty Thieves. Clown—Allnutt.

The following Copies of original Letters may prove interesting:—

From J. HARRIS, Esq.

March 7th, 1874.

My dear Levey,

This is too bad ; not a man but has deserted the ex-Manager. I did hope for something better from the Fiddler. Well, I must bear it, I suppose. I am better to-day. I suppose you would come despite this grumblelation as a plague upon you. No one for the dinner.*

Yours truly,

J. HARRIS.

R. M. Levey, Esq.

* Mr. Harris had some friends at dinner every Saturday.

From CHARLES MATHEWS, Esq.

Jury's Hotel,
April 14th, 1874.

My dear Levey,

There are few things I wouldn't do to please you; but sit for my photograph, never more. It is just the *one* thing that I wouldn't do even to please *you*, though I am always

Faithfully yours,

C. J. MATHEWS.

I'll see you to-morrow night, and then I won't.

From J. B. BUCKSTONE.

Theatre Royal, Haymarket,
18th January, 1876.

My dear O'Shaughnessey Lavey,

I send you my likeness as promised. I hope you will not think it too flattering. I send it with pleasure, as I do not know when I may see dear old Dublin again ; still I cannot forget the many happy days I have passed in that city.

Faithfully yours,

JOHN B. BUCKSTONE.

From SIR JULIUS BENEDICT.

February 20th, 1872.

My dear Mr. Levey,

I hasten to inform you that the Norwich Festival will begin on Monday, September 23rd, terminating on the Friday in the same week. I am always glad to see your handwriting, and should be happy to shake hands with you once more at Dublin, though my poor music seems to be tabooed by all your authorities; but what cannot be cured must be endured.

Ever, my dear Mr. Levey,
Your old friend,
JULIUS BENEDICT.

R. M. Levey, Esq.

From SIMS REEVES, Esq.

Grange Mount, Upper Norwood,
May 13th, 1877.

My dear Levey,

A few lines before leaving your musical city, to thank you warmly for your very great kindness in carrying out, under somewhat trying circumstances, my wishes. I hope shortly to have again the pleasure of singing with you. And with our united kind regards, and every good wish for your continued health and prosperity,

Believe me
Yours sincerely,
J. SIMS REEVES.

From J. W. CALCRAFT (COLE), Esq.

The Dutch House,
March 9th, 1869.

My dear Levey,

I have received both your letters and newspapers you were so kind as to send me. I should have written an acknowledgment sooner, but I have been assailed during the last week by a sharp attack of gout in my right hand, so that I was disabled from writing, and can only now with some difficulty hold a pen. I have been much interested by the account you gave me of your own family affairs. Taking the *vicissitudes of life* as they usually run their course, I think you may consider yourself, as Macbeth says of his predecessor, the Thane of Cawdor, "a prosperous gentlemen," and I hope you will long continue so. Poor old ——————! It was strange enough that his death should occur so immediately you were asking about him. I am sorry he got under a cloud in his latter days; but it was all his own fault. I do not think he could have been 84, as the papers state, or even 80—about 76, according to what he always told me; but people, even when *very ancient*, have a strange propensity to reduce their real *anno domini*.

Believe me yours very truly,
Although almost illegibly,
JOHN W. COLE.

PART II.

Italian Opera in Dublin.

THE Italian Opera proper commenced at Hawkins-street in the year 1829. Many old playgoers will insist that the "Don Giovanni" at Crow-street might claim the priority; but the cast was not complete, the troupe not perfect, nor was the Opera produced in its integrity. Much misapprehension also exists with reference to the number of nights of the "run." It has been seriously asserted that it amounted to "hundreds of nights;" but facts are stubborn things, and in referring to the bills of the day, it is found that twelve or fifteen nights make up the whole amount.

Were it not for the name of Ambrogetti, whose great performance of the Don created such a *furore*, all recollection of the event might have passed away. It may not be out of place to repeat here the legend with reference to Signor Ambrogetti. It is recorded that during the performance of the last scene, when the Don descends to "Hades," one demon more than the regulation number appeared on the stage. Ambrogetti referred to the prompter, who told him there should be six. The Signor saw seven. This occurred night after night. The event so worked on his imagination, that he retired to the convent of La Trappe, where he ended his days.

The engagement of Pasta, in August, 1827, may also be passed over, as only detached scenes were given, and one Act of " Romeo e Giuletta."

A "scratch" Company appeared when "Don Giovanni" was produced, on January 7th, 1828. Madame Cornega and Signor Begrez were the principals, the other characters having been filled by members of the Stock Company—Messrs. Latham, Brough, &c., &c.—except Masetto, by Signor Giovanolo, from the " King's Theatre." On this occasion the pronunciation was certainly not *la lingua Toscano in Bocca Romana*, but a strange mixture. The bills of the next day announced that "' Don Giovanni' was received on its production last evening by a brilliant and fashionable audience, with a degree of enthusiasm not surpassed by any previous musical performance in the metropolis." But after the third night, the following appeared in the bills :—" Mozart's *chef d'œuvre*, 'Il Don Giovanni,' has been received with the utmost favour, and admitted by the professors of Dublin to be the most perfect musical production ever represented in this metropolis; but having nevertheless totally failed in attraction, it will be represented for the two last nights, this evening and Thursday."

Madame Catalani commenced an engagement on the 14th March, 1829, concluding April 11th. She was the sole musical attraction, and sang " Rode's Air," and other *morceaux*, during the interval between play and farce.

Her great *piece de resistance* was "Rule Britannia," the first word of which she always made two syllables, "ru-le."

The first properly organized Italian Opera Company in Dublin commenced then on the 14th October, 1829, under the management of Signor de Begnis; and many will doubtless learn for the first time of the production of such Operas in Dublin as Paer's "Agnese," Rossini's "Il Turco in Italia," "Tancredi," "Italiani in Algiere," "Otello," "La Gazza Ladra." The Company consisted of Madame Blasis (prima-donna), Castelle (seconda), Signor Curioni (tenor), Signor de Angeli (baritone), Signor Giubilei (basso), Signor de Begnis (buffo). Leader, Signor Spagnoletto; Prompter, Signor Rubbi. The campaign commenced with "Il Barbiere," then at the height of its popularity. Rosina, Blasis; Beita, Castelli; Almaviva, Curioni; Figaro, De Begnis; Bartolo, De Angeli; Basilio, Giubilei; Fiorello, Rubbi, who retired to his prompt-box after the first scene. The upper gallery, although not so boisterous as now, would have their joke, and the very commencement of the Opera offered an opportunity. Signor Rubbi possessed a nasal organ of great dimensions, and the colour was indeed rubicund. It fell to his lot to sing the first note, and when he had chanted, "*Piano, pianissimo,*" a voice called aloud from the gallery: "Misther Ruby!" The latter, unaccustomed to such an interruption, ceased for a moment and looked up, but soon recommenced: "*Piano, pianissimo.*" Again, "Misther Ruby!" still louder from above. The poor artist was completely at a loss, looked up again, looked at Spagnoletti, and muttered: "*Perche 'l diavolo si chiama cosi?"* He was about to proceed the third time, when the voice called out: "Bedad, Misther Ruby, the full of your nose of snuff would be worth sixpence." The effect may be easily imagined.

Signor de Begnis was considered the best Figaro in the world. His "*Largo al factotum*" was, indeed, a most artistic effort, not alone vocally, but in a dramatic point of view. He possessed the *vis comica* to an extraordinary degree; and the rapidity of his pronunciation in the "*Ah, bravo, Figaro; bravo, bravissimo,*" while dancing from one end of the stage to another, was very remarkable, every syllable telling. De Begnis was deeply marked from the effects of small-pox, but on the stage this did not show, or diminish the effect of his otherwise favourable appearance and most telling eye. Although very active in his professional capacity, he was otherwise indolent. He lived in D'Olier-street, but should have a car to drive round the corner to the stage-door. He was frequently remonstrated with on this unnécessary proceeding, but without effect.

Madame Blasis was a finished artiste, and had made a success at His Majesty's Theatre, where the troupe had been performing. Curioni was a careful tenor, with a sweet voice, of no great compass. (The music of Sonnambula would have astonished him.) De Angeli was an excellent musician, and had a daughter (also his pupil), whom we shall find later on a *prima-donna*. Giubilei was a good basso: so the "cast" was strong. Signor Spagnoletti led with his bow, playing his violin at intervals (the conductor's baton had not as yet been introduced).

He was a great master of his instrument, and for years had kept together with a firm and powerful hand the fine band-chorus and principals of the Italian Opera House in London. He had, however, two great lieutenants, Lindley (violoncello), and Dragonetti (double bass). Signor Spagnoletti, in addition to his great musical genius, had a keen sense of the ridiculous, and frequently amused the members of his orchestra with some witty observation or droll action. On one occasion, after rehearsal, he descended from his elevated seat, stooped, and was observed to search closely as if under the music-stand of the violin players. W. Vincent Wallace (who, at this time, played from the same desk as Spagnoletti) asked him what he was looking for; when the Signor replied—"Ah, for a great many notes which I missed from some of the violin parts. I suppose I shall find them after two or three nights more." He added, at the same time, addressing Wallace —"You did't drop any." The future eminent composer was a most accomplished violinist, and received much praise, and a *souvenir* from Signor Spagnoletti at the termination of the season. It will be new to many to learn that Rossini's "Il Turco in Italia," and " La Gazza Ladra" were produced during this engagement; also "Il Fanatico per la Musica," in which De Begnis seemed to revel.

On the 8th of December, 1831, we find the Italian troupe again with De Begnis, who reigned as manager for many years. Curioni, Giubilei and Rubbi continued— Signor Albertini, Signor Masi and Miss Waters were the soprani; and the novelties in the male department were

Signor Deboccini and Antonio Sapio. The latter afterwards settled in Dublin. Catherine Hayes became his pupil, and under his auspices appeared at the Anacreontic Society, getting at first five guineas, and after some time seven, eight, and perhaps ten guineas. She boldly took her flight from Ireland, having first, as she herself intimated, secured all her money in the lining of her corset, and was shortly after in the receipt of £50, £60, and sometimes £100 per night. "Il Barbiere," as usual, opened the season. Rosini, Masi; Bartolo, Sapio—the others as before. On the 17th of December was produced " Agnese," by Paer, which was then announced " Agnese di FitzHenry; or, the Father and Daughter," taken from Mrs. Opie's celebrated tale of the same name. The following explanatory notice appeared in the bills:—
" The deeply interesting tale by Mrs. Opie, ' The Father and Daughter,' proved too powerful to be confined within the limits of one country and one language. It forced its way shortly after publication into various parts of Europe, and in Italy was converted into a *semi-seria* drama in prose, by Filippo Casari, under the title of 'Agnese di FitzHenry.' This becoming extremely popular, was adopted for the lyric stage by Luigi Burnavogha, who, omitting some characters and scenes, in order to facilitate the musical performance, and shorten the representation, delivered it into the hands of Paer, the celebrated composer, and this joint production, which has met with the most distinguished success abroad, is now introduced into this country."

The audience discovered an old friend in the overture,

as it had often been played as an "Occasional," or between the acts, also at the Society's Concerts. The music of the Opera is full of merit, good sterling stuff, in the composer's best vein, but not calculated to make a lasting impression on the public.

The cast was as follows: Conte Alberto (Father of Agnese), Signor De Begnis; Agnese (his daughter), Signora Albertini (her first appearance); Ernesto (Lover of Agnese), Signor Curioni; Don Pasquale (Governor of the Hospital for Lunatici), Signor Giubilei; Don Givolamo (Chief Physician), Signor Sapio; Vergina, Mdlle. Waters; Keeper of the Hospital, Signor de Boccini. Agnese met with a *succes d'estime*, and was not repeated.

On Saturday, September 24th, 1834, Signor De Begnis commenced the season with his Italian troupe, with Signora Kintherland as *prima-donna*—the other artistes nearly as before. Maestro al Piano, Signor Aldobrande; Leader of the Orchestra, Mr. Geo. Stansbury. The last-named gentleman had succeeded Mr. William Penson as leader and director of music. He was a most versatile musician, a good vocalist, excellent pianist, fair violinist, and frequently ascended from the orchestra to the stage, fulfilling a part in Opera with great effect. On such occasions he entrusted the baton to the care of Mr. Levey, whom, at the termination of his engagement, Mr. Calcraft placed in the position of leader.

As a matter of course De Begnis commenced with the eternal "Barbiere." Kintherland, Rosina; Destri, Fioriello—rest as before. The bills announced: "A Complete Italian Chorus are engaged for the occasion." At the end of the Opera the Italian Company will sing the National Anthem of "God Save the King."

On Tuesday, September 23rd, 1834, was produced Rossini's Grand Opera of "Otello." Otello, Curioni; Rodrigo, Arrigotti (his first appearance); Desdemona, Kintherland. The Opera was fairly successful; the duet between Otello and Rodrigo (two tenors) making a good effect. On Thursday, September 25th, the "Barbiere" was repeated; and on Saturday, September 27th, 1834, was produced, for the first time, Rossini's Grand Opera Seria of "Tancredi." Tancredi, Signora Cesari (from the Scala, her first appearance); Amenaide, Signora Kintherland; Argirio, Signor Curioni; Orbasano, Signor Giubilei; Isaura, Signor Crampini. Signora Cesari was an immense success. She looked the part to perfection, possessed a fine and flexible contralto voice, and produced a wonderful effect in the opening recitative, "Oh! Patria;" and at the enthusiastic demand of the entire audience, she had to sing the aria, "Di tanti palpiti" three times every night.

The name of Cesari still lives in the recollections of many surviving opera-goers of old Hawkins-street.

"Otello" was repeated on Monday, September 29th; also repeated on Wednesday, October 1st.

On Thursday, October 2nd, 1834, were given the first Act of "Il Barbiere," the second Act of "Tancredi," and the third Act of "Otello."

On Saturday, October 4th, 1834, "Il Fanatico per la Musica." Cast as before, except Donna Aristia, Signora Cesari.

The same bill on Monday, 6th October.

On Tuesday, October 7th, 1834, was produced for the first time, Rossini's Comic Opera, "Il Turco in Italia." Selim, Signor Sapio; Donna Fiorilla, Signora Kintherland; Don Geronio, Signor De Begnis; Don Narciso, Signor Arrigotti; Prosdecimo, Signor Destri; Zaida, Mdlle. Waters; Albazon, Signor Troyano. "Il Turco" (possessing no special pieces of interest to the audience) created no sensation; it was announced for repetition on the following Saturday, but has never since been given. The first performance in Dublin of "Semiramide" took place on Thursday, October 9th, 1834. The bills were headed thus: "Signora Cesari returns her best thanks to the public for the flattering reception she has met with in Dublin, and begs to inform the nobility, gentry, the military, and the public generally, that her benefit and last appearance will take place on Thursday, October 9th, 1834, when will be performed for the first time the Opera of 'Semiramide.' (This Opera is the *chef d'œuvre* of the celebrated Rossini.) Semiramide, Madame Kintherland; Arsace, Signora Cesari; Assur, Signor Sapio; Idreno, Signor Arrigotti; Oroe, Signor Giubilei; Ghost of Ninus, Signor Cevallos." The overture to "Semiramide" had already been popular, having been frequently heard at the Anacreontic and Philharmonic Societies. It was, however, encored on this occasion. The orchestra was strengthened by the addition of Signor Cavallini, the celebrated performer on the clarionet, who was bandmaster of the 18th Royal Irish, then stationed in Dublin. He performed a solo of his own composition, accompanied by Signor Aldobrandi, between the acts of the Opera. The services of Mr. S. J. Pigott, the eminent violoncellist, were also secured, whose exquisite tone, faultless execution, and classic style must still linger in the memory of the few surviving lovers of really good music, now becoming small by degrees and beautifully less. In the good old time a complete *ensemble* attracted; now-a-days, a combination of angels would be useless without one great name—" a star !"

The cast of the Opera was excellent, although not including a *star*-tling name : Semiramide, Madame Kintherland; Arsace, Madame Cesari; Assur, Signor Sapio; Idreno, Signor Arrigotte; Oroe, Signor Giubilei; Ghost of Ninus, Signor Cevallos. It would be no exaggeration to say that the music of Rossini's *chef d'œuvre* was perhaps as well interpreted on this occasion as on any other to the present time. Madame Kintherland was a welltaught and accomplished soprano, voice a little hard; but in the " Bel Raggio " the scales and passages were faultless. In the celebrated duet she also displayed a thorough knowledge of the composer, and in those passages in Rossini's music which, on repetition, admit of change, her variations were judicious and musician-like.

It may also be stated with confidence that, until the advent of Madame Alboni and Trebelli-Bettini, no contralto produced so great a sensation in Dublin as Cesari. A fair estimate may therefore be formed of her Arsace.

On Saturday, October 11th, and on Tuesday, October 14th, "Tancredi" was repeated, with the first Act of " Il Fanatico." On the latter evening was the benefit of Signora Kintherland. On Thursday, 16th, " Semiramide " was given, after which the third Act of the celebrated Opera Seria of "Anna Bolena." Anna, Signora Kintherland. Signora Kintherland gave still further proof of her high artistic qualities, both in her performance and interpretation of the beautiful music which the composer has given to Anna in the third Act.

The last night of the season (moderately successful) took place on Saturday, the 18th of October, "Under the Patronage of their Excellencies the Lord Lieutenant and the Marchioness Wellesley," when were performed the first Act of, "Il Barbiere," the second Act of "Tancredi," and the second Act of "Il Fanatico."

The year 1835 passed without an Italian Opera. However Signor de Begnis gave some Concerts at the Rotundo, assisted by Miss Waters (his pupil); Signor Arrigotti (tenor); Signor A. Sapio (baritone); the leader being Signor Chaves, a Spanish violinist then resident in Dublin. Principal violoncello, Mr. Pigott; principal second violin, Mr. Robert Barton; double bass, Mr. Harrington; flute, Mr. Richard Powell; oboe, Mr. Mazzocchi, and viola, Mr. Ford; pianoforte, Mr. W. S. Conran. Signor Chaves was an accomplished violinist. Mr. Pigott, who ranked with Lindley (then the greatest of English violoncellists), has been before alluded to. Robert Barton held for years the post of *repetiteur* or deputy-leader at the Theatre Royal, under his brother, James Barton, who commenced at Crow-street, continued at Hawkins-street, and held the post of leader up to about the year 1825 or 1826, with credit to himself and advantage to the public. "Bob," as he was familiarly called by the gods, was very popular. In addition to music he cultivated what was then entitled the "noble art of self-defence;" most unobtrusive and inoffensive by nature, he still, on some occasions, was called on to display his accomplishment. An athletic, powerfully-built frame favoured his studies "under the best masters." Tom Reynolds, the then celebrated champion of "light weights," had a tavern in Abbey-street, near Sackville-street, and contributed to Bob's education by careful training. As already remarked, although most peaceful in disposition, he had (many times in the cause of others) defeated sturdy opponents. He therefore obtained the sobriquet of "Boxing Bob," by which title he was frequently greeted when he made his appearance in the orchestra. It must be recorded that at this period the art of self-defence was not in such bad odour as at present, but was cultivated generally by almost all classes, even the "upper ten," as a necessary accomplishment. Pierce Egan's drama of "Tom and Jerry; or, Life in London," gave a still greater impetus to the study of the art. One of the scenes represented the establishment of a celebrated "champion," and a regular "set-to" took place very often between two of the most renowned professors, to the great delight of all parts of the house; so that Bob only followed the prevailing fashion. It may be added that he instilled some of the power of his pugilism into his violinism, for he had indeed a powerful tone. Mr. Harrington had been a student in the Royal Academy of Music, London, an excellent double-bass player. His wife (also an academician), was a good harpist, and taught the instrument in

Dublin with success. Richard Powell was well-known as a flautist of first-rate capabilities. He was, indeed, the best local performer on the flute that Dublin, to that period, had " turned out "—a diligent and conscientious student. He possessed a beautiful tone, perfect intonation, and finished execution. He frequently practised from eight to ten hours a-day, never allowing a difficulty to conquer him. He would persevere at a few bars for weeks, to make them perfect. He was the first to perform in Dublin the beautiful flute obligato in the charming three-eight "Ranz de Vache" movement in the overture to " William Tell " at the Anacreontic Society. He served his apprenticeship to a well-known musician in Dublin, familiarly called " Tommy Robinson," and sometimes " The Doctor ;" for although he had never obtained the degree of Mus. Doc., his friends considered him worthy of the title.

Richard Powell was also a fair organist, having obtained his knowledge of the king of instruments from "The Doctor," who was organist of Bride's Church. Powell was also a perfect French scholar, speaking the language with fluency. He was professor of that language in Edinburgh. Mazzocchi was oboist of the Theatre Royal—a thorough master of his difficult instrument.

Edward Ford (tenor) will be remembered by Hawkins-street playgoers as the most respectable member of the orchestra, where he was principal viola, from about 1823 until his death, only a few years since. He was brother to Miss Ford, the original Agnes in " Der Freischutz," in Hawkins-street. This lady possessed a magnificent soprano voice, was an excellent actress; her appearance was most prepossessing, and her manner was simple and fascinating. She was a particular favourite, and " moved " amongst the *elite* of Dublin society. She joined the Haymarket Company in October, 1827, and remained in London. The other members of the Dublin Theatre who were engaged with her at the Haymarket on this occasion were Mr. James Barton, leader; Mr. John Fallon, violin; Mr. R. M. Levey, violin; Mr. E. Ford, Mr. Robert Barton, Mr. John Mulligan, horn. Mr. John Mackintosh, also a "Dublin Boy," was second leader, having been engaged sometime previously for Drury-lane, by Tom Cooke (one of the writer's illustrious predecessors). The Haymarket Theatre was then under the proprietorship of Mr. Morris, and the duration of the season was only four months, from about the 15th of June to the 15th of October, which allowed the members of the Dublin Company to return in time for the winter season.

This digression from the regular Italian Opera chronicle will, under the circumstances, be excused, also what follows with relation to one of the greatest of lyric artistes—Madame Malibran De Beriot. On the 13th of September, 1836, the following announcement appeared:—

"Mr. Calcraft begs respectfully to announce that he has, with great difficulty and at a most unprecedented expense, effected an engagement with that unrivalled artiste, Madame Malibran De Beriot, for six nights only, to commence on Tuesday, September 20th, 1836. In consequence of the very heavy expense attending the engagement, the prices on this occasion will be as

THEATRE ROYAL, DUBLIN. 87

follows :—Boxes, 6s.; pit, 4s.; first gallery, 2s.; second gallery, 1s. 6d.; no half-price. Mr. Templeton, first singer of the Theatre Royal, Drury-lane, is expressly engaged to support Madame Malibran. On Tuesday evening, 20th September, will be performed the Opera of ' La Sonnambula.' Amina, Madame Malibran; Elvino, Mr. Templeton. Further particulars in future announcements."

On the 20th September the following advertisement appeared :—

" Theatre Royal, Dublin.

" Mr. Calcraft regrets extremely to be under the painful necessity of stating to the public that having on Thursday received a letter from Manchester, informing him that Madame Malibran De Beriot has been suddenly seized with alarming illness, was unable either to finish her engagement there or come to Dublin, he immediately repaired to Manchester, where the accompanying certificate was placed in his hands by the medical gentlemen whose names are signed to it.

"'CERTIFICATE.
"' Manchester, 10 o'clock,
"' 16th September, 1836.

"'Madame Malibran De Beriot has passed a very restless and distressing night, and the symptoms of her complaint require confinement to her room. It is our decided opinion that Madame Malibran De Beriot cannot undertake the voyage to Dublin without danger to her life. We think it necessary to add that from the nature of her complaint there is no probability of her being able for some considerable time to resume the duties of her profession.

"'T. A. BARDSLEY, M.D.
"'JOHN HULL, M.D.
"'HENRY THOMAS WORTHINGTON, Surgeon

"Mr. Calcraft regrets still further to add that, in consequence of the very precarious state of Madame Malibran's health, he is at present quite unable to say when her engagement in Dublin can be resumed."

The *Saunders* of the 1st October contained the following notice:—

"Madame Malibran De Beriot is to be interred this day in the cemetery of the principal Roman Catholic chapel in Manchester. The mournful procession was to leave the 'Mosley Arms' at ten o'clock, a.m. Several noblemen and gentlemen notified their intention of attending the obsequies of this unrivalled artiste."

It was during the Manchester Festival (at which the writer was also engaged) that this sad event took place. Nothing could equal the consternation it caused in the town. She sang a duet with Caradori in magnificent style, and on her return to the hotel was seized with her fatal illness. The writer was to have returned with De Beriot and his distinguished wife. All was arranged for a pleasant journey: but what a change! Poor Mr. Calcraft was met near the "Mosley Arms" without his hat, which, in his distraction, he had forgotten. When he was convinced of the truth of the melancholy affair, he hastened back to Dublin, and was obliged to return nearly one thousand pounds at the box-door; and it may safely be stated that he never financially recovered the shock.

On the 3rd of January, 1837, an Italian Opera Company commenced an engagement. The artistes were—La Signora Contessa Degli Antonj, Mdlle. d'Angioli, Signor Antonio de Val, Signor Berrettoni, Signor de Angioli, Signor Galle, Signor Paltoni, and Signor De Begnis.

THEATRE ROYAL, DUBLIN. 89

Conductor, Signor Gabussi; Leader, Mr. Levey. De Begnis still continued *impresario*. A Dramatic Company was "on" the establishment at the same time, which would naturally increase expenses considerably. Much curiosity was excited by the announcement of a "Real Countess" as *prima-donna*. The usual rumour of the Count, her husband, having been addicted to gambling, losing all his fortune, and ever encroaching on the professional earnings of the Countess, was widely spread, and that she was obliged to resort to all sorts of stratagem to secure even sufficient to pay her way. The report may or may not have possessed a particle of truth, for a mania for play has often been attributed to vocalists and actors, most unjustly, and without the slightest foundation. The same remark applies to the vice of intemperance, for which, in the writer's experience, many distinguished vocalists, one in particular, received a reputation without the most remote cause. The Countess was an excellent mezzo-soprano, nearly contralto, and made a marked impression during the engagement. This lady afterwards became Duchess of Cannizaro.

On January 3rd was performed "La Cenerentola." Prince Ramin, Signor De Val; Don Magnifico, Signor De Begnis; Aliano, Signor D'Angioli; Dandini, Signor Berrettoni; Cenerentola, Signora Contessa Degli Antonj; Clorinda, Miss M. Hamilton; Tisbe, Miss A. Hyland. Miss M. Hamilton was a member of the Stock Company, an excellent soprano, and a great favourite with the Dublin audience. She left the stage on her marriage with Hugh Maguire, a gentleman of very handsome appearance and good property. Miss A. (familiarly called Alley) Hyland was also an especial favourite, an accomplished artiste (soprano), and good musician. She performed all the principal soprano parts with Braham, with great success, in an English Operatic engagement on the occasion of his farewell visit to Dublin in 1839. The Hylands were a most gifted family. The eldest Miss Hyland will be remembered by old stagegoers as a highly accomplished vocal and histrionic artiste, with a most attractive appearance. She possessed a cultivated soprano voice, and as an actress alone, could have commanded high terms in London. She made a successful appearance at Covent Garden, under the auspices of the late John Barton (then an eminent singing-master in Dublin). Miss Hyland shortly after retired, on her marriage with Thomas Hayes, the well-known and much-respected stockbroker of Westmoreland-street. The stage, indeed, experienced a loss from the retirement of this lady. The youngest sister, Jane, was also exceedingly clever : indeed a versatile genius. With her sister "Alley" she sang duets, which, from relationship of voice and careful practice, were rendered with great perfection. She also performed Doctor O'Toole in the "Irish Tutor," dancing the Irish jig in capital style.

To return to "Cenerentola," the Clorinda and Tisbe of the above-mentioned young ladies received great encomiums in the press, and the strongest expressions of praise from the Countess Degli Antonj.

On Thursday, January 5th, the Opera was "La Gazza Ladra." The Podesta, Signor De Begnis; Fernando,

Signor Berrettoni; Fabrizzio, Signor D'Angioli; Isacco, Signor Galli; Giannetta, Signor Antonio De Val; Ninetta, Mdlle. D'Angioli; Pippo, Miss Jane Hyland; Lucea, Miss E. Hamilton. The performance of Pippo, a most important *role*, will sufficiently prove the extraordinary versatility of Miss Jane (popularly called "Jenny") Hyland. Pippo is concerned in some of the most important music of the Opera, and the part was, in every particular, up to the mark.

On Tuesday, January 10th, "La Sonnambula" was to have been given, but in consequence of the illness of Signor Berrettoni, the "Barbiere" was substituted, with De Begnis, Figaro; De Val, Count; Galli (Bazilio); Mdlle. D'Angioli, Rosina; Miss E. Hamilton, Berta; and Mr. Eaton, Fiorello. Mr. Eaton was chorus-master to the Theatre.

On Friday, the 13th January, 1837, the Opera was "Tancredi." Tancredi, Signora Contessa Degli Antonj; Argirio, Signor Antonio De Val; Orbazzano, Signor Berrettoni; Amenaide, Mdlle. D'Angioli; Isaura, Miss M. Hamilton; Ruggiero, Signora Galli.

On Tuesday, January 17th, "Sonnambula" was given. Amina, Mdlle. D'Angioli; Lisa, Miss M. Hamilton; Elvino, De Val; and Rodolpo, Berrettoni.

On Friday, the 20th, "Cenerentola," as before.

On Tuesday, 24th January, 1837, was produced Rossini's grand Melodramatic Opera, "La Donna del Lago," founded on Scott's celebrated poem of "The Lady of the Lake." James (King of Scotland), Signor De Val; Roderic Dhu, Mr. Barker (his first appeaaance in Italian Opera);

Douglas, Signor Berrettoni; Ellen (The Lady of the Lake), Mdlle. D'Angioli; Malcolm Græme, Signora Contessa Degli Antonj; Albina, Miss A. Hyland; Serino, Signor Galli. The band of the 71st Highlanders assisted, "by permission of the Hon. Lieut.-Col. Grey." Much effect was produced in the finale of the 1st Act by the combination of orchestra and military band, more especially at the end, where the two subjects are so well worked together—one a pompous march, the other a quick movement in two-four time.

Mr. Barker, who performed "Roderick Dhu," was a member of the Stock Company, a very sweet ballad-singer, and composer of some popular songs. Without his aid the Opera could not have been produced; at least without sending to London for a second tenor, as Roderick is nearly as important as James—the duet in the second Act for the two tenors forming one of the most important features of the work. Barker was quite capable in the part, and received congratulations on his first effort in Italian Opera.

In social life "Little Barker," as he was called, was a great favourite. He "dressed" to perfection (in his daily life). Indeed he was regarded something like the Count D'Orsay. As a model in that particular, it was said he changed his dress three or four times a day. He wore patent leather boots in all weathers, by which he obtained the friendly sobriquet of "Polish Barker."

On Friday, the 27th, "La Gazza Ladra" was repeated.

On Saturday, January 28th, 1837, was produced Bellini's Grand Opera Seria of "I Capuletti e Montecchi," founded on Shakspeare's Tragedy, "Romeo and Juliet." Capulet, Signor Berrettoni; Juliet, Mdlle. D'Angioli; Romeo, Contessa Degli Antonj; Tybalt, Signor De Val; Lorenzo, Signor D'Angioli.

The Contessa gave a thoroughly Shaksperian reading to Romeo, displaying tragic powers of great force. She was much applauded, and repeatedly "called out" during the performance. Mdlle. D'Angioli, in Juliet, made also a most favourable impression, in a histrionic point of view; her graceful figure and beautiful face according well with the idea of what Juliet might have been. The Opera, musically, was a success; Berrettoni's fine, deep basso-profondo contributing much to the very excellent *ensemble*.

On Tuesday, January 31st, "La Sonnambula" was given in lieu of "La Donna del Lago," originally announced; the change taking place in consequence of the illness of the Countess.

On Friday, February 3rd, "La Donna del Lago" was repeated.

On Saturday, February 4th, 1837, was produced, for the first time in Dublin, Bellini's Grand Opera, "I Puritani," with the following cast:—Lord Walton, Signor D'Angioli; Sir George, Signor De Begnis (who has obligingly undertaken the part on this occasion); Lord Arthur Talbot, Signor A. De Val; Sir Richard Forth, Signor Berrettoni; Sir Bruno Robertson, Signor Galli; Henrietta of France, Miss M. Hamilton; Elvira, Mdlle. D'Angioli.

It will be perceived that the names of the characters

are in English. Signor De Begnis and Mr. Calcraft, with their "heads together" in council, decided on this course, and also added a description of each—for example, Lord Walter Walton was Governor-General, a Puritan; Lord Arthur Talbot, a Cavalier, and partisan of the Stuarts, &c., &c. The performance of "I Puritani," although not equal to what was witnessed in Dublin many years after, with such wonderful casts, deserved and received much praise. Mdlle. D'Angioli giving her "Son Vergin Verzozza" with much elegance and finish, singing the chromatic passages to great perfection. She was a pupil of her father (Lord Walton in the cast), Signor Angioli, who was an experienced musician and a most competent singing-master.

The now well-known duet, "Suoni la Tromba," then heard for the first time on the stage, created quite a sensation. De Begnis' voice was sufficiently heavy; that of Berrettoni still more so, and when they both joined in unison, the *fortissimo* was indeed tremendous—the brassy tone of two trumpets playing the melody adding much to the effect. For it must here be noticed that the cornet had not then come into so much use. It is a great addition to the modern orchestra, but is often substituted for the trumpet, when the latter would be much more in place. Balfe deserves the credit (indeed he boasted) of having "brought out" the "cornet-a-piston" in his celebrated, song "The Light of other Days," belonging to the Opera of "The Maid of Artois."

On Thursday, February 9th, repetition of "I Capulette e Montecchi," after which "Ole Bull," the celebrated

Norwegian violinist, performed three of his most celebrated compositions.

On Friday, February 10th, repetition of " Puritani."

On Saturday, February 11th, 1837, was produced, for the first time in Dublin, Rossini's Grand Opera Seria of " Otello " (for the benefit of Signor De Val). Otello, Signor De Val; Rodrigo, Mr. H. Bedford (his first appearance in Italian Opera); Iago, Signor Berrettoni; Elmiro, Signor Berrettoni (who had undertaken the two characters on this occasion); the Doge, Signor Galli; Emilia, Miss A. Hyland; Desdemona, Mdlle. D'Angioli.

Mr. H. Bedford, who came into the breach for Rodrigo, was the " Stock " tenor, and a most useful member of the Company. He was brother of the celebrated Paul Bedford, and father of the well-known low comedian, Harry Bedford, who, after a successful engagement at the Haymarket, returned to Dublin, and died in the midst of a most promising career. H. Bedford (*père*) had a good tenor voice and was an excellent musician, having commenced his career as a violinist. He possessed much of the natural humour which prevailed in the family. He would frequently, by some twitch of the eye, or a peculiar movement of the shoulder, set the members of the orchestra in a roar in the midst of their duties. Signor De Val's performance of Otello, although not equal to what we have seen since, was a well-studied and praiseworthy effort. The same remark will apply to Mdlle. D'Angioli's interpretation of Desdemona.

" Tancredi " was repeated on Tuesday, the 14th : Mr. Ole Bull again performing on the violin.

On Friday, February 17th, "La Donna del Lago" as before.

On Tuesday, 21st, "La Gazza Ladra" was given; as also on Friday, 24th February, 1837, the last night of the engagement, when the second Act of " Cenerentola," and the Opera of " Puritani" were performed for the benefit of Signor de Begnis. Mr. Macready, the great tragedian, was fulfilling an engagement at the same time, and performed on the non-opera nights. His benefit took place on Monday, February 27th, when Signor De Begnis sang his celebrated scena from " Il Fanatico per la Musica."

On Tuesday, February 27th, 1838, an Italian Opera Company, under the management of Mr. Mitchell, commenced an engagement, announced thus :—" Mr. Mitchell, Manager of the Opera Buffa, London, begs respectfully to announce that he has made arrangements with Mr. Calcraft for a series of twelve representations, at this Theatre, of the most popular Italian Operas recently performed in London." Accordingly, on Tuesday, February 27th, was produced, for the first time in Dublin, Donizetti's Opera Buffa, " L'Elisire d'Amore." Nemorino, Signor Catone; Belcore, Signor Bellini; Dulcamara, Signor F. Lablache; Adina, Madame Franceschini; Giannetta, Mdlle. Vermani; Conductor, Signor Negri; Leader, Mr. Levey. The representations will be selected from the following Operas : " L'Elisire d'Amore," Donizetti ; " Eliza e Claudio," Mercadante ; " Le Nozze de Figaro," Mozart; " L'Italiani in Algieri," Rossini ; " Betly," Donizetti; " Il Campanelli," Donizetti; " Nina,"

"Pazza per Amore," Copola; "Un 'Aventura di Scaramuccia," Ricci. Mr. Mitchell, of Bond-street, was the enterprising theatrical agent and publisher. This was his first effort as an *impresario*, and the pecuniary success was not equal to the merits of the productions. The season of Lent interfered, to some extent. A more perfect quartet of voices has seldom come together, even in later times, than on this occasion. Mdlle. Schieroni (who appeared on the second night) was a charming vocalist, very youthful and fascinating in appearance. Some old opera "goers" (unfortunately not many) will remember the lovely, pure tenor of Catone. His delivery of the "Una furtiva Lagrima," really enchanted his hearers. Indeed all through the work he carried the audience by storm. It may safely be recorded that, with the exception of Mario, Rubini, and Giuglini, no tenor ever created such an effect as Catone on the Dublin stage. Unfortunately, this was his first and last engagement, as he was killed some time after by a fall from a window in Naples. F. Lablache, son to the giant (in talent and person) of the same name, was, and happily is well known as a first-rate vocalist and musician. Signor Bellini, an artist of perhaps the very highest class, completed the excellent quartet. This was the first occasion of augmenting the prices for Italian Opera. The prices of admission were announced thus: "Reserved stalls (dress boxes), 10s. 6d.; reserved stalls for twelve representations, 5 guineas; dress circle, 7s.; and notwithstanding the great expense incurred, there will be no advance to the other parts of the Theatre."

On Saturday, March 3rd, an Operetta in one Act, by Donizetti, was produced, entitled "Il Campanello." Seraphina, Madame Franceschini; Madame Rosa, Mdlle. Vermani; Henry, Signor F. Lablache; Don Hannibal, Signor Sanquirico; Spiridione, Signor Bellini; after which Donizetti's admired Opera of "Betly." Daniel, Signor Catone; Max, Signor F. Lablache; Betly, Mdlle. Schieroni, This charming work was most successful, the only fault being its brevity. The very pretty sleeping duet, at the end of the first Act, between Daniel and Betly, was given with such true artistic skill by Catone and Scheroni, that it produced quite an agreeably somnolent effect on the audience. An English version of this work was produced by Madame Vestris, under the title of "Why don't she Marry?"

On Tuesday, March 6th, 1838, was presented, for the first time in Dublin, in Italian, Mozart's Opera—"Le Nozze di Figaro." Count Almaviva, Signor Lablache; The Countess, Madame Franceschini; Susanna, Mdlle. Schieroni; Figaro, Signor Bellini; Cherubino, Mrs. Fitzwilliam (her first appearance in that character); Basilio, Signor Catone; Bartolo, Signor Sanquirico; Marcellina, Mdlle. Vermani; Antonio, Mr. Eaton. Mrs. Fitzwilliam, then one of the most popular of English artistes, was playing a "starring" engagement, acting on the three non-opera nights during the week. It will be sufficient evidence of her talent and versatility to record her perfect success in "Cherubino." By a curious coincidence, the same part was performed by Madame Vestris at the Italian Opera House, London, some time before.

N.B.—Bishop's version of "The Marriage of Figaro" had been performed in Dublin, but it is, as all amateurs are aware, only a mere sketch.

On Thursday, March 8th, repetition of "Le Nozze." Saturday, March 10th, "L'Elisire d'Amore." Tuesday, March 13th, "Campanello" and "Betly." Thursday, March 15th, "Le Nozze" and "Betly." This night was extra, not included in the subscription; an attempt to increase the rather limited exchequer.

On Saturday, March 17th, 1838, was produced, for the first time, Copola's Opera Semi Seria, in two acts, called "Nina." Count Rodolph, Signor Bellini; Nina, Mdlle. Schieroni; Henry (in love with Nina), Signor Catone; Doctor Simplicio, Signor Sanquirico; Mariana, Mdlle. Vernani; George, Mr. Eaton. Although some of the music of "Nina" had been popularized by pianoforte arrangements of Henri Herz, then the most favourite of pianists, still the Opera produced no lasting impression. Auber's overture to "Fra Diavolo" was performed by the band between the acts of the Opera, but the "gods" insisted on "Patrick's Day," which request was complied with, as it was the festival day.

On Tuesday, March 20th, 1838, another new work was presented to the Dublin public, viz.: Ricci's Opera Buffa, in two acts—"Un 'Aventura de Scaramuccia." Scaramuccia, Signor F. Lablache; Selio, Signor Catone; Domenico, Signor Sanquirico; Tomaso, Signor Bellini; Count de Pontigny, Mdlle. Parigiani (her first appearance); Sandrina, Mdlle. Schieroni; Elena Mdlle. Vernani.

The plot of this Opera turns on the adventures and vicissitudes of a poet and director of an Italian Company (Scaramuccia). He engages two performers, Lelio and Domenico, who give him all sorts of annoyance, and make love to his servant, Sandrina, a country girl (Schieroni), she in her turn becoming bitten with the mania for acting. It is amusingly worked out. The light and sparkling music is well adapted to the subject, and is the joint production of two brothers (Ricci), who "collaborated" with much success, and whose works are still popular in some parts of Italy. One duet in particular became very popular in Dublin.

Mdlle. Parigiani was a good contralto, created a most favourable impression, and contributed much to the completeness of this very efficient Italian Company.

On Thursday, March 22nd, "Scaramuccia" was repeated, "in consequence," as the bills announced, "of the very general demand for its repetition."

On Saturday, March 24th, 1838, was performed a selection from "Il Barbiere," after which, for the first time in Dublin, Rossini's admired Opera, "L'Italiani in Algieri." Mustapha (Dey of Algiers), Signor Bellini; Isabella (an Italian Lady), Mdlle. Schieroni; Zulma, Mdlle. Vermani; Taddeo, Signor Sanquirico; Lindor (a young Italian), Signor Catone.

The overture to "L'Italiani" has been made familiar by frequent performance at the Concerts and in the Theatre. The music of the Opera cannot, however, be recorded as a success. The celebrated trio, " Papa taci," being perhaps the only feature which created much notice. Catone, however, introduced a cavatina, "Languir per una bella," accompanied on the violoncello by Mr. Pigott, which was much admired.

On Tuesday, March 27th, Copola's Opera of "Nina" was repeated. On Wednesday "L'Italiani" and "L'Elisire" for Catone's benefit. On Thursday, March 29th, "Betly."

On Saturday, March 31st, 1838, was produced, for the first time in this country, Mercadante's Opera Seria in two acts, entitled "Eliza e Claudio," with the following cast:—Eliza, Mdlle. Schieroni; Carlotta, Mdlle. Parigiani; Claudio, Signor Catone; Count Arnaldo, Signor F. Lablache; the Marquis Fritstzio, Signor Sanquirico; Lucca, Signor Bellini; Silvia, Mdlle. Vermani; Celso, Mr. Eaton.

From the rapid production of so many new works, it may well be supposed that the performances would be far from perfect; but under the circumstances, they were most creditable, Signor Negri and Mr. Mitchell bearing frequent testimony to the fact. The principal instruments in the orchestra were in the hands of very excellent (some first-rate) artistes. Mr. Pigott was a host in himself. Mr. Powell (flute), Harrington (double bass), Tighe (clarionet), Mulligan (horn), &c., &c.: all expert "readers at sight." No more than one, or at most two, rehearsals could possibly be devoted to each work, to which in London, or on the Continent, weeks are sometimes allowed. If this fact, which sometimes prevails at the present day, were considered, it might considerably lessen the sting of hasty or hostile criticism. The Opera, "Eliza e Claudio," contains some of Mercadante's original and beautiful conceptions, but did not make any great *furore*.

Mdlle. Schieroni's benefit took place on Monday, April 2nd, 1838, when "Scaramuccia" was repeated, and " Eliza e Claudio."

On Tuesday, April 3rd, for the benefit of Signor F. Lablache, was performed, " Eliza e Claudio," with some detached pieces, which included Moore's melody, " Oft in the Stilly Night," sung by Signor Catone and Signor Lablache, as a duet, and which received a tremendous encore. The voices blended exquisitely, and the slightly broken English seemed to lend additional interest to the music.

On Thursday, April 5th, 1838, Mr. Mitchell had his benefit, when were performed a selection from " Le Nozze di Figaro " and the first Act of " L'Elisire d'Amore," and " by particular desire," a repetition of " Oft in the Stilly Night," concluding with " Betly."

The last performance took place on Saturday, April 7th. By command of His Excellency the Lord Lieutenant and the Countess of Mulgrave, " God Save the Queen " was sung by the Company, after which " La Sonnambula," the duet, " Oft in the Stilly Night," and other pieces ; and Signori Catone and Lablache again repeated their duet on Monday, April 16th, after the Drama of " Therese, the Orphan of Geneva."

On Tuesday, April 17th, 1838, the following announcement appeared :—" Mr. Calcraft has the honour to announce that, in compliance with the wishes of numerous parties of distinction, and the general desire of the public, he has made an arrangement with Mr. Mitchell and the Italian Opera Buffa for four nights only."

On Tuesday, April 17th, was performed " La Sonnambula " (as before).

On Thursday, April 19th, was produced for the first time a new Opera, by Donizetti, called "Torquato Tasso," with the following " Argument," on the bills :—
" The illustrious name of Torquato Tasso and his misfortunes are too well known to require any comment; still it is necessary to say thus much for the illustration of this drama, that he lived in the sixteenth century, and that he arrived at the highest degree of honour and reputation as a literary man, a poet, and a politician. His immortal poem, ' Jerusalem Delivered,' raised the envy of his enemies, and the favour which he enjoyed at the Court of Ferrara, incited them to annoy and persecute him whenever they could. Unfortunately for Tasso, they succeeded in discovering the secret of an attachment which he had conceived for the Duke of Ferrara's sister, Countess Eleonora, who distinguished him and gave him unequivocal marks of her affection and highest esteem. He was banished the Court and City of Ferrara, exiled from the States, and even imprisoned as a man whose mind was out of order; but some powerful and influential friends of Tasso obtained at last that he should be released. He went to Rome at the invitation of his numerous and noble friends, who gave him that reception which his high reputation deserved, and decreed him the same honours which were paid to Petrarch, by crowning him as the prince of poets on the Capitol; but the illus-

trious poet, consumed by an ardent passion which his heart could not stifle, and broken-hearted through the unjust treatment he met at the hands of persons whom he had never injured, but who were jealous of his merits, expired on the eve of his coronation, April 25th, 1595." The cast was thus:—Alfonso (Duke of Ferrara), Signor Bellini; Eleonora (his Sister), Signora Schieroni; Countess of Scandinavia, Mdlle. Vermani; Torquato Tasso, Signor F. Lablache; Roberto Geraldini (Secretary to the Duke), Signor Catone; Don Gherardo (a Courtier), Signor Sanquirico; Ambrozzio (Servant to Tasso), Mr. Eaton.

One Act of "Eliza e Claudio" was performed on Thursday, with "Betly;" and a repetition of "Torquato Tasso" on Saturday, April 21st, 1838, concluded the four nights of this re-engagement. The repetition of the latter Opera was given in consequence of its eminent success; but, with the exception of two or three pieces, no great effect resulted, and the Opera has not held possession of the stage like the immortal "Favorita," "Lucia," "L'Elisire," &c., &c.

Mr. Mitchell then visited Belfast with his Company, taking several members of the Dublin orchestra:—Mr. Pigott, Mr. Levey, Mr. Harrington, Mr. Powell, &c., &c., in his suite. A rather strange incident occurred on the occasion. Mr. Mitchell was the last to arrive in Belfast; he was always solicitous as to the personal comforts of his Company, and he visited the different residences where they were located, to make sure they were "all right." He found out all but Mr. Pigott, and as he was an especial favourite, he should see him. On inquiry, Mr. Mitchell learned that Mr. Pigott had gone to the "Temperance Hotel," whence Mr. Mitchell repaired. He entered a rather dingy parlour, rang the bell, no answer; rang again, with like result. He proceeded to the drawing-room (it was Sunday evening), rang three times, some minutes intervening between each sound. At length a very ruddy-visaged waiter staggered in, saying, in broken accents— "D-d-id you r-r-ing, sir? wh-wh-who d-d-d-i-u want?" and fell right down on Mr. Mitchell's arm in a glorious state. Mr. Mitchell, who was rather slow and formal in expression, was naturally surprised, and asked, "Is not this the 'Temperance Hotel?'" "O-o-f c-u-u-r-se it is," was the reply. The *impresario* made the best of his way out, and never forgot the event, as he renewed the recollection at a dinner-party at Mr. Bussell's table on his last visit to Dublin, about 1865.

The next Italian engagement occurred in September, 1838, when Signor De Angioli announced that, " in compliance with many applications from distinguished parties, and the general accommodation of the public, he has engaged the Theatre Royal from Mr. Calcraft for one night only, this present Thursday, 6th September, 1838, on which occasion the performance will include an unprecedented combination of musical talent—Madame Persiani (Cantante di Camera di S. M. I. e R. L'Imperatore di Austria), and Signor Rubini (being his last season previous to his retirement from the stage), Signor Nigri (Basso Cantante from Naples), and the violinist, Signor Emiliani."

A grand vocal and instrumental Concert commenced

the musical entertainment, which concluded with the first and third Acts of Donizetti's new Opera of "Lucia di Lammermoor," described as never represented in this country, and founded on Walter Scott's celebrated romance of "The Bride of Lammermoor." Lucia, Mdlle. Persiani ; Edgardo, Signor Rubini ; Enrico, Signor Nigri.

Madame Persiani was, perhaps, one of the most acomplished vocalists who ever appeared on the lyric stage. No second opinion existed as to the perfection of her scale singing, diatonic and chromatic ; and it is not too much to assert that her performance of Lucia has seldom been equalled and never excelled. Rubini was up to that period the most wonderful of tenors. His voice was of most extraordinary compass, with flexibility equalling that of a soprano. The ordinary "break" did not occur (at least apparently) in passing from one register to another, and his delivery of the now well-known "Fra poco" was surpassingly touching and beautiful ; the effect on those who heard it for the first time, under such circumstances, may be well imagined. The "tremolo," now so often abused, he used judiciously and in the right places. The "Tu Vedrai" ("Pirata"), which he sang in the Concert, gave ample opportunity for the display of his marvellous qualities, the opening cantabile showing the extreme power of sostenuto and wondrous pathos, while, in the second movement, the most florid passages came forth with the precision of a flute or violin played to perfection. Truly Rubini was a wonder ; but there was one just then beginning a career which would equal, if not excel, this great star, whose name will appear by-and-by.

Signor Emiliani's violin-playing was chiefly remarkable for power and purity of tone. He possessed a superb "Cremona," which, it is needless to say, lent additional charm to his performances.

The Company performed a second night, "in consequence of the brilliant success which attended the representation on Thursday, and of many applications from parties who were prevented from attending on that occasion;" therefore, on Saturday, 8th September, 1838, a repetition of the Concert and the first and third Acts of "Lucia" took place.

No Italian Opera Company appeared in the year 1839, which was remarkable by the farewell appearance of Braham, the celebrated veteran English tenor, who commenced an engagement of six nights on Monday, July 22nd, 1839.

Thalberg performed at the Theatre Royal on the 14th and 15th October, 1839, at which Mrs. and Mr. Balfe appeared.

In 1840 commenced what may be styled the Augustan period of Italian Opera in Dublin. The first troupe, under the auspices of the celebrated house of Beale and Co., Regent-street, London, and managed by Mr. Willert Beale, who, at an early age, displayed remarkable qualities as an *impresario,* combining with a thorough knowledge of music and a keen appreciation of artistes, all the coolness and judgment necessary for such a part. Willert, as his numerous friends in Ireland called, and still continue to call him, accompanied his troupe here for many years. He was, indeed, the "right man in the right place." Never was there a more efficient manager. An excellent linguist, he possessed the power of arranging any little differences which might and will occur with the best regulated companies, in a decided but quiet manner; all submitting to his decree, which they felt was always just. In his social capacity he was a universal favourite, and his society was much sought for. Great regret was felt when he discontinued his operatic speculations in Dublin; but his "troops of friends" have the satisfaction of knowing that "Walter Maynard" is still well and flourishing, and that they may, at intervals, have the pleasure of seeing their old friend, the *impresario*, for many years to come.

An engagement for three nights only commenced on September, 8th, 1840, with the following artistes: Madame Grisi, Signor Tamburini, Signora Ernesta Grisi, Signor Brizzi. Mr. Benedict, conductor. The "charming, the incomparable Guila Grisi," as the London *Times* styled her, made her first appearance in Dublin on Tuesday, September 8th, 1840, Mr. Calcraft having announced that he had made the engagement "at an enormous expense." It is almost unnecessary to record the sensation created by this wonderful artiste, whose efforts of genius are still fresh in the memory of the Dublin audience, before whom she appeared for so many successive years, and whose due appreciation of her great talent created a lively impression, as she always looked forward to her visit to Ireland with the greatest pleasure. Tamburini was the prince of baritones. To a magnificent voice, possessing the finest quality and great compass, he added the highest cultivation, which displayed itself in a remarkable manner in the opening scene of the Opera, "Semiramide." His singing in Assur forming a model for all future aspirants to the part. His perfect execution of the very difficult and florid passages written by Rossini for a baritone, was indeed something to remember. Signor Brizzi was a nice tenor, and Signora Ernesta Grisi a good *seconda donna*.

On Thursday, September 8th, 1840, was performed, in two Acts, "Semiramide." Arsace, Signora Ernesta Grisi; Assur, Signor Tamburini; Semiramide, Madame Grisi. Pasta had made Semiramide "her own" until the advent of Grisi, who continued to hold the crown until near her retirement, when one worthy successor appeared in the person of Teresa Tietjens. This was Mr. Benedict's first appearance in Dublin. Happily Sir Julius Benedict still lives to enjoy his well-earned title.

On Wednesday, September 9th, 1840, was performed "La Sonnambula." Count Rodolpho, Signor Tamburini; Amina, Madame Grisi; Elvino, Signor Brizzi; Lisa, Signora Ernesta Grisi; Allessio, Mr. J. Penson; Teresa, Miss M. Hamilton; Notario, Mr. Shean. Of course the quartet was perfection. Mr. J. Penson, who performed Allessio, was brother to William Penson, formerly leader of the orchestra. J. Penson was "stock" low comedian, a fair musician and good actor. Miss M. Hamilton, before alluded to, was efficient in everything she undertook. Mr. Shean (the immortal "Dan"), when cast for the Italian part of Notario, expressed great surprise, and made a strong appeal that he might be permitted to sing his part in English; this was, of course, refused, on the grounds that when the notary came to ask Elvino with what worldly goods he would endow Amina, Elvino would not understand him. "Well," Dan replied, "That will occur, in any case: for if I try the Italian, I'll puzzle him a great deal more. I cannot get over their *cheese.*" Dan alluded to the Italian pronunciation of the letter *c*. Dan, however, "got through" the notary without damage.

On Thursday, September 10th, was performed "Semiramide," with cast as before; and on Friday, September 11th, 1840, was produced, for the first time in this country, Donizetti's Grand Opera Seria of "Anna Bolena." King Henry VIII., Signor Tamburini; Lord Richard Percy, Signor Brizzi; Smeaton, Signora Ernesta Grisi; Anna Bolena, Madame Grisi; concluding with "Il Barbiere," compressed into one act. Mr. Benedict performed a pianoforte fantasia on popular national airs between the Operas.

Grisi's performance of "Anna Bolena" was indeed something never to be forgotten. It brought the historic description of the beautiful and unfortunate queen to life. Indeed, if the reality was equal to the "counterfeit presentment," Henry's infatuation was not to be wondered at; and all this, without the additional charm of the singing, which, it is unnecessary to say, was perfection itself. Tamburini's representation of the Bluff King Hal was also a study. From the wonderful "make-up" one could see him "in his habit as he lived."

The last night of the engagement was that of Saturday, September 12th, 1840, with "La Sonnambula" (as before), and a Concert.

On Monday, August 30th, 1841, the following announcement appeared:—

"Mr. Calcraft begs respectfully to announce that he has (at an unprecedented expense, considerably exceeding two thousand pounds) been enabled to effect an engagement for the production of Italian Operas on a scale superior to any which has hitherto been attempted in this country. The Company includes the following artistes:— Madame Grisi, Signor Lablache (the far-famed bass singer, his first appearance here), Signor Mario (first tenor of the Queen's Theatre, the undoubted successor of Rubini), Signor F. Lablache, Signora Ernesta Grisi, and Signor Puzzi (the celebrated horn-player). Conductor, Mons. Benedict; Leader, Mr. Levey. No alteration or prolongation can possibly take place, in consequence of the previous arrangements of the parties engaged."

On Monday, August 30th, 1841, "I Puritani." Sir George, Signor Lablache; Lord A. Talbot, Signor Mario; Sir Richard Forth, Signor F. Lablache; Henrietta, Signora Ernesta Grisi; Elvira, Madame Grisi.

This should be a memorable date in our musical annals—the first appearance of perhaps the greatest tenor the world has yet seen or heard. "The undoubted successor of Rubini," Mario, in some points alike, possessed qualities in many respects superior. It would require a musical Plutarch to give a parallel description of the two wonders. Rubini, as before alluded to, possessed a marvellous range of voice, without a break, making constant use of what Italian singing-masters term the *voce di testa*—head voice. In the "Ah perche," in "Sonnambula," he reached F sharp in alt with great ease, singing the scena in D natural as written by Bellini. The voice was also capable of much dramatic power; indeed the general impression prevailed that Rubini was matchless, and that years might elapse before another could approach him. The star, however, appeared, and only those who then heard Mario, and witnessed the occasion, can judge of the effect. There is possibly no position in the lyric world which requires so many qualities combined in a single individual as a perfect Italian tenor. Of course the same will apply to an English artist; but it cannot be denied that the language of Italy is peculiarly adapted to musical sounds. Well, all the various talents necessary to make perfection were concentrated in Mario, with one trifling exception (which he always tried to overcome by high-heeled boots), he was slightly below the standard in stature. In every other respect perfection is not too strong a word to apply to him. With an appearance of the most manly beauty, he possessed a grace of form and a fascination of manner which made him the "observed of all observers." An artist as well as a nobleman by nature, he studied costume to a degree, and in all his characters was most exact in this particular, to the very "buckle of his shoe." The sound of his marvellous voice (he used the chest-voice more than Rubini) still lingers in our ears. The quality, the high training, the exquisite *timbre*—shall we ever hear the like again? And as an actor, fortunately many well remember his Raoul in "The Huguenots," in which it would be difficult to say which was the better, the acting or the singing. Few are aware that he performed (once only) in Dublin in Rossini's "Otello," which was, independent of the vocalism, a magnificent display of histrionic power, and parts of which were compared with the impersonation of the great Edmund Kean. In 1841, the date of this engagement, Mario was in his zenith; it will therefore be understood that his very appearance at the end of the first Act of " Puritani " created a sensation; but when the first liquid notes of the "A te o Cara" commenced, a death-like stillness (without the slightest exaggeration) prevailed, and at the conclusion of the movement there was a "shout" (for this is the word) of delight, the like of which it is difficult to hear out of Dublin. No words could give an adequate idea of his "Crede a misera," in which he reached the F in alt, thus equalling his great predecessor in range of voice, while exceeding him in power. The duet, also, "Vieni," with Grisi in the third Act, enraptured the audience. Thus commenced the Grisi and Mario era of Opera in Dublin, which continued for so many years to the delight of the Dublin public. Well might Sheridan's beautiful words from the "Duenna" be applied to the two:—

> "Ah, sure a pair were never seen
> So justly formed to meet by nature."

This was also the first appearance of The Lablache, enormous in size as in talent. His voice came forth " as from a mountain." The death of this wonderful artiste left a blank which has never been filled up. Although of such immense dimensions, his every movement was a model for students of the art. He was an exception to the general rule of Italian vocalists, who, for the most part, devote (perhaps wisely) their whole time and attention to the cultivation of the voice, without giving much trouble to the study of music as a science. Lablache was an excellent musician, a good double bass player, and would sometimes, for a change, come to the orchestra and take a part on that instrument. So consummate an artiste was Lablache on the stage that his performance of even a second-rate part (to which he sometimes descended) would make it unusually prominent and important, as all who remember his "Doctor Bartolo" will bear witness to. He also "essayed" Figaro, a grand performance, in which he danced about the stage as lightly as a gossamer, although his reputed weight was twenty-five stone. Lablache indeed "astonished the natives" with his wondrous combined powers. When the voice rolled out in the "Suoni la Tromba," the comparatively weak organ of his son Fred, even combined with the whole power of the orchestra, was "nowhere!" The same effect is recorded of one of the musical festivals in England, in which, during the combined efforts of an enormous chorus and band of perhaps 1,000 performers, Lablache's D thundered prominently over all. This great artiste's face was, as it were, "chiselled" in the highest classic form, and is said to have been taken as a model by several great sculptors. In social life he sometimes delighted his friends by kneeling at the end of a table, placing his head between two lights, and depicting the passions—rage, envy, despair, love, revenge, pity, &c.—a really magnificent exhibition of facial expression and refined art.

Signor Puzzi, who performed fantasies on the horn in the course of the evenings during this engagement, was an eminent performer and principal horn-player at all the English musical festivals. He played on the simple horn— the valve horn had not as yet come into general use ; and it is still doubtful if the application of the valve, while it has the effect of equalizing the scale, has not taken from the effect of the natural pure horn notes.

Mr. William Murphy, announced as "Assistant-Chorus-master," was then a most promising young student (of composition and orchestral scoring), and lent much aid in the preparation of the Operas, which at the time demanded several weeks of preliminary rehearsals; the chorus and band being supplied from local resources. Mr. Murphy gained his degree of Musical Bachelor in Trinity College some years afterwards, for which degree he passed a most creditable examination, and on which occasion a choral and orchestral work of great merit was performed.

On Tuesday, August 31st, 1841, "Norma." Pollione, Mario; Oroveso, Lablache; Adalgisa, Ernesta Grisi; Norma, G. Grisi.

This was Grisi's first appearance here in the great *role*, the wonderful performance of which bestowed on her the title of "Queen of Song." Her majestic form and commanding expression of feature were sufficiently impressive as she entered, with the measured and dignified step to which we became so well accustomed

The recitative "Seditiose Voce" followed, and at the long-sustained A flat on the first syllable of the last word "mieto" (which appeared endless), the house, of course, "came down." Her delivery of "Oh non tremare" was fittingly described as "terrible" by a listener in the pit. It was supposed that "Norma" would die with Grisi.

Pollione is not a favourite part with tenors in general, the music is ungraceful, and the character not calculated to impress the audience favourably. Mario only performed it with Grisi, and it is unnecessary to say that he made the most of a weak part.

The Oroveso of Lablache was simply grand. In the third bar of the opening recitative—"Ite sul colle o Druide"—he had the chance of thundering out that wonderful D of his; also in the "Si parlera," and "Tremendo," the last word was, indeed, appropriate to the tremendous tone of the voice. A "roaring" encore was the result, which rarely occurs with the opening chorus of Norma.

On Thursday, September 2nd, 1841—"La Sonnambula." Count Rodolpho, Signor F. Lablache; Amina, Madame Grisi; Elvino, Mario; Lisa, Signora Ernesta Grisi; Teresa, Mrs. T. Hill; Alessio, Mr. J. Penson; Notary, Mr. Shean.

Of late years Mario has "given up" Elvino, but his singing of the music at this period was superb. Grisi was, as usual, perfection. It will be perceived that "Dan" held possession of "Il Notario," until a season or two afterwards, when it was filled by a Frenchman, whom Dan regarded with sovereign contempt, remarking, " Well, come, my Irish-Italian is as good as that fellow's French-Italian any day." Mrs. T. Hill (Teresa) was one of the " Stock " Company—an excellent actress, who had received a good musical education.

" La Prova d'un Opera Seria " concluded the entertainment, in which Lablache gave his most amusing representation of " Campanone."

On Saturday, September 4th, " Puritani " was repeated.
On Monday, September 6th, " Norma."
On Tuesday, September 7th, " Sonnambula."
On Thursday, September 9th, " La Gazza Ladra," compressed into one Act, after which a Concert, concluding with the second Act of " I Puritani."

During the concert a pianoforte duet was performed by Mr. Benedict and Mr. W. S. Conran. William Conran was a most brilliant pianist, almost attaining to greatness. Had he proceeded to the Continent, as was intended, and devoted his exclusive time to his instrument, he would probably have obtained a world-wide reputation, as he possessed all the qualities for a great performer; but he marred his hopes, like many young artistes, by marrying too early, and had to devote his whole time to the slavery of giving lessons from one week's end to another, often devoting the nights, after a hard day's work, to severe practice. Mr. Conran had a large and talented family, one of whom (Mdlle. Conrani) is a distinguished lyric artiste of European fame. It is sufficient proof of Conran's merit that Benedict and Thalberg looked upon him as a worthy coadjutor.

An extra night was given on Friday, September 10th,

with "Il Barbiere," Mario giving his unrivalled impersonation, Count Almaviva. Who that heard the "Ecco ridente," could ever forget it? Grisi introduced "Rode's Air and Variations," first written for the violin, and adapted for the voice by Bochsa.

The Operatic season closed with "I Puritani," for Grisi's benefit, and "God save the Queen," sung by all the artistes.

The next Italian Opera engagement commenced on September 5th, 1842, the expenses still increasing. The following announcement appeared:—" Mr. Calcraft begs respectfully to announce that he has (at an unprecedented expense, nearly amounting to three thousand pounds), been enabled to effect an engagement for the production of Italian Operas on a scale fully superior to those which gave so much satisfaction last year." The Company consisted of Madame Grisi, Signor Lablache, Signor Mario, Signor F. Lablache, Signora Ernesta Grisi, " with various competent auxiliaries." Leader, Mr. Levey; Prompter, Signor Salabert (of Her Majesty's Theatre); Assistant Chorus Master, Mr. William Murphy; Conductor, Signor Costa (Musical Director of Her Majesty's Theatre). This was the first and only appearance of Signor Costa in Dublin. It is unnecessary to record that it is due to the skill and tact of this eminent musician that the London Italian Opera Band, from his powers of selection and organization, has arrived at a perfection unsurpassed, perhaps unequalled, in the world. Amidst all the changes which have taken place in the musical world within the last quarter of a century, Sir Michael Costa still holds his position as first of conductors; and the universal feeling of all members of the profession who have come in contact with him, and who judge justly and without prejudice, is that Sir Michael may live long to enjoy his well-deserved dignity. Should he again visit Ireland, he will meet with the reception to which his merits fully entitle him.

On Monday, September 5th, 1842, was given "I Puritani," with the same cast as in 1841, which, therefore, will demand no further remarks. Unfortunately Madame Grisi was seized with severe illness from affection of the throat, and on Tuesday, Wednesday, Thursday, Friday, and Saturday, Concerts were given; but the absence of the great *prima-donna* made a serious difference in the receipts, although all the other artistes assisted.

Madame Grisi, having recovered from her severe indisposition, made her re-appearance on Monday, September 12th, 1842, in "Norma" (cast as before, with the same artistes).

On Wednesday, September 14th, "Anna Bolena" was given, announced, through mistake, as "for the first time in Dublin." Lablache's representation of Henry VIII. was quite in keeping with every character undertaken by that consummate artiste. Mario was Lord Richard Percy; Grisi, Anna Bolena; Smeaton, Miss A. Hyland; Lord Rochfort, Signor Salabert; Sir Harry, Mr. Sala. Mr. Sala was a member of the Stock Company, and an artiste of much promise. He inherited much of the musical talent of his distinguished mother, Madame Sala, possessed dramatic ability of a high degree, with great imitative capacity, often excited in the green-room to the great delight of his hearers. On one occasion, whilst giving a life-like imitation of Charles Kean (during one of his engagements), the tragedian suddenly and quietly entered the green-room. The mimic having his back towards the door, still proceeded, and the effect may be imagined when he suddenly turned and met the original face to face. Sala, who died young, was a relative of the immortal George Augustus.

Signor Salabert ascended from his prompt box for Sir Harry. Salabert was indeed most useful. In figure, however, he was very short and stout. His sword went awkwardly between his legs on one occasion, and some one called out from the gallery—" Bravo, ould Slabertashe!" Of course he retained the sobriquet.

On Thursday, "I Puritani" was given as before; on Friday, "Il Barbiere," and on Saturday, "Anna Bolena."

On Monday, September 19th, 1842, "La Sonnambula" was announced for the benefit of Mario, and last night of the engagement, ending with "God Save the Queen." The illness of the great *prima-donna* was a sad blow to this engagement, causing a loss of perhaps thousands of pounds in the receipts, and was one of those unforeseen strokes of "bad luck" which Mr. Calcraft had unfortunately so often to encounter.

No Italian Opera engagement took place in 1843. Mr. Calcraft issued the following notice at the foot of the bills, dated August 10th of that year: "In answer to many inquiries, the public is respectfully informed that the engagement with the Italian Opera Company has been abandoned, from various unexpected difficulties, and will not take place this season.

The next Italian Opera Company commenced an engagement of ten nights on the 9th September, 1844. Artistes : Madame Grisi, Signora Favanti (her first appearance), Signor Mario, Signor Carelli (his first appearance), Signor Pultoni (his first appearance), Signor F. Lablache ; Conductor, Signor Schira ; Leader, Mr. Levey ; Prompter, Signor Salabert.

The chief novelty in this troupe was Signora Favanti, an English lady, who had studied for some time in Italy, and who had created an impression in London. Her voice was supposed to be contralto, and had great scope, ranging from F below to D in alt. Much difference of opinion existed, however, as to her artistic powers. The higher and lower portions of the voice possessed much power and brilliancy; but the middle range, if it ever existed, had been sacrificed. Sometimes a dash of genius would display itself, and then a feeling of disappointment ensue. It was really a case which puzzled the critics, who were relieved of their anxiety by the early death of Mdlle. Favanti, whose splendid appearance and great extent of voice made a sensation for the time.

Some friend asked Tom Cooke his opinion with reference to Favanti. Tom was silent and shook his head— "Well (said the friend), but has she not a wonderful voice?" Cooke looked doubtful. "Is it not very high?" "H-m-m," muttered Tom—"and very low?" continued the friend. "Yes (said Cooke), and very middling!"

On Monday, September 9th, 1844, was given " La

Sonnambula;" and on Tuesday, September 10th, "Semiramide." Arsace, Signora Favanti; Semiramide, Grisi; Idreno, Corelli; Assur, F. Lablache; Oroe, Paltoni.

Favanti met with a favourable reception, looking well in male attire, and getting through the music satisfactorily, with periodical flights of talent.

On Thursday, September 12th, "Don Pasquale" was performed for the first time in Dublin. Don Pasquale, Signor Paltoni; Malatesta, Signor F. Lablache; Ernesto, Signor Mario; Norina, Madame Grisi.

Of Grisi's singing the music of this charming work it is quite unnecessary to write, but her acting proved her a light and "eccentric" *comedienne* of the very first order. Her by-play in the scenes with Pasquale set the audience in a roar. The Opera was, indeed, a "hit"—Mario's "Com' e Gentil." "We shall never hear the like again."

The bills announced, "To-morrow, Friday, there will be no dramatic performance whatever. The entertainment will consist of Rossini's Grand Oratorio, entitled 'The Stabat Mater,' which most certainly cannot be repeated." The announcement of "The Stabat Mater" to be performed in a theatre created a great sensation amongst the religious portion of the public. Mr. O'Connell, then a political prisoner in Richmond Bridewell, after reading the advertisement, wrote a letter to Mr. Calcraft, protesting strongly against the performance of so solemn a work in a dramatic temple, and requesting that it should be abandoned. Places had been taken, and a change would have entailed a severe loss. An embassy, consisting of the musical director and other officers of the

Theatre, was despatched in all haste to Richmond with the view to set matters right. It was explained to the "Liberator" that no dramatic performance whatever would take place on the same evening; also that the Theatre had been used for the performance of "The Messiah," "The Triumph of Faith," and other sacred works, on the occasion of the Dublin Musical Festival. These statements prevailed to some extent; but when Mr. O'Connell was told that Mr. Calcraft (for whom he had a great respect) would be a severe loser by any change, he yielded, kindly remarking that he was sure Mr. Calcraft would not sanction any performance in his establishment contrary to public morality. Accordingly, on Friday, September 13th, 1844, Rossini's "Stabat Mater" was given, in which Grisi, Favanti, Mario, Corelli, Paltoni, and Fred Lablache took parts. The overture to Mendelssohn's "Hymn of Praise" was performed by the band in the course of the evening.

On Saturday, September 14th, 1844, was performed Rossini's Grand Opera of "Otello." Otello, Signor Mario (his first appearance in this part); Elmiro, Signor Paltoni; Rodrigo, Signor Corelli; Iago, Signor F. Lablache. This was Mario's first and only appearance in Otello, a performance which might well be termed wonderful in every particular. Nothing could exceed the powerful tragic force displayed in the impassioned scenes with Iago. As before stated, they were compared by some old play-goers to Edmund Kean's extraordinary efforts in the same scenes. A more Shaksperian reading (as far as an Opera would allow) of the part was perhaps never witnessed. Grisi was a worthy Desdemona. Indeed, only one opinion existed as to the unqualified success of the two great artistes; but those who remember Mario's Otello can never forget it, and it has always remained a mystery that he never again essayed the part in Dublin.

On Monday, September 16th, " Norma " was given.

On Tuesday, September 17th, " Semiramide " and the last Act of "Lucia," with Mario's Edgardo; and on Wednesday, September 18th, " Cenerentola," with the following cast :—Cenerentola, Favanti; Ranviro, Corelli; Don Magnifico, F. Lablache; Tisbe, Miss Fitzgerald; Clorinda, Signora Corri. Favanti had sufficient opportunity of displaying the high and low portions of her voice in the "Non piu mesta," of which she took full advantage, dashing through brilliantly enough, but without much regard for the perfection of scale-singing, which is so essential in this finale. The majority of the audience, however, let this pass and applauded. Signora Corri (Clorinda) was a daughter of Haydn Corri (before alluded to), a popular singing-master, and organist for many years of the Metropolitan Roman Catholic Church. Miss Fitzgerald (Tisbe) was one of the local choristers, and was soon afterwards engaged to lead the soprani in one of the Italian Opera Houses, proving most useful in the performance of " small parts " when required. It would surprise many to be aware of the many members of the choral and orchestral department Dublin has contributed to the London musical forces. To the present day we frequently discover the home accent in perhaps the leader of the Italian bassi, or one of the principal instrumentalists (bassoon, for example), in the orchestra who, not very long ago, belonged to the staff of the " Old Royal."

On Friday, March 20th, 1844, " Don Pasquale," and one Act of "Cenerentola," were given for Mario's benefit; and on Saturday, 21st September, 1844, the programme included " Norma," a Scena from " Roberto Devereux," "Largo al factotum," by Paltoni, and the last Act of " Lucia ;" concluding with "God save the Queen." The performance was for the benefit of Madame Grisi. This was the last night of a very successful season.

The year 1845 passed without an Italian Opera, but was remarkable by the appearance of Mons. Duprez, the celebrated French tenor, who, with Madame E. Garcia, appeared at the Theatre Royal on two nights, Thursday, May 22nd, and Saturday, May 24th; on the first night in two Acts of " Lucia," and on the second night in the third Act of " Lucia," the third Act of " Sonnambula," and the last scene of " Guillaume Tell." This year was also remarkable by the appearance in October of Mr. Sims Reeves, who, with Mr. and Mrs. Alban Croft, fulfilled an operatic engagement; the Operas performed being " Lucia " (in English), " Sonnambula," " Love in a Village," " Fra Diavolo," " Bohemian Girl," " Beggar's Opera," " Der Freischutz," and " Guy Mannering."

On Monday, August 31st, 1846, the following Company commenced an engagement :—Madame Castellan, Signora Corbari, Signor Marras, Signor Ciabatta, and

Signor Fornisari. Conductor, Signor Orsini. Leader, Mr. Levey. Prompter, Signor Salabert.

Madame Castellan was a good and successful *primadonna;* Signora Corbari, a competent and artistic contralto. Signor Marras, who had established himself as a singing-master in London, was possessed of a light, sweet tenor voice, but (as sportsmen say) it could not "stay." During the first, or sometimes as far as the second Act of an Opera, if not very trying, Marras contrived to please his audience, but towards the conclusion the weakness would sometimes display itself lamentably. On one occasion, in the " Ah perche non posso " ("Sonnambula"), in which, when sung in D flat, the singer must ascend suddenly to the F above, Marras missed the note, but raised his first finger very much above his head, evidently under the impression that the audience would either hear the note or be compensated for its absence. This weakness of voice was a misfortune, not a fault, for Signor Marras was an experienced musician and most pleasing concert singer. Ciabatta was a fair baritone, of handsome appearance. The criticisms of Signor Fornasari were conflicting; some indicating that he was the greatest artiste that had ever appeared in London ; other reports were of a nature directly the contrary. He had certainly made a sensation in "Belisario," his success in which was attributable to his acting more than to his singing—indeed, like "Single-speech Hamilton," Fornasari might have been entitled "One-part Fornasari," for in no other character did he produce any particular effect. To the title of "vocalist" he could have no pretension, for it was a good extensive voice "gone mad," showing no cultivation or careful training. His was a somewhat parallel case to the Signora Favanti before mentioned— a short, flashy career, and then "heard no more."

On Monday, August 31st, 1846, the engagement opened with "Lucia." Lucia, Castellan; Edgardo, Marras; Enrico, Fornasari; Raimondo, Ciabatta. The performance called for no special notice: Castellan bearing away the palm. Marras, artistic and correct, but as usual weak at the finish.

On Tuesday, September 1st, was performed "Sonnambula," with Castellan as Amina, Marras as Elvino, Fornasari as Rodolpho, and Corbari as Lisa.

On Thursday, September 3rd, 1846, was presented for the first time in Ireland, Donizetti's grand Opera Seria in three Acts, called "Belisario." Cast—Antonia, Madame Castellan; Irene, Signora Corbari; Alamiro, Signor Marras; Giustiniano, Signor Ciabatta; Belisario, Signor Fornasari.

In witnessing Fornasari's performance of "Belisario" one could not suppose the artiste could have failed so much in other characters. He represented the blind General most powerfully, and in the last scene, when reduced to beggary, he really displayed remarkable dramatic ability. He seemed inspired even in his interpretation of the music, for his singing in this part (and in this only) was faultless, and, more particularly in the pathetic scenes, his hearers would suppose him a vocalist of the highest cultivation. His appearance was much in his favour; he looked indeed a "noble Roman." The Opera itself is not one of the composer's best efforts, and is seldom performed. It would be, perhaps, correct to say that no other artiste has undertaken the part in England since Fornasari.

On Saturday, the 5th September, "I Puritani" was given. Sir George, Fornasari; Lord Arthur, Marras; Sir Richard, Ciabatta; Henrietta, Corbari; Elvira, Castellan. The duet "Suoni la tromba" was about the best feature in the performance.

On Monday, the 7th September, "Norma" was performed—Norma, Castellan; Adalgisa, Corbari; Pollio, Marras; Oroveso, Fornasari. Norma was not suited to Castellan's powers. Pollio required a *tenore robusto* of which Marras was not possessed. Fornasari looked the part of Oroveso well. Adalgisa was the best of the quartet.

"Belisario" was repeated on Tuesday.

On Wednesday, September 9th, "Sonnambula" was performed by command of the Lord Lieutenant. Cast as before.

On Friday, 11th September, "I Puritani" as before, for the benefit of Signor Marras; and on Saturday, September 12th, "Norma," for Madame Castellan's benefit, and last night of the engagement, which did not prove very profitable.

The year 1847 passed without an Italian Opera.

On Tuesday, August 29th, 1848, the following Company appeared:—Madame Grisi, Signora Vera, Signor Mario, Signor Ciabatta, Signor Galli, Signor Tagliafico. Conductor, Mons. Benedict; Leader, Mr. Levey; Prompter, Signor Salabert.

On Tuesday, 29th, "Norma" was performed, with the following cast :—Norma, Grisi; Adalgisa, Signora Vera; Pollio, Mario; Oroveso, Tagliafico; Flavio, Galli. Grisi and Mario, now at the very pinnacle of their glorious career, were indeed magnificent in each Opera during this engagement. Tagliafico, then *primo-basso* at the Royal Italian Opera, displayed all the artistic capabilities which he has sustained through his long and successful career. He is now the efficient stage-manager of the Royal Italian Opera.

On Wednesday, 30th August, "Puritani" was given. Elvira, Grisi; Enrichetta, Vera; Arturo, Mario; Ricardo, Ciabatta; Walton, Galli; Georgio, Tagliafico.

On Friday, September 1st—"La Gazza Ladra." Ninetta, Grisi; Pippo, Vera; Gianetto, Mario; the Podesta, Tagliafico; Fernando, Ciabatta. Grisi's Ninetta was something never to be forgotten. On this occasion, when the officers of justice were about to take her to prison for stealing the silver spoons, &c., an occupant of the upper gallery called out, "Ah, sure, it was the magpie that took them; bring her back!"

On Saturday, September 2nd, was produced "La Sonnambula." Amina, Grisi; Lisa, Signora Vera; Elvino, Mario; Rodolpho, Tagliafico; Teresa, Miss Mason; Allessio, Galli.

On Monday, September 4th, "Don Pasquale" was the Opera. Norina, Grisi; Ernesto, Mario; Malatesta, Ciabatta; Don Pasquale, Tagliafico; Notario, Galli. Tagliafico's Pasquale was an excellent performance. Although the "giant" Lablache had created the part and

I

made it "his own," still Tagliafico's reading was full of original humour, and the fact of having been chosen to succeed such an original was proof of the confidence reposed in his capabilities, and, as the result proved, with justice. Mario, on this occasion, had to come on the stage three times to repeat the " Com 'e gentil," his singing of which never has been, or perhaps never will be, equalled.

On Tuesday, September 5th, " Norma " was repeated. On Thursday, September 7th, " Puritani," and third Act of " Don Pasquale " were given for Mario's benefit ; and on Saturday, September 9th, " La Sonnambula " was played for Grisi's benefit, and last night of the season.

Now succeeded perhaps the most remarkable operatic engagement which has ever taken place in Dublin. Mr. Calcraft, after much difficulty, and with the exertion of great diplomacy, succeeded, after much competition, in forming an engagement for the appearance of " Jenny Lind " at the Theatre Royal. Many tempting offers had been made from local speculators for her appearance in concerts ; but her managers (for she had many) wisely decided that she should open in Opera. The reports of her wonderful career in London had given rise to great expectations indeed, and never, perhaps, were great expectations so fully realized. Her terms were fabulous— £500 per night. With the addition of vocalists qualified to sing with such an artiste, a corresponding orchestra, chorus, &c., &c., it can with truth be asserted that the nightly expenses were enormous. It was indeed a bold experiment in the year of famine; but the result proved most satisfactory to Messrs. Lumley, Knowles, and Calcraft, each of whom made a considerable sum. After much deliberation, the prices fixed were as follows:—Dress Boxes, £1 10s.; Second Circle, £1; Pit, 12s. 6d.; First Gallery, 7s. 6d.; Second Gallery, 5s.

On Tuesday, October 10th, 1848, was announced the first appearance of Jenny Lind, the Company including the following artistes:—Mons. Roger, the celebrated tenor from the Grand Opera, Paris, and Italian Opera, Covent Garden; Signor Belletti, Signor F. Lablache, *primi-bassi* from Her Majesty's Theatre, Haymarket; Signora Grimaldi, Signor Bottura, Signor Guidi, and, in addition to the chorus of the establishment, the following also from Her Majesty's Theatre, viz.: First soprano, Miss Renaud, Mdlle. Payne, Mrs. Hughes, and Miss E. Thompson; contralto, Miss Kennedy and Miss Henly; $1^{mi.}$ tenori, Signor Benzi, Signor Grimaldi; $2^{d.}$ tenori, Mr. Thompson, Mr. C. Taylor; bassi, Signor Brigg, Herr Hengler; principal instrumental performers—leaders, Mons. Nadaud (from Her Majesty's Theatre), and Mr. Levey; first violin and solo, Monsieur Herrmann; second violin, Mons. Oury; viola, Mr. Hughes; violoncello, Signor Piatti; contra-basso, Mons. Anglois; grand flute, Mons. Remusat; piccolo, Mr. King; oboe, Mons. Lavigne; clarionet, Signor E. Belletti; bassoon, Signor Tamplini; horn, Herr Sleglick; trumpet and cornet, Herr Zeiss; trombone, Mons. Marin; drums, Mr. R. Hughes; music librarian, Mr. Mapleson; prompter, Mons. Crippa—all from Her Majesty's Theatre. Conductor, Mr. Balfe.

The above names, joined with the local force, formed

indeed an attractive and most effective combination. A glance at some of the names cannot fail to prove interesting. Mons. Roger had only just started as an Italian vocalist, having been for years the first and favourite tenor at the Grand Opera (French) in Paris. After a successful career he returned to the French Opera, where he continued to a recent date, delighting his audiences by his pure style of vocalism and excellent acting. Belletti was a highly-finished artiste, and has long since left the stage. Frederick Lablache (son of The Lablache), is now a professor of the London Academy of Music—by-the-way, an Irish pupil of his, Miss Landore, has made several most successful appearances in Dublin. Mdlle. Payne, first soprano in the chorus, became the wife of Mr. Aynsley Cook, the favourite vocalist, a most careful student and painstaking artist. Mr. Cook has succeeded in making several parts "his own"—Devilshoof amongst the rest. Mrs. Aynsley Cook was soon emancipated from chorus-singing, and became a valuable second soprano, and was the original in Wallace's Opera of "Lurline." In addition to her musical and dramatic capabilities, Mrs. Cook is an accomplished *danseuse*, and so thoroughly versed in the Terpsichorean art, as to materially assist in the production of the incidental ballets. That Mrs. Cook and " Old Aynsley," as he is affectionately entitled, may have a long and prosperous career, is the wish of all their professional brethren and "sistern!" Mons. Nadaud was the favourite leader of the ballet, in which department he was without a rival. The ballet at this period formed as great an attraction as the Opera. Indeed, with some, it was the feature. Mons. Nadaud was an especial favourite with Taglioni, Fanny Ellsler, and all the great artistes of "La Danse." He possessed the peculiar qualities necessary for his post, unvarying attention to the feet of the performer, having the music always by heart. He never had occasion to look at the book, so that the eye was ever fixed upon the stage, and a perfect sympathy appeared to exist between the artiste and the leader. Young conductors would do well to follow the example of Mons. Nadaud, by so closely studying the music they have in hand as to obviate the necessity of constantly bending the head over the book. Mons. Nadaud was also "Chef d'Attaque" in the Italian Opera. Mons. Herrmann (first violin), was one of the four brothers Herrmann, who so successfully appeared in Dublin as quartet performers. Giving the works of Beethoven, and other classics, with great precision, it might indeed with safety be asserted that those wonderful creations of genius were by them first interpreted in Dublin according to the intentions of the author. In addition to the instrumental attraction, the Brothers Herrmann also performed vocal quartets, and introduced many of the pieces now forming portions of the Orphean collection; and although not one of the four possessed a solo voice, the effect produced, from constant practice together, and extreme care in amalgamation (so to speak), viz., in the observance of pianos, extreme pianissimos, crescendos, fortes, &c., the effect was indeed wonderful; clearly proving what might be done if those possessing great voices were to bestow as much care and conscientiousness in the preparation of their concerted music. One of the four brothers settled afterwards in Dublin, Mr. Lidel Herrmann, better known by the single title "Lidel," and remained for several years fulfilling the post of principal violoncello at all the concerts, and, on special occasions, at the Theatre. He was an admirable soloist, and an especial favourite in private circles. He is still well, and holds a high professional position in London. His place is now worthily filled in Dublin by Herr Elsner, who followed closely on Lidel's departure. Mons. Oury (principal second) was an eminent violinist, and husband to Madame Oury, a very popular and accomplished pianist. Signor Piatti is so well known as the Prince of Violoncellists that it is only necessary to give his name. More than thirty years have passed, and he still holds the very first rank against all comers. Lavigne, the great oboe performer, also still retains his lip, his fingers, and his faculties, to the delight of all who hear him. All the other instrumentalists in this list have passed away, except the present writer, who still struggles to "beat time." The music librarian, Mr. Mapleson, was father to Mr. J. H. Mapleson, whose reputation as manager of Italian Opera is world-wide, and to whom the Dublin public are so much indebted for the production of the works, in particulars and in detail, only to be equalled in London. Michael William Balfe was conductor. He filled the same post at Her Majesty's Theatre, and came to Dublin *ex officio*. "No man is a prophet in his own country." His presence evoked nothing like the enthusiasm he merited. His reception was certainly good, but no more.

Several eminent composers have failed in wielding the conductor's baton; but Balfe possessed all the qualities—great decision, "an eye to threaten and command," a faultless ear, ready to discover the slightest inaccuracy, and, above all, an intelligible and decisive beat, without which all the other attributes are as nothing; indeed none but the initiated can have an idea of the importance of the movements of the "small white wand" to those whom it is intended to guide. Much mischief may be done by a moment's distraction on the part of the holder. He may be compared to a skilled "whip." He has not only four, but perhaps forty, yea, one hundred "in hand" (now-a-days the number is illimitable), and even a temporary indecision may do much harm. Perhaps no other occupation demands greater "strain" of brain or steadiness of hand for the time being than that of an operatic conductor. And, as remarked above, many of the greatest composers, from lack of the peculiar talent, have been obliged to "pass the torch" (baton) to another for the conduct of their own works. Balfe was "all there." Every man under his jurisdiction knew what he meant, and at what part of the bar he might be, so that, as far as the numbers would admit, all went well. Before giving the list and cast of Operas in connection with this most remarkable engagement, it may not be out of place to record that Jenny Lind stayed at Morrison's Hotel. Mr. Lumley, the then great *impresario*, the vocalists, and Mr. Balfe also remained at the same hotel. Two "off nights" occurred during the engagement, and on each of those vacant evenings the great "stars" had a reunion amongst themselves, the writer receiving a special invitation, as "one of the family." It would be difficult, indeed, to imagine any unstudied or unrehearsed entertainments more delightful and unconventional than those two, of which music formed but a limited portion, dancing, forfeits, and cards (for very small stakes) filling nearly all the time. Jenny Lind could dance nearly as well as she could sing. Balfe inherited the art, and was capital on the "light fantastic." A mock ballet was organized, the great soprano fulfilling the *role* of the Maiden, and the composer and conductor that of the Lover. The "corps de ballet" consisted of the company (Mick, the waiter, being once pressed into the service when he entered in his professional capacity). Mr. Lumley, a model manager in appearance, was placed on a throne to decide on the merits of the aspirants, and was supposed to offer an engagement to the most accomplished. The ballet proceeded most seriously, Mons. Nadaud and the writer contributing the music alternately, each, as he passed the "fiddle" to the other, joining the dancing group. At the end a discussion occurred, carried on most gravely, as to the respective merits of the two principal characters. The great manager was undecided. His means would only allow the engagement of one. The question was put to the vote (a plebiscite). The votes were equal. What was to be done? The manager decided that one great trial of skill should take place, each to perform an elaborate solo. Balfe led off, and danced "like an angel." Then "enter Jenny Lind" with all the air and grace of a Taglioni. She proceeds—

an "adagio" and fascinating allegro, tripping "solo" to follow, astonish all the lookers-on. Rounds of applause, bouquets, &c., &c., and, to conclude, great Jenny "wins the day." The evening concluded with a set of quadrilles, Mdlle. Lind singing the quadrilles, seated in a corner on the music stool. These evenings might well be placed amongst the "Noctes Ambrosiani."

On Tuesday, the 10th of October, 1848, was performed "La Sonnambula." Amina, Jenny Lind; Lisa, Mdlle. Payne; Teresa, Signora Grimaldi; Elvino, Mons. Roger; Count Rodolpho, Signor Belletti; Allessio, Signor Guidi; and Notario, Signor Bottura.

The receipts on this night reached £1,600, a sum never equalled before or since in the Theatre Royal, Dublin. The question has often been asked, "Was Jenny Lind so great?" The simple answer is "Yes." A sort of feeling of disappointment prevailed with some at first. The voice was not what might be termed "great," the personal appearance not startling, still the impression made way that a wonderful artiste was present. The "Come per me" was listened to with breathless silence, and all doubt vanished at the end of the cabaletta, "Sovra il sen." Indeed the success of the whole performance was complete; but description fails to give an idea of the effect produced in the last Act. In the sleeping scene it is no exaggeration to state that the "Ah non credea" displayed as great an effort of genius as was ever witnessed on any stage. The audience seemed absolutely entranced. It was indeed a singing somnambulist. The whole movement was *sotto voce*, the eyes unconsciously fixed (it was particularly remarked without blinking) on one imaginary object; the cadenza at the climax, long, most original and wailing, was simply electrifying. A burst of applause about to commence was immediately hushed down, lest the "sleeper" should be awakened."

The other parts were well and efficiently filled, Mons. Roger displaying all the care and finish of the French school, and Belletti creating a deep impression as a most finished artist in every particular.

On Thursday, October 12th—"I Puritani." Elvira, Jenny Lind; Enrichetta, Signora Grimaldi; Arturo, Mons. Roger; Sir Richard Forth, F. Lablache; Sir George Walton, Signor Belletti; Lord George Walton, Signor Bottura; Bruno, Signor Guidi. Although not the most attractive of her impersonations, some preferred the Elvira of Jenny Lind to her other characters; but Grisi had "created" the part, and her singing of the music was fresh in the recollection of all. However, on this occasion, the performance of the celebrated polacca, "Son Vergin verzozza," was particularly fine, the chromatic ascending and descending scales coming out with extraordinary precision. The lovely duet, "Vieni" (in the third Act), for soprano and tenor, was also an *encore;* but nothing could possibly efface the impression produced by Grisi and Mario in the same duet.

On Saturday, 14th October, was given "La Figlia del Reggimento." Maria, Jenny Lind; La Marchesa, Signora Grimaldi; Tonio, Mons. Roger; Ortenzio, Signor Bottura; Il Corporale, Signor Guidi; Il Sergente Salpizio,

Signor F. Lablache. It was in this Opera that the famous songstress made her great "hit" in London. Indeed, the work was, in consequence, magnified to an importance it did not before possess. Wondrous versatility, combined with consummate art, rendered Jenny Lind's Maria most fascinating. The "Ciascun lo dice" and "Egli'e la" were full of life and vivacity. In the "Rataplan" the artiste accompanied herself on her own small "side drum," playing like an experienced "tambouriere," and creating the greatest possible amount of merriment, amounting to enthusiasm, at the marching off with her companions. Then the "Convien partir" (in finale, first Act), when obliged to part from her "Fathers," was given with such exquisite tenderness that white pocket-handkerchiefs came extensively into use. But the climax arrived at the performance of the singing-lesson, opening the second Act, "Sorgera." The instructions in the scene attached to this *morceau* are thus: "Questo ritornello deve eseguirsi con caricatura." And well were the instructions carried out, commencing with the antiquated "motivo" for a certain time, then gradually (to the great horror of the ancient relative who accompanies), introducing snatches of "The Song of the Regiment," presently breaking into elaborate variations, and concluding with the most extraordinary vocal feats ever ventured on, and for the performance of which the only term appropriate is "wonderful." All the solfeggi of all the masters seemed heaped into one. In fact, every possible display of which the "human voice divine" is capable, was developed in this effort, never equalled before or since.

On Monday, 16th October, "Lucia di Lammermoor" was the opening. Lucia, Jenny Lind; Alice, Signora Grimaldi; Edgardo, Mons. Roger; Enrico, Signor Belletti; Bidebent, Signor F. Lablache; Arturo, Signor Guidi; Normanno, Signor Bottura. The special feature of Mdlle. Lind's "Lucia" was her great interpretation of the mad scene, at the end of the third Act, the cadenza with the flute, concluding the "Alfin son tua," amounting to perfection; while the exit, at the end of "Spargi d'amor," was worthy of a Siddons.

A re-engagement for two nights took place, the Opera being "Sonnambula," on the 19th, and "La Figlia," on the 24th October, 1848. The prices for those two nights were :—Dress Boxes, £1; Second Circle, 15s.; Pit, 10s. 6d.; First Gallery, 7s. 6d.; Second Gallery, 5s.

A Concert took place at the Rotundo on Saturday, the 21st. The receipts of this speculation were something enormous, all the more so taking into consideration that a famine prevailed in the land. The excitement produced at the first announcements was extraordinary, and communications from all quarters of Ireland arrived rapidly to secure places, some only containing the amount necessary, which, as a matter of course, were the only ones attended to; and many were the disappointments which arose in consequence, as some who had not enclosed the money arrived expecting unreasonably that the places were secured; but much inconvenience would have followed such arrangement, as many who wrote letters never came. The music-sellers were overwhelmed with commissions; some anxiously demanding places to be secured for four or five for every night, the letter containing no remittance. When it is considered that the amount for one family of four would be £40, it would have required a good capital to have carried out those requests to a large extent. Many cases of "outrunning the constable" occurred; indeed, a regular "Jenny Lind mania" prevailed for the time.

The success of this great artist was not obtained without the most severe study. Not the music alone, but each character, in its most minute particulars, must have been sedulously and deeply contemplated—no one but a close observer of nature could combine the qualities necessary to pourtray the opposite feelings of mirth and grief in the same *role*. As before observed, the "Convien partir" was sung with such wondrous pathos that the audience were affected even to tears; then the singing-lesson, when Maria branches suddenly off to "The Song of the Regiment," recalled to mind by the presence of the sergeant one of her "Fathers" evoked roars of laughter. It would be unjust to conclude this hasty sketch of an artist of whom a volume might be written, without recording an act of charity performed by her after her departure from the stage.

About the year 1854 or '55 an application was made that she would come to Dublin and sing at a Concert to be given for the joint benefit of "Mercer's Hospital" and the "Irish Musical Fund Society." Consent was most kindly and promptly given. The "Messiah" was performed at the Antient Concert Rooms. The resident local artists gave their gratuitous services on the occasion;

Mdlle. Lind singing the principal soprano music with marvellous effect—indeed, it is only necessary to state that in sacred music she excelled quite as much as in the dramatic school. "I know that my Redeemer liveth" was indeed a splendid effort, and held the listeners spellbound; and in the performance of the difficult "Rejoice greatly," the wondrous versatility of the artist shone forth peculiarly, the brilliant passages being given with marvellous precision and ease. The London critics held but one opinion of the extraordinary merits of Jenny Lind's singing in Handel's great work. The result of the concert was indeed most satisfactory for the two charitable institutions: a sum of about £940 remained (after all expenses) to be divided, to the great gratification of all concerned, and to none more than the great artiste herself.

The next Italian engagement commenced on Thursday, August 13th, 1849, with Mdlle. Alboni, Mdlle. Corbari, Mdlle. A. Corbari, Madame Valle, Mr. Sims Reeves, Signor Bartolini, Signor Galli, Signor Polonini, Signor Tagliafico. Conductor, Mons. Benedict. Leader, Mr. Levey. Prompter, Signor Salabert.

On Thursday, 13th, was given "La Cenerentola." Cenerentola, Alboni.

On Friday, 14th, "La Figlia" (ending with the singing-lesson), and the second Act of "Cenerentola."

On Saturday, 15th, "Don Pasquale," with selections from the first Act of "Linda di Chàmouni."

On Monday, 17th, "La Sonnambula." Amina, Alboni.

On Tuesday, 18th, the first Act of "Linda" and two Acts of "Cenerentola."

On Wednesday, 19th, a Concert was given, and Selections, in consequence of the illness of Mr. Sims Reeves.

On Thursday, 20th, "La Sonnambula" was given, with Alboni as the heroine; Elvino, Bartolini.

On Friday, 21st, "Il Barbiere" (compressed into one Act), and two Acts of "Lucia."

On Saturday, 22nd, the first Act of "La Figlia," after which Alboni sang the brindisi from "Lucrezia Borgia;" the second Act of "Cenerentola;" and the third Act of "Sonnambula," for the benefit of Alboni, and last night of engagement.

The illness of Mr. Sims Reeves caused considerable changes in the casts during this engagement. However, the singing of Alboni created of course a *furore*. Enormous in size as well as talent, she possessed the most wonderful contralto voice perhaps ever heard up to her advent; it was cultivated to the very highest degree. "Cenerentola" in particular was indeed something to remember. The andante introducing the finale was entrancing; and in the "Non piu mesta," the simple melody was sung with wondrous effect, and in the variations no instrument could equal the perfection of the scales, extending, as sung by Alboni, from the C below to C above—the equality of *timbre* being most remarkable. The huge dimensions of this great artiste sometimes called forth some amusing remarks from the "gods," especially when she appeared in her regimental suit in "La Figlia." Her gigantic figure was also scarcely appropriate to the part of "La Sonnambula." On one occasion, when getting into the bed in the sleeping scene, an excited beholder called out, "Begorra, that bed 'll break down!" The engagement was but moderately successful.

We now arrive at a rather remarkable epoch in Dublin lyric art, viz., the first appearance of a native artiste in Italian Opera.

Miss Catherine Hayes, a native of Limerick, who had a few years before left Dublin for Italy, with all her worldly wealth sewn up in her corset, commenced an engagement in company with the following artistes:— Herr Damcke, Signor Paglieri (tenor); Signor Bardini (basso); Signor Galli (baritone); Miss Norman (contralto). Prompter, Signor Salabert. Leader, Mr. Levey.

Catherine Hayes came heralded with a great Continental reputation, having created the greatest sensation in all the principal cities of Italy and France. The most flattering and exciting criticisms from the leading journals had been translated and inserted in the "locals," and London having *fiated* her success, it is no wonder that she fulfilled all the anticipations of her "compatriots," although the voice had been a little "thinned" from extreme study and hard work. She had evidently placed herself with a great vocal master—Garcia, it was said, with whom Jenny Lind had also studied; indeed, the similarity of style in both artistes was evident, clearly proving the importance of finding an experienced and careful teacher; for many voices have been ruined, even in Italy, by would-be teachers, who knew nothing of the correct placing of the vocal organ. Unfortunately Catherine Hayes on this occasion was not well supported. On the first night of performance ("Lucia") the tenor broke down in the duet at the end of the first Act, and this event gave rise to a very remarkable occurrence. Mr. Sims Reeves (whose engagement concluded the night previous) was sitting in one of the upper private boxes; he was, of course, recognised by the audience. The curtain had descended in consequence of the weakness of Edgardo, from cold or nervousness, or perhaps both combined. The audience called out lustily for "Reeves! Reeves!!" and a long delay ensued, the calls still increasing. At last Mr. Calcraft made his appearance, and, after apologizing for Signor Paglieri, and learning the anxiety of the house that Reeves should finish the part of Edgardo, he proceeded to the box in order, if possible, to persuade the great tenor to "come to the breach." However, contrary to the manager's customary diplomatic reserve, he made the request to appear rather as a demand, and Reeves refused point-blank. Still the cry increased. Mr. Calcraft reappeared, and told the audience that Mr. Reeves had declined to comply with their wishes. Almost immediately Mr. Reeves appeared side by side with the manager, and an extraordinary scene was the result. Reeves stated that he had been asked in a most autocratic manner to appear. Mr. Calcraft denied this. Then the tenor replied. The manager of course defended his position, and a dialogue of some minutes' duration continued—one asserting, the other denying. Reeves concluding by the observation, "that he would not be browbeaten by Mr. Calcraft, or anyone else." At last, at the instigation of the audience, a reconciliation took place. The two disputants shook

K

hands, amid the universal plaudits of the house, and Sims Reeves proceeded to the dressing-room, made up for Edgardo, and finished the Opera, of course to the great delight of all. It should here be mentioned that a report existed about this time that the distinguished tenor and Catherine Hayes were engaged to be married. The success of the native songstress was complete. " Lucia " never received, perhaps, a more poetic impersonation than in the hands of Catherine Hayes. Her acting, particularly in the mad scene, reached the highest standard, and her singing equalled any of the Italian artistes in style and finish.

On Wednesday, November 7th, " Norma " was given. Norma, Miss C. Hayes ; Adalgisa, Miss Poole ; Pollio, Herr Damcke ; Oroveso, Burdini ; Flavio, Galli ; Clotilda, Miss Fitzgerald.

Poor Herr Damcke was no great improvement on Paglieri, and did not distinguish himself very greatly in the *role*. The gallery "lads" made sad havoc of the name, parodizing it in all sorts of ways. When singing somewhat out of tune, a voice called out—"What damn key are you singing in now?" Another said— "Bravo Coal-quay" (the tenor was of very dark complexion).

On Thursday, November 8th, " Norma " was repeated ; and

On Friday, " Norma," and the mad scene from " Lucia." Catherine Hayes singing " The Harp that once," in the interval. The poverty of the Company did not admit of an extended *repertoire*, so Norma had to be repeated on Saturday, the 10th, for the benefit of Catherine Hayes. A short Concert concluding, in which she sang "Kathleen Mavourneen" and a ballad entitled "The Return to Erin," composed expressly for her by Mons. Benedict. As may be supposed, the weight of the attraction lay entirely with the soprano during this engagement; but she carried it nobly through, the pecuniary success encouraging the management to form another engagement, which could not arrive for a few months; accordingly

On Thursday, February 21st, 1850, the following Italian Company commenced an engagement:—Miss Catherine Hayes, Miss Poole, Mr. Travers (tenor), Signor Polonini (basso), Herr Mengis (baritone). Conductor, Signor Vera. Prompter, Signor Salabert. Leader, Mr. Levey. This was a great improvement on the former Company. Mr. Travers, a young English artiste, who had for years studied in Italy, and appeared there with much success, possessed a pure and well-cultivated tenor voice, and made at once a favourable impression in Dublin. With a good presence and gentlemanly demeanour, he did not depend entirely on his vocal efforts, for he was a capital actor. The contrast from the *fiasco* of the former engagement was much in his favour. Signor Polonini was a thorough artist, and continued for years a reigning favourite in Dublin. Herr Mengis was also a competent and experienced vocalist. So the soprano was fairly supported now by a well-balanced troupe, and relieved of the responsibility of having the weight entirely on her devoted shoulders.

On Thursday, February 21st, 1850, "Linda di Chamouni" was given. Linda, Miss Hayes; Pierotto, Miss Poole; Madelina, Miss Norman; Carlo, Mr. Travers; Il Marchese, Signor Polonini; Antonio, Herr Mengis; Il Prefetto, Signor Salabert; L'Intendente, Mr. Houghton. Miss Hayes had created a great sensation in the part of Linda during her Continental tour. Indeed the character was peculiarly suited to her capabilities, at once lively and pathetic—qualities which her Celtic nature portrayed with admirable effect. All the other parts were efficiently filled, and the performance was a marked success. On Saturday, 23rd, " Linda " was repeated.

On Monday, February 25th, " Norma " was the Opera. Norma, Miss C. Hayes; Adalgisa, Miss Poole; Pollio, Mr. Travers; Oroveso, Polonini; Flavio, Mr. Houghton. Mr. Travers, whose voice was a *tenore robusto*, made a hit in the *role* of Pollio, the music of which requires much power from beginning to end.

On Tuesday, February 26th, "La Sonnambula" was given. Amina, Miss C. Hayes; Lisa, Miss Norman; Teresa, Miss Fitzgerald; Elvino, Mr. Travers; Rodolpho, Polonini; Alessio, Mr. Coleman. This was Miss Hayes' first appearance as Amina. "La Sonnambula" was then in the zenith of its popularity. The simplicity of the story, and the complete and happy adaptation of the melodies to the plot, certainly charmed the world for years. Perhaps no other Opera, except " Trovatore," has been so many times given. All the great soprani ambitioned to excel in Amina, and nearly all had been heard in Dublin in the Opera. The climax of perfection seemed to have been reached in Jenny Lind's version. It was, therefore, a trying ordeal for the native soprano, coming so soon after the "Swedish nightingale." Doubts were entertained as to the result, but all uncertainty vanished after the first scene. " Care Compagni " was faultless, and the " Sovra il sen " enchanted the audience. The sleeping scene was considered by some equal to that of the fair Swede—it certainly did not suffer by comparison—and the finale, " Ah, non giunge," was a triumph. There cannot be a doubt but that the performance of Amina alone would have sufficed to establish Catherine Hayes as a great lyric artiste. All the other characters were well filled; but, unfortunately, at that period the travelling Italian companies were not so complete as at the present day, and we were obliged, as will be perceived by the cast, to "fill up" the small parts. Poor Coleman, who played Alessio on this occasion, has been before alluded to. He was a most useful member of the chorus—indeed leader of the basses—a good reader, and frequently performed small parts in English Opera. Alessio is a comic part, and John was not funny. When he entered, one pit-goer asked another: "Who the d—l is that?" The other answered: " I know him well—he is a fishmonger." And so he was; at six o'clock in the morning he might be seen in Pill-lane, "knocking down" an immense "lot" of cod or haddock, as the case might be. At twelve he would be at the Theatre, assiduously rehearsing his part, and punctually again at his post in the evening. He was for several years *primo basso* in the Catholic Cathedral,

Marlborough-street. To return to his Alessio. He danced merrily on with Lisa, and all was smooth until, at Amina's entrance, all turned to greet her. Alessio turned round with the rest, and at the moment a "lad." called out: "Hallo, Fish, there's a hole in your stockin'!" Of course, a universal shout of laughter followed, in which Miss Hayes heartily joined.

On Thursday, February 28th, "in compliance with repeated applications, and in consequence of the overflowing house which witnessed its repetition on Saturday," Linda was repeated.

On Saturday, March 2nd, "Lucia" was given. Lucia, Miss Hayes; Edgardo, Travers; Ashton, Mengis; Raymond, Polonini; Norman, Salabert; Arturo, Houghton.

Monday, March 4th, there was a repetition of "Sonnambula;" on Tuesday, March 5th, "Norma;" Thursday, March 7th, "Linda," after which "Terence's Farewell to Kathleen," written by Lady Dufferin, was sung by the *prima-donna*. Friday, "Lucia;" Saturday, "Sonnambula"—last night; but on Thursday, the 21st, Mr. Calcraft announced that "he had been enabled to effect a re-engagement with Miss Catherine Hayes for two nights only, on her return from the South of Ireland, previous to her appearance at Her Majesty's Theatre in London." On Thursday, 21st March, "La Sonnambula" (as before), and on Saturday, "Linda" were performed to crammed houses.

Catherine Hayes visited Cork and Limerick during the interval, where she, as might be expected, received great ovations. In Cork the Theatre was not sufficiently large to accommodate the numbers. But in Limerick the excitement was indeed great. It was her native city. At a very early age she displayed rare musical promise, and had been endowed by nature with a wonderful soprano voice. The good Bishop of Limerick (with whom the mother of the artiste resided in the capacity of housekeeper) discovering those qualities, contributed a sufficient sum to allow of their cultivation; and accordingly Catherine proceeded to Dublin, and became a pupil of A. Sapio, under whose auspices she appeared at the Anacreontic and other musical societies with great success; and after some time proceeded to Italy. She quickly advanced, and gained a Continental reputation, which, of course, rapidly spread to England, and the most lucrative engagements ensued, managers vying actively to secure her services.

Naturally the public of Limerick were proud of sending forth the first great Irish *prima-donna*, and expectation was at the highest pitch when the announcements appeared. Places were all secured in advance, and, like that at Cork, the Theatre was not sufficiently large for the demand. "La Sonnambula" was the first Opera. A rather strange scene occurred on the occasion. When the orchestra commenced the introduction to the Opera, the occupants of the pit and gallery called out for "Garryowen" (their national tune). Of course, no notice was taken; the music proceeded, but the uproar increased until it became hopeless to continue, and "Garryowen! Garryowen!" was the cry. The leader turned round and remonstrated with some respectable-looking young men in the pit, asked them what they wished. They replied, "We all want 'Garryowen.'" The leader argued and said: "Surely you won't force us to play 'Garryowen' as an overture to an Italian Opera! What will the musical world say of your taste should such an occurrence take place?" The spokesman seemed to see the force of the argument, and conversed with those around him; then said: "It's no use, Mr. Levey; they must have 'Garryowen.'" A long parley ensued between the leader of the band and the leader of the malcontents; the latter turning first to the orchestra and then towards his friends with the *pros* and *cons*, and evidently trying to make peace. At last, after a long diplomatic discussion, a compromise was effected, by which it was conceded, on the part of the management, that "Garryowen" should be played after the first Act. This arrangement was carried out amidst the most vehement applause, the tune proceeding while Catherine Hayes was on the stage, having, of course, received a universal "call" after the first Act.

One of the most agreeable occurrences of the Limerick engagement was a grand pic-nic given to the star by the Messrs. Beale, to which several distinguished citizens of Limerick were invited. Both the Beales were present—Fred, as the celebrated and popular *impresario* was familiarly called, and his no less talented son, Willert, everybody's favourite. There were also Dr. Joy, acting manager, who made hosts of friends wherever he went; James Price (then editor of the *Evening Packet*), who came expressly from Dublin to collect materials for a biography of Miss Hayes; Michael Joseph Barry, then editor of the Cork *Southern Reporter;* Mr. Calcraft; the present writer, &c., &c. It was, indeed, a day to remember. The "spread" took place *al fresco* on the banks of the glorious Shannon, at Castleconnell. Mrs. Hayes, the worthy mother of Catherine, was, of course, present. Toasts, songs, glees, orations, &c., &c., were the order of the day. M. J. Barry gave the health of the "star" in his own felicitous style, infusing therein some of the burning thoughts of his writings in the "Spirit of the Nation." Wild hurras followed. Catherine was "a jolly gay fellow;" she was familiarly associated with "all good lasses," &c., &c. She responded herself, and gave "The Last Rose of Summer." The "feast of reason and flow of soul" prevailed. J. Price, who had been sitting beside Mrs. Hayes, said to her: "You should be proud of this scene; few mothers possess such a daughter. Do you not feel happy?" Mrs. Hayes replied, with ecstasy: "Oh! my dear Mr. Price, *I'm at the summit of my climax.*"

Miss Hayes had a short and successful re-engagement, commencing Monday, October 21st, 1850. There was a repetition of the usual *repertoire.*

"Italian Opera for seven nights only, commencing on Monday, February 10th, 1851," was thus announced: "The unrivalled *prima-donna,* Mdme. Grisi, supported by the two eminent tenors, Mr. Sims Reeves and Signor Ricciardi; Mdlle. Bassano, Herr Mengis, Signor Pattoni, &c., &c. The first four nights will be Monday, 10th,

Tuesday, 11th, Thursday, 13th, and Saturday, 15th. In consequence of the unprecedented expense attending this engagement, the prices will be as follows :—Dress Circle, 8s.; Second Circle, 5s.; Pit, 3s.; Middle Gallery, 2s.; Upper Gallery, 1s. Conductor, Mr. Lavenu; Leader, Mr. Levey."

The following notice appeared on Friday, 7th: " Mr. Calcraft regrets exceedingly to state that he has most unexpectedly received a medical certificate from Dr. Tyler Smith, Bolton-street, Piccadilly, London, stating that Madame Grisi has been taken suddenly ill, and is totally unable to fulfil any professional engagement. The Italian Opera will commence with Mr. and Mrs. Sims Reeves, Mdlle. Bassano, Herr Mengis, Signor Pattoni, &c., &c., on Monday next, as announced, with the favourite Opera of 'Lucia di Lammermoor.' In consequence of the disappointment, the following scale of prices will be adopted :—Dress Circle, 5s.; Second Circle, 3s.; Pit, 2s.; First Circle, 1s.; Upper Gallery, 6d."

On Monday, the same announcement, but stating the engagement would commence on Wednesday, and Signor Ricciardi's name withdrawn.

On Friday, the 13th, the following appeared :—

"Theatre Royal, Dublin.

"The following telegraphic message has been forwarded from Harrowgate, dated Monday evening : 'Mrs. Sims Reeves is ill in bed. The doctor says she cannot leave this until Wednesday morning. Send the libretto.' Mr. Calcraft, in announcing, as he does with much regret, the above additional disappointment, thinks it right to state in the most explicit terms that not the slightest blame can be attached to any person whatever for a casualty which could not possibly be foreseen or provided against. The first Italian Opera is, therefore, unavoidably postponed until Saturday next, the 15th inst., when will be performed 'Lucia di Lammermoor.' The appearance of Mr. and Mrs. Sims Reeves at the Philharmonic Concert on Friday will, it is hoped, sufficiently satisfy the public that no further delay will take place."

On Friday, 14th, the following appeared :—

"Mr. Calcraft again regrets to be under the necessity of stating that another communication has been received, to the effect that Mrs. Sims Reeves will not be sufficiently recovered to leave Harrowgate until this day (Friday). The Opera of 'Lucia di Lammermoor,' announced for to-morrow (Saturday), is therefore unavoidably postponed until Monday next, the 17th inst."

The next announcement as follows :—

"Theatre Royal, Dublin.

"Mr. Calcraft has much pleasure in announcing that Mr. and Mrs. Sims Reeves (late Miss Lucombe) have arrived in Dublin. The series of Italian Operas will, therefore, commence this evening (Monday, 17th). The Company includes" (&c., &c., as before). "'Lucia di Lammermoor.' Edgardo, Mr. Sims Reeves ; Lucia, Mrs. Sims Reeves ; Colonel Ashton, Herr Mengis ; Raimondo, Signor Pattoni, &c. Tuesday, 18th, 'La Sonnambula.' Amina, Mrs. Sims Reeves ; Elvino, Mr. Sims Reeves ; Count Rodolpho, Herr Mengis. Thursday, 20th, 'Lucia,' as before. Saturday, 22nd, 'I Puritani.' Lord Arthur Talbot, Mr. Sims Reeves ; Elvira, Mrs. Sims Reeves ; Sir George Walton, Signor Pattoni ; Sir Richard Forth, Herr Mengis. Monday, 24th, 'Ernani.' Ernani, Mr. Sims Reeves ; Elvira, Mrs. Sims Reeves ; Don Carlos, Herr Mengis ; Don Ruy Gomez, Signor Pattoni. Wednesday, 26th, 'I Puritani,' as before. Friday, 28th, 'La Sonnambula.' Cast as before, with the addition of—Lisa, Miss Norman ; Teresa, Miss Fitzgerald. Saturday, March 1st. Benefit of Mr. and Mrs. Sims Reeves. Commencing with Third Act of

'Lucia;' after which the Second Act of 'I Puritani.' To conclude with (in two Acts) 'The Beggar's Opera.' Captain Macheath, Mr. Sims Reeves; Mat of the Mint, Herr Mengis."

On Friday Evening, September 17th, 1852, the following Company commenced an engagement, announced for six nights only :—Madame Grisi, Mdlle. Bertrandi, Signor Mario, Signor Galvani, Signor F. Lablache, Signor Lusini, Signor Galli, Signor Salabert. Conductor, Mr. F. Mori. Leader, Mr. Levey. The following were the casts :—

Friday, September 17th. "Lucrezia Borgia." Lucrezia Borgia, Madame Grisi; Maffio Orsini, Mdlle. Bertrandi; Alfonso, F. Lablache; Gennaro, Mario; Astolfo, Benelli; Petrucci, Galli; Gazella, Lavini; Rustighello, Salabert; Liverotto, Casaboni; Vittellozzo, Fiorini; Gubetta, Susini.

Saturday, September 18th. "Norma." Norma, Grisi; Adalgisa, Bertrandi; Pollio, Mario; Oroveso, Susini; Clotilda, Miss J. Braun; Flavio, Galli.

Monday Evening, September 20th, "I Puritani." Elvira, Grisi; Henrietta, Miss J. Braun; Walton, Galli; Sir George, Susini; Talbot, Mario; Forth, F. Lablache; Bueno, Casaboni.

Tuesday, September 21st. "Don Pasquale." Norina, Grisi; Ernesto, Mario; Malatesta, F. Lablache; Don Pasquale, Susini; Notary, Galli. Concluding with the last Act of "Lucia." Lucia, Mdlle, Bertrandi; Edgardo, Signor Galvani; Bidebent, Susini.

Friday Evening, September 24th. "Don Giovanni." Don Giovanni, F. Lablache; Don Ottavio, Mario; Don

Pedro, Galli; Leporello, Susini; Masetto, Salabert; Donna Anna, Grisi; Zerlina, Bertrandi; Donna Elvira, Miss Clarke.

Saturday Evening, September 25th. " Norma " (cast as before); concluding with the last Act of "L'Elisire d'Amore." Nina, Mdlle. Bertrandi; Gianetta, Miss J. Braun; Nemorino, Galvani; Doctor Dulcamara, Susini; Sergeant Belcore, F. Lablache.

The following announcement appeared the following Monday: " Farewell Engagement of Madame Grisi.— Mr. Harris has the honour to announce the re-engagement of the Italian Company for three performances only, and begs to state that this is the last opportunity Madame Grisi can possibly have of appearing in Dublin." Accordingly, on Monday evening, October 4th, 1852, was given " Don Giovanni," with cast as before; after which Signor Mario sang "Com 'e gentil," from " Don Pasquale." On Tuesday, " I Puritani " was given, as before. On Wednesday, October 6th, the first and second Acts of " Lucrezia Borgia," with cast as before, and the last Act of " Lucia ;" the last Act of " La Sonnambula " (Amina, Bertrandi; Lisa, Miss Clarke; Teresa, Miss J. Braun; Rodolpho, F. Lablache; Elvino, Mario); concluding with the last Act of " L'Elisire d'Amore," as before.

This was the first engagement of Italian Opera under the management of Mr. Harris, and proved a great success. It was under the special patronage of the Lord Lieutenant and the Countess of Eglinton, and was remarkable for the earliest announcement of the *last* appearance of Grisi. Several others to the same effect subsequently took place; at last repeated too often for the fame of the then acknowledged Queen of Song. Miss Clarke, who performed Donna Elvira in "Don Giovanni," and Lisa in "Sonnambula," was a pupil of Gustavus Geary, the popular tenor vocalist of Dublin, and then a vicar of the Cathedral churches. Miss Clarke's voice was a pure soprano, and well cultivated. She acquitted herself most creditably, and to the entire satisfaction of the public, although having undertaken the part at a short notice, in consequence of the disappointment of one of the Italian artistes. Miss J. Braun was also a resident of Dublin, daughter of a bandmaster.

No Italian Opera engagement took place during 1853; but on Monday, September 11th, 1854, a most attractive Company commenced a series of Operas. The artistes were:—Mdlle. Sophie Cruvelli, Mdlle. Marai, Mdlle, Albini, Mdme. Albini, Signor Tamberlik, Signor Tagliafico, Signor Fortini, Signor Polonini, Signor Luchesi, Signor Santi, Signor Monterosi. Regisseur, Mr. A. Harris; Conductor, Mr. Alfred Mellon (Mr. Benedict's name had been announced, but was withdrawn); Leader, Mr. Levey.

The chorus on this occasion was much strengthened by the addition of several members of the Covent Garden choral department. The dresses were also from the same establishment, and the Operas were consequently produced on a scale of great completeness. They were announced "under the patronage of their Excellencies the Lord Lieutenant and the Countess of St. Germains." The following were the casts:—

Monday, September 11th, 1854. "Norma." Norma, Cruvelli; Adalgisa, Mdlle. Marai; Clotilda, Mdme. Albini; Pollio, Signor Tamberlik; Oroveso, Signor Tagliafico; Flavio, Signor Santi.

Tuesday, September 12th. "Sonnambula." Amina, Mdlle. Marai; Teresa, Mdme. Albini; Lisa, Mdlle. Albini; Rodolpho, Polonini; Elvino, Signor Luchesi.

Wednesday, September 13th. "Otello." Otello, Tamberlik; Desdemona, Mdlle. Cruvelli; Elmiro, Signor Fortini; Rodrigo, Signor Luchesi; Iago, Signor Tagliafico; Emilia, Mdlle. Albini; Doge, Signor Polonini.

Thursday, September 14th. "Fidelio." Leonora, Mdlle. Cruvelli; Margarita, Mdlle. Marai; Rocco, Signor Fortini; Pizarro, Signor Tagliafico; Il Ministro, Signor Polonini; Jacquino, Signor Santi; Ferdinando, Signor Tamberlik.

Friday, September 15th. In consequence of numerous inquiries, "Il Barbiere di Siviglia." Rosina, Mdlle. Marai; Bertha, Mdlle, Albini; Count Almaviva, Signor Luchesi; Bartolo, Signor Polonini; Basilio, Signor Fortini; Fiorello, Signor Santi; Figaro, Signor Tagliafico. Concluding with one Act of "Massaniello." Massaniello, Signor Tamberlik; Borella, Polonini; Pietro, Signor Tagliafico; Fenella, Mdlle. Ernestine St. Louin.

Saturday, September 16th. "Ernani." Ernani, Signor Tamberlik; Ruy Gomez, Signor Tagliafico; Charles V., Signor Fortini; Riccardo, Signor Santi; Iago, Signor Polonini; Elvira, Mdlle. Cruvelli; Giovanna, Mdlle. Albini.

Monday, September 18th. "Norma" was repeated, for the benefit of Mdlle. Cruvelli.

On Tuesday, 19th, there was a repetition of "Otello," for the benefit of Signor Tamberlik—last night of the engagement.

The Operas on this occasion were performed in a style worthy of London. The chorus was more numerous and complete than on former occasions; and the dresses, from the Covent Garden wardrobe, perfect. Sophie Cruvelli appeared like a brilliant meteor, and during her short and extraordinary career, astonished and delighted the musical world. The impression left on those who had the good fortune to hear and see her could never be obliterated. Her voice—a mezzo soprano of great compass—seemed to contain all the perfections of every register of the female voice concentrated. It bore no comparison to that of any other artiste. It was rich beyond compare, and the equality "all round" was wonderful, the highest notes never losing in quality. In fact, words must fail in describing the qualities of this great artiste, who too soon disappeared from the lyric stage. Coming after Grisi, Cruvelli had a severe ordeal to undergo, commencing with "Norma;" but her rendering was so totally different and original, that universal delight took the place of comparison. The career of this great artiste was of short duration, but her many friends had satisfaction in knowing that she had made an exalted marriage.

On Tuesday, May 15th, appeared an Italian Opera Company, including Mdme. Alboni, Mdlle. Jenny Bauer,

Herr Reichart, Signor Susini, Signor Lorenzo. Violinist, Herr Ernst; Conductor, Signor Li Calsi.

On Tuesday, 15th, was given "Il Barbiere." Rosina, Alboni; Almaviva, Herr Reichart; Figaro, Signor Lorenzo; Bartolo, Signor Susini.

On Wednesday, 16th, "La Cenerentola" was performed. Cenerentola, Alboni; Dandini, Lorenzo; Don Magnifico, Susini; Ramiro, Reichart; Clorinda, Miss J. Cruise; Thisbe, Miss F. Cruise.

The Misses Cruise proved themselves equally capable in Italian as in English music. They were highly complimented by Alboni on their finished style; she remarked that she had never sung with such good "ill-natured" sisters. The Misses Cruise studied with Mr. Thomas Blanchard, perhaps one of the most careful and efficient vocal masters in existence. Happily he still resides in Dublin, to impart the secrets of his art to those who are fortunate enough to place themselves under his tuition.

Then followed, on Thursday, May 17th, "Lucia." Lucia, Mdlle. Bauer; Aston, Signor Lorenzo; Edgardo, Herr Reichart; Raimondo, Signor Susini. On Friday, a repetition of "Cenerentola." On Saturday, "La Sonnambula." Amina, Alboni; Lisa, Miss F. Cruise Teresa, Miss J. Cruise; Elvino, Herr Reichart; Conte, Signor Lorenzo; Alessio, Mr. Stinton.

This was Signor Li Calsi's first visit to Dublin, when he gave ample proof of the efficiency and experience which have since caused his name to be welcomed in Ireland whenever it appears on a list of Italian artistes.

Herr Reichart also appeared for the first time—an excellent vocalist; he was, besides, composer of some popular songs—" Thou art so near and yet so far," amongst others. It was likewise the *debut* here of Susini, a first-rate *basso profondo*, who won golden opinions during his stay. Mr. Stinton was one of the stock : "Good-natured Jack" was his kindly title amongst his fellows. He had a nice tenor voice, was a fair musician, and could assist with his brush in the scene-painter's room; indeed, a most useful member, as he proved by acquitting himself tolerably in small Italian Opera parts. He married the daughter of the celebrated Pierce Egan (author of " Life in London "), who was the stock " chambermaid " and " soubrette " of the Company, and a favourite with the Dublin public.

The Opera was each night agreeably and delightfully varied by the performance of Herr Ernst, then the most finished of living violinists, whose wonderful playing was fully appreciated. This great artiste combined with his remarkable musical abilities the most accomplished mind and fascinating manner. He had just returned from a long visit to Sir E. Lytton Bulwer, who was his ardent and enthusiastic friend and admirer.

The next Italian Company commenced an engagement on Monday, August 6th, 1855. The bills were headed " Last performance of Madame Grisi in Dublin." The troupe consisted of Madame Grisi, Madame Gassier, Madame Dediee, Mdlle. Sedlatzek, Madame Heinrich, Signor Mario, Signor Lorini, Signor Gassier, Signor Susini, Signor Galli, Signor Sante.

Conductor, Signor Li Calsi. The following Operas were given :—

Monday, August 6th. "Norma." Norma, Grisi; Adalgisa, Mdlle. Sedlatzek; Clotilda, Madame Heinrich; Pollio, Signor Lorini; Flavio, Signor Sante; Oroveso, Signor Susini.

Tuesday, August 7th. "La Sonnambula." Amina, Madame Gassier; Lisa, Mdlle. Sedlatzek; Teresa, Madame Heinrich; Elvino, Signor Mario; Count Rodolpho, Signor Gassier.

Wednesday, August 8th. "Lucrezia Borgia." Lucrezia, Grisi; Orsini, Mdlle. Dedice; Gennaro, Mario; Don Alfonso, Susini.

Thursday, August 9th. "Don Pasquale." Norina, Madame Gassier; Ernesto, Signor Mario; Malatesta, Signor Gassier; Pasquale, Susini.

On Friday, August 10th, "La Sonnambula" was repeated; and

On Saturday, August 11th, "Semiramide" was produced. Semiramide, Grisi; Azema, Mdlle. Sedlatzek; Arsace, Mdlle. Dediee; Idreno, Signor Lorini; Assur, Signor Gassier; Oroe, Signor Susini.

On Monday, August 13th, "Lucrezia Borgia" was repeated, for the benefit of Signor Mario; and

On Saturday, "Norma" (as before), for the benefit of Madame Grisi.

Grisi and Mario left, and a re-engagement for three nights took place with the remainder of the Company, August 20th, 21st, and 22nd; but the absence of the great luminaries caused apathy with the public, although the prices were lowered, the houses were not up to "concert pitch." Madame Gassier was, however, a most accomplished soprano, with an extraordinary compass of voice, more particularly in the upper register. She frequently touched A in alt in her scale-singing, which was very perfect. Her husband was also one of the best of baritones. He had formed himself on the great Tamburini, and his wonderful flexibility displayed itself remarkably in the difficult music of Assur (Semiramide). He astonished the instrumentalists of the orchestra by the perfection of a descending scale, which he introduced in the first movement of "Vieni la mia Vendetta" (Lucia). Gassier was most amusing in private circles; he imitated closely with his voice all instruments, frequently causing merry interruptions at the rehearsals by coming over to the orchestra and playing the bassoon on his walking stick, the laughter of the performers causing much delay. He was, of course, "pulled-up" by the stage-manager, but the applause of his auditors fully recompensed him. One day, after dinner, at the hospitable house of a well-known and much-respected medical gentleman, Gassier went to the door of the dining-room (which opened inwards), stood on a chair, held the door above with his left hand, grasped an imaginary bow with his right hand and scraped away at the door, imitating at the same time the double-bass to perfection. Gassier died a few years ago in Italy, and was much regretted by the profession, of which he was an ornament, as well as by many personal friends.

First performance of "Il Trovatore."

The next Italian Opera engagement was, indeed, in many ways, one to be remembered. The bills were headed: "Royal Italian Opera, Covent Garden, under the patronage of his Excellency the Lord Lieutenant. Arrangements having been effected by Mr. Harris and Messrs. Cramer, Beale & Co. with the above great lyric establishment, for the performance of Operas by the same artistes as at the Theatre Royal, Covent Garden, it is respectfully announced that a series of Italian Operas will be given, commencing on Monday, September 3rd, and terminating on Tuesday, September 11th, assisted by the following eminent artistes:—Madame Viardot Garcia, Mdlle. Marai, Mdlle. Heinrich, Signor Tamberlik, Signor Gardoni, Signor Graziani, Signor Polonine, Signor Tagliafico, Signor Santi. Conductor, Mr. Alfred Mellon; Prompter, Signor Monterasi; Regisseur, Mr. A. Harris. There will be an important addition to the orchestra and chorus from the Royal Italian Opera, and the Operas will be produced on a scale of greater magnificence than hitherto attempted."

On Monday, September 3rd, 1855. "The last new Opera, as produced in London with such brilliant success, 'Il Trovatore,' with new scenery, dresses, &c., &c., and the Operas produced with the same completeness as at the Royal Italian Opera, Covent Garden. Leonora, Mdlle. Marai; Azucena, Madame Viardot Garcia; Manrico, Signor Tamberlik; Il Conte di Luna, Signor Graziani; Ferrando, Signor Polonini; Riuz, Signor Santi." This was, of course, the first performance of " Trovatore " in Dublin—and such a performance! Although a great number of years have elapsed, many survive who were present, and still bear witness to the extraordinary impression created on this occasion. The music of "Young Italy" had scarcely yet been heard, at least interpreted, as it was in this instance. "Ernani" had been done in English; but Verdi's great work, which, however captious critics may condemn it, still holds its ground, was indeed a novel and startling event in Dublin. Glorious representatives of all the characters have since appeared, but first impressions go a great way. Certainly the Azucena, as an "all round" performance, has never been equalled; but all the lyric world with one consent submit to the matchless genius of Viardot. The effect produced by Graziani was also extraordinary; a new era in baritone singing seemed to have commenced—the wonderful beauty, extent, and equality of his voice astonished and delighted all. In the "Il Balen," which was sung in the original key (B flat), the G above was taken and sustained with extreme accuracy, and in exquisite tune, a note usually heard only from tenors. The remembrance of this first appearance of Graziani is still fresh in the minds of those who were present on the occasion. Marai was an excellent Leonora, and one can imagine Tamberlik, then in his zenith, singing and acting Manrico. Although the "Ut de portrine" had not appeared in the 'Di quella pira," still the performance all through was marked with wonderful force and vigour. Polonini and Santi contributed in no small degree to the almost perfect performance.

On Tuesday, September 4th, "Il Barbiere" was performed. Rosina, Viardot; Berta, Heinrich; Bartolo, Polonini; Basilio, Tagliafico; Fiorello, Santi; Almaviva, Gardoni; Figaro, Graziani. This Opera was remarkable for the excellence of the *ensemble*.

On Wednesday, September 5th. "Lucia de Lammermoor." Lucia, Mdlle. Marai; Edgardo, Gardoni; Raimondo, Polonini; Arturo, Santi; Normanno, Mattoni. Concluding with second Act of "Massaniello." Massaniello, Tamberlik; Pietro, Tagliafico; Borello, Polonini.

On Thursday, September 6th, was produced, for the first time in Dublin, Meyerbeer's grand Opera of "Le Prophete," with the dresses, decorations, suits of armour, and appointments from the Royal Italian Opera. Fides (her original part, being expressly composed for her), Madame Viardot Garcia; Bertha, Mdlle. Marai; Jean of Leyden, Tamberlik; Zacharia, Tagliafico; Jonas, Santi; Mathisen, Polonini; Count D'Oberthal, Graziani. This was, perhaps, the most complete representation which ever took place in the Theatre Royal, not only with reference to the artistes engaged, but to the accessories, the *mise en scene*, &c., &c. It required a vocal and dramatic genius, such as Viardot, to grasp the character of Fides. It cannot give offence to say that all succeeding attempts have been imitations, and the nearer they approached the original "creation" the more successful. The same remarks will apply to Tamberlik's performance of "The Prophet," a rare combination of marvellous power and art. The music was rather "advanced" to please the general public of the day, but all gave willing testimony to the rare merits of the work.

On Friday, September 7th, "I Puritani." Elvira, Marai; Henrietta, Madame Heinrich; Lord Walton, Polonini; Sir George, Tagliafico; Sir Richard Forth, Graziani; Bruno, Santi; Lord Talbot, Gardoni.

On Saturday, September 8th, "Otello." Desdemona, Viardot Garcia; Emilia, Madame Heinrich; Elmiro, Tagliafico; Iago, Graziani; Rodrigo, Gardoni; Il Doge, Polonini; Otello, Tamberlik. It was in this Opera that Tamberlik startled the musical world by his C sharp from the chest. Duprez had already become celebrated by his wonderful "Ut de portrine" in "William Tell," but Tamberlik's effort eclipsed that of the great French tenor. The C sharp had a pure metallic ring about it, and the pitites stood up from their seats in wondering amazement. Viardot's Desdemona was a study in every particular.

On Monday, September 10th, "Il Trovatore" was repeated (cast as before); and

On Tuesday, September 11th, there was a repetition of "Le Prophete."

This brilliant engagement concluded with an extra night, Saturday, September 15th. "Don Giovanni." Donna Anna, Viardot; Donna Elvira, Madame Marai; Zerlina, Madame Sedlatzek; Don Giovanni, Graziani; Leporello, Tagliafico; Il Commendatore, Polonini; Ottavio, Tamberlik. A glorious performance of "The Don."

On Monday, September 15th, 1856, Mr. Harris arranged with the firm of Cramer & Beale for a series of Italian Operas. The following artistes formed the Company:—Mdme. Grisi, Mdme. Lorini, Mdme. Zedlatzek,

Mdme. Amadei, Mdme. Gassier, Signor Mario, Mr. Tennant, Signor Lorini, Signor Albicini, Signor Luigi Mei, Signor Gregorio, Signor Graziani, Signor Rovere, Mons. Gassier, Herr Formes. Conductor, Signor Li Calsi; Leader, Mr. Levey; Prompter, Signor Galli.

The Operas were :—Monday, Sept. 15th, " Ernani." Elvira, Mdme. Lorini (first appearance); Ernani, Signor Lorini; Carlo, Graziani; Silva, Mons. Gassier.

Tuesday, September 16th. "Lucrezia Borgia." Lucrezia, Grizi; Orsini, Amadei; Gennaro, Mario; Duca, Gassier; Gubetta, Signor Rovere (his first appearance); Rustighello, Signor Albicini (his first appearance).

Wednesday, 17th. "Il Barbiere." Rosina, Mdme. Gassier; Almaviva, Mario; Bartolo, Rovere; Figaro, Mons. Gassier; Basilio, Herr Formes.

Thursday, 18th. "Norma." Norma, Grisi; Adalgisa, Mdlle. Lorini; Pollio, Signor Lorini; Oroveso, Herr Formes.

Friday, 19th. "Don Pasquale." Norina, Mdme. Gassier; Ernesto, Mr. Tennant (his first appearance); Don Pasquale, Rovere; Malatesta, Gassier.

Saturday, 20th. "La Favorita." Grisi, Mario, Graziani, and Formes.

Monday, 22nd. "Il Trovatore." Leonora, Grisi; Azucena, Mdme. Amadei; Manrico, Mario; Conte di Luna, Graziani; Ferrando, Gassier.

Tuesday, 23rd. One Act of "Ernani" (as before); the second Act of "Il Barbiere," and last Act of "Don Pasquale" (as before).

Wednesday, 24th. "Norma" (cast as before).

Thursday, 25th. "Il Trovatore" (repeat).

Friday, 26th. One Act of "Puritani"—Elvira, Mdme. Lorini; Arturo, Mario; Ricardo, Graziani; Georgio, Formes; concluding with "La Sonnambula"—Amina, Mdme. Gassier; Teresa, Mdlle. Belosio; Elvino, Albicini; Rodolpho, Gassier.

Saturday, 27th. For the benefit of Mdme. Grisi and Signor Mario. "Lucrezia Borgia." Cast as before. Concluding with the second Act of "Il Barbiere."

Nothing worthy of remark occurred during this engagement, except the appearance of Mr. Tennant, who had been known as a "distinguished amateur" in Dublin. He possessed a nicely cultivated tenor voice, but not sufficiently powerful for the lyric stage. He was, however, making some way, when his career was cut short by an early death.

An Italian Opera engagement for four nights, commencing on October 14th, 1856, with—Mdlle. Piccolomini, Mdlle. Borgaro, Signor Rossi, Signor Belletti, Mdlle. Berti, Signor Pierini, Signor Kinni, and Charles Braham. Conductor, Signor Bonetti.

On Tuesday, October 14th, 1856, was produced Verdi's Opera, "La Traviata." Violetta, Mdlle. Piccolomini; Floria Bervois, Mdlle. Borgaro; Amiria, Mdlle. Berti; Alfredo, Mr. Charles Braham; Dottori Grenvil, Rossi; Baron Dauphol, Signor Pierini; Marchese D'Obigny, Kinni; Germont, Signor Belletti.

The Opera of "La Traviata" had created a great sensation in London, in many ways. The subject, taken from the celebrated French novel, "La Dame aux Camelias," gave much offence to the fastidious portion of the music-loving public. The Opera at first rather "flagged," notwithstanding Piccolomini's extraordinary representation of Violetta. Some strong letters appeared in the *Times* and other journals, condemning the subject as entirely unfit for the stage, being calculated to excite sympathy with immorality, &c., &c. Replies to those epistles appeared from Mr. Lumley, then Manager of Her Majesty's. A long correspondence, very animated on both sides, was the result. This had the effect of exciting public curiosity to such an extreme degree, that the houses "pulled up" considerably; and at last crowds rushed nightly to see "La Traviata." It was rumoured by some of the manager's kind friends that he was the author of all the letters, *pro* and *con*—an assertion never proved. However, the success must not be altogether attributed to this newspaper controversy, for Piccolomini was a genius in her way. She was not a great vocalist; her scale singing was defective, but her beautiful sympathetic voice carried her through the music; and her acting, particularly in the tragic scenes, was fine beyond precedent, compared with lyric artistes. Her assumption of the consumptive cough was most distressingly natural; and the death-scene produced quite as much sympathy, and caused as death-like a silence, as the best of our tragedians in the last scene of "The Gamester." A rumour, circulated in Dublin, that the young artiste was related to the Cardinal of the same name, added much to the success of the engagement.

Charles Braham was a son of the veteran tenor; his

voice in many particulars resembled that of his father; and although possessing some of the imperfections of his great parent, he was in marked favour with the public.

Signor Belletti was one of the most accomplished artistes of the day—a highly-finished vocalist and a sound musician.

The character of Violetta has been essayed with much success by many great artistes, but there was a specialty attached to Piccolomini's version which left a lasting impression. It would be unjust not to record the great capacity of Signor Bonetti as Conductor. This was his first and only visit to Dublin; he enjoyed an extended Continental reputation.

On Wednesday, October 15th, "La Figlia del Reggimento" was given. Maria, Mdlle. Piccolomini; La Marchesa, Mdlle. Borgaro; Tonio, Mr. C. Braham; Corporale, Signor Kinni; Sulpizio, Signor Belletti.

Piccolomini's Maria was highly characteristic and animated, but, as might be supposed, the vocalism fell far short of that of Jenny Lind.

On Thursday, October 16th, "Don Pasquale," was performed. Norina, Piccolomini; Ernesta, Charles Braham; Malatesta, Belletti; Don Pasquale, Rossi; Notaro, Mariani.

On Saturday, October 18th, the engagement concluded with a repetition of "La Traviata." Cast as before.

Piccolomini's fascinating manner attracted many friends, and during her short career her engagements were most profitable to her managers and to herself.

In March, 1857, the following announcement appeared: " Mr. Harris has the honour to announce that, in compliance with the earnest solicitations of her numerous admirers, and the express wish of the public in general, he has made arrangements with the celebrated artiste, Miss Catherine Hayes, to appear for a limited number of nights in Italian Operas, supported by an efficient Company, selected from the principal Opera-houses of Europe. *Prima-donna*, Miss Catherine Hayes; Contralto, Mdlle. L. Corelli; Tenors, Signori Volpini (his first appearance), Mr. W. J. Tennant; Baritones, Signor Badiali (from La Scala, Milan; his first appearance), Signor Pierini; Buffo, Signor Maggiorotti (his first appearance); Signor Mariani. Conductor, Herr Anschuez; Prompter, Signor Galli; Stage Director, Mons. Martini. The orchestra and chorus will be considerably augmented, under the direction of Mr. Levey."

On Monday, March 16th, 1857, " Lucia di Lammermoor." Lucia, Miss Hayes; Aston, Signor Badiali; Edgardo, Signor Volpini; Raimondo, Signor Pierini; Arturo, Signor Mariani.

On Thursday, March 19th, " Don Pasquale." Norina, Catherine Hayes; Ernesto, Mr. Tennant; Malatesta, Signor Badiali; Don Pasquale, Signor Maggiorotti.

On Saturday, March 21st, " Norma." Norma, Catherine Hayes; Adalgisa, Miss Julia Cruise; Pollio, Signor Volpini; Flavio, Mariani; Oroveso, Signor Badiali.

On Monday, March 23td, " Linda di Chamouni." Linda, Miss C. Hayes; Pierotto, Mdlle. Corelli; Carlo,

Mr. Tennant; Intendente, Signor Mariani; Antonio, Signor Badiali; Marquis, Maggiorotti.
Thursday, March 26th. "Norma." Cast as before.
Saturday, 28th. "Linda." As before.
Monday, March 30th, 1857. "Lucrezia Borgia." Lucrezia, C. Hayes; Orsini, Mdlle. Corelli; Gennaro, Volpini; Alfonso, Badiali; Gubetta, Signor Magiorrotti; Petrucci, Pierini; Rustighello, Mariani; Gazella, Dunelli; Vitellozzo, Hortinelli; Liverotto, Benelle; Astolfo, Casaboni.

Although the Lucrezia of Catherine Hayes lacked the power of other great artistes who had and have since appeared in the part, still, in dramatic conception, it was in every respect a study of high artistic merit. The change of hair, naturally light, to a very dark colour, made a striking alteration in Miss Hayes' appearance; her classic features and commanding figure lending additional effect. The tragic scenes were given with much force; and, indeed, the performance, as a whole, proved that the Irish *prima-donna* was equally at home in the heavier as in the lighter *rôles* of the lyric drama. The name Dunelli (attached to the part of Gazella) was an excusable change from Dunn, the possessor of which was a member of the company pressed into the service, and who had a capital bass voice. Hortonelli was also a member of the "stock" (Horton). Such changes are not more startling than Foli (Foley), Bentami (Bentham), Campobello (Campbell), &c., &c.

Some of the Italian *impresarii* found it difficult to Italianize the name of Hayes; so it appears to have been compromised, as in some foreign programmes the name appears as "Katarina Hayes." The name of Balfe was, during his sojourn in Italy, Signor Balfi.

Thursday, April 2nd, "La Sonnambula." Amina, Catherine Hayes; Lisa, Miss F. Cruise; Elvino, Volpini; Rodolpho, Badiali.

A more effective performance of this work has seldom been witnessed in "the Royal." Amina caused enthusiasm from beginning to end. The *finale*, "Ah, non giunge," fully equalling any other effort either before or since. Miss Fanny Cruise (then at her best), a highly-finished vocalist—a pupil of T. Blanchard, as before stated —was, perhaps, as efficient a representative of Lisa as ever "trod the boards." Volpini's Elvino was blameless; and the Rodolpho of the veteran Badiali was something to remember—a study in every particular for all aspiring young artistes.

Saturday, April 4th, 1857. Two Acts of "Don Pasquale," and two Acts of "Lucia." Casts as before. Miss Hayes singing between the Operas "The Harp that Once," and "Home, sweet Home," with extraordinary success.

The Company proceeded to Cork and Limerick, where—in the latter city especially—a great ovation again naturally awaited the appearance of the native *prima-donna*.

A re-engagement of the Catherine Hayes' Company took place for three nights only, commencing on Tuesday, April 21st, 1857, with "Trovatore." Leonora, C. Hayes; Azucena, Mdlle. Corelli; Manrico, Volpini;

Conte di Luna, Badiali; Ferrando, Pierini. An excellent performance "all round," but especially remarkable by the wonderful singing and acting of the immortal Badiali. Comparisons are at all times odious, more particularly in matters of art; but the great old man suffered nothing whatever even in comparison with the most eminent of baritones who had preceded him—Graziani. All the freshness of voice and beauty of style of the younger artist seemed concentrated, even improved, in the "old man eloquent." All living witnesses who were present on the occasion will vouch for the truth of this not exaggerated criticism of Signor Badiali.

Thursday, 23rd. "Trovatore" repeated. Saturday, 24th. "Lucrezia Borgia," as before.

The next Italian Opera Company was, indeed, a strong one, and consisted of Mr. Gye's Covent Garden troupe, being the first and only speculation in Dublin of that distinguished *impresario*. The list included Madame Bosio (her first appearance), Madame Didier, Madame Tagliafico, Mdlle. Parepa, Mdlle. Victoire Balfe (her first appearance), Signor Gardoni, Signor Neri Baraldi (his first appearance), Signor Graziani, Signor Tagliafico, Herr Zegler (his first appearance), Signor Polonini, and Signor Ronconi (his first appearance). Conductor, Mr. Alfred Mellon; Prompter, Signor Monterasi; Acting and Stage Manager, Mr. A. Harris; Leader, Mr. Levey. The orchestra and chorus were strengthened by "considerable additions from the Royal Italian Opera." The magnificent costumes and appointments of the Covent Garden establishment were also made available on this occasion.

Monday, August 3rd. "Lucia di Lammermoor."
Lucia, Mdlle. Victoire Balfe (her first appearance); Alice,
Mdme. Tagliafico; Enrico, Graziani; Raimondo, Zegler;
Normanno, Polonini; Arturo, Cherricci; Edgardo, Neri
Baraldi.

Tuesday, August 4th. "Rigoletto." Gilda, Bosio;
Madelena, M. Didie; Giovanna, Mdme. Tagliafico;
Duca, Neri Baraldi; Sparafolle, Signor Tagliafico; Monterone, Signor Polonini; Rigoletto, Ronconi.

Wednesday, August 5th. "Sonnambula." Amina,
Victoire Balfe; Lisa, Mdme. Tagliafico; Teresa, Mdme.
Cherricci; Rodolfo, Ronconi; Alessio, Polonini; Elvino,
Signor Gardoni.

Thursday, 6th. "Fra Diavolo." Zerlina, Mdme. Bosio;
Lady Allcash, Mdme. Parepa; Fra Diavolo, Gardoni;
Lorenzo, Neri Baraldi; Matteo, Polonini; Beppo, Tagliafico; Giacomo, Herr Zegler; Lord Allcash, Signor
Ronconi.

Friday, 7th. "La Favorita." Leonora, Mdme. Didie;
Inez, Mdme. Tagliafico; Alfonso, Signor Graziani; Baldassare, Zegler; Gaspardo, Polonini; Fernando, Neri
Baraldi.

Saturday. "Trovatore." Leonora, Mdme. Bosio;
Azucena, Mdme. Didie; Inez, Mdme. Tagliafico; Il
Conte di Luna, Graziani; Ferrando, Signor Tagliafico;
Ruiz, Signor Cherricci; Manrico, Neri Baraldi.

Monday. "La Traviata." Violetta, Mdme. Bosio;
Florio Bervois, Mdme. Tagliafico; Amiria, Mdme. Cherricci; Alfredo, Gardoni; Grenvill, Zelger; Dauphol, Polonini; D'Obigny, Signor Tagliafico; Germont, Graziani.

Tuesday. "Puritani." Elvira, Mdlle. Victoire Balfe; Henrietta, Mdme. Tagliafico; Sir R. Forth, Graziani; Sir George, Tagliafico; Lord Walton, Polonini; Arthur Talbot, Gardoni. After which a Scene from "Lucrezia Borgia"—"Il Segreto," by Mdme. Didie—concluding with the last Act of "La Favorita."

Wednesday. "Trovatore," as before.

Thursday, August 13th, 1857, for the benefit of Mdlle. Victoire Balfe. The First and Third Acts of "La Sonnambula;" cast as before. Followed by a Concert, as follows:—"Kathleen Mavourneen," Mdlle. Parepa; "The Flowers of the Forest," Signor Neri Baraldi; "Ah, mon Fils," Mdme. Didie; Ballad, "You'll remember me," Gardoni; Ballad, "I dreamt that I dwelt in Marble halls," Mdlle. Victoire Balfe. On this occasion, Mr. M. W. Balfe presided at the piano, it being announced as "his first appearance these ten years." The performance concluded with "L'Elisir d'Amore," compressed into one Act. Adina, Mdlle. Parepa; Gianetta, Mdme. Tagliafico; Nemorino, Neri Baraldi; Belcore, Tagliafico; Dulcamara, Ronconi.

Friday, 14th. "Fra Diavolo," "in consequence of the unprecedented success of the Opera."

Saturday, August 15th, 1857, for the benefit of Mdme. Bosio, "Lucrezia Borgia," with (as announced) "the following unprecedented cast, viz.:—Lucrezia Borgia, Mdme. Bosio; Maffio Orsini, Mdme. Didie; Gennaro, Neri Baraldi; Don Alfonso, Ronconi; Rustighello (for this occasion only), Graziani; Petrucci, Polonini; Gubetta, Signor Tagliafico; Vitellozo, Herr Zegler.

This was the last night of the most complete Italian Company which ever had been heard up to that date in the Royal. The chorus and band had formerly been supplied from local resources; now some of the "pick" of both departments, from the most perfect choral and orchestral organization in Europe—nay, we might say, in the world—joined with their powerful aid. The costumes and appointments in every department were perfect; the dresses of the chorus, and all the minor parts, being supplied from the wonderful wardrobe of Covent Garden. It was, indeed, a novelty here to behold so perfect an *ensemble*. In addition, the combination of principal artistes was unprecedented. Of course much curiosity existed with reference to the first appearance of Victoire Balfe, who, as may be perceived, was accompanied by her celebrated father. He was not attached to the Company, but was naturally intensely interested in her success, and travelled with her all through the tour, playing the piano accompaniments when required. She was, as may be supposed, an accomplished artiste, and had studied with Garcia, Jenny Lind's professor. Added to a most prepossessing appearance, her figure was graceful and elegant; and in her acting she displayed a premature ease and knowledge of the stage remarkable, considering her youth, as she was then only about eighteen or nineteen years of age. After a short and successful career, she retired, and, as is well known, married Sir John Crampton, then English ambassador at Madrid.

The first appearance of Bosio was also an event to be remembered. This wonderful creature seemed to combine all the qualities, "all the talents" of all the great ones who had appeared before, and, it might be said, of any who have since been heard. Like Cruvelli, she only paid one visit to Dublin, and the impression created by each of those great artistes was very much alike, both possessing many similar artistic qualities. Notwithstanding the great success of Piccolomini in "Traviata," the Violetta of Bosio was considered by critics a performance of a much higher class; and from a musical point of view, no doubt could exist of the justice of this decision. The harrowing death-scene was not so melodramatic, but not the less telling.

The name of Parepa added great strength to this list of distinguished vocalists. With all the qualifications of a great lyric artiste—a magnificent voice, of wonderful compass and the highest cultivation, dramatic capability equal to any "walk," tragic or comic, a commanding figure, and highly classic features—Mdlle. Parepa was a "host in herself." It is hardly necessary to say that she became Mdme. Parepa-Rosa by marriage with the renowned *impresario*, Carl Rosa, and, to the great grief of her husband, and to the extreme regret of the whole musical world, she was prematurely taken away at a comparatively early age, and at the very meridian of a brilliant and splendid career.

Mdme. Didie was a contralto of first-rate capacity. Gardoni, elegant in appearance, and then at his best, was, amongst a large portion of the *élite* of London and Paris, *the* favourite tenor. Neri Baraldi created quite a sensation in Dublin. Graziani had already made his mark. Ronconi (first appearance), the greatest artiste of the day, not alone as a vocalist, but as an actor, completed the list of this remarkable combination. The Operas, as already remarked, were mounted in a style of unprecedented perfection; and the result—heavy loss! So bad, that the late Mr. Gye never could be induced to try again his luck in Dublin.

It would be fruitless to enter into the cause of this; but after a long experience, it is unfortunately too true that a great musical *ensemble* is not sufficiently appreciated in Dublin; that is to say, a "star"—one name placed in large letters at the head of the bills will "draw," when a number of names, if not well known, will fail; and the pecuniary result will show a large balance in favour of the starring system. In proof of this fact, the Piccolomini engagement, shortly before and after, with a comparatively weak troupe to support her, produced nearly double the sum. Matters may have since improved somewhat, but not sufficiently so that we may congratulate ourselves. Several recent instances might be quoted in support of this view.

Monday, September 21st, 1857, the following Italian Opera engagement commenced :—Mdme. Grisi, Mdme. Alboni, Mdme. Gassier, Mdme. Gramaglia, Mdlle. Baillon, Signor Dragone, Mr. George Perrin, Signor Annoni, Signor Benedetti, Mr. Tennant, Signor Mario, Signor Baillon, Signor Kinni, Signor Gabussi, Signor Deriviz. Prompter, Signor Galli; Conductor, Signor Stanzieri.

Monday, September 21st, 1857. "La Traviata." Violetta, Mdme. Gassier; Alfredo, Signor Mario; Germont, Signor Dragone.

Tuesday, 22nd. "Il Trovatore." Leonora, Mdme. Grisi; Azucena, Mdme. Alboni; Inez, Mdlle. Baillon; Conte di Luna, Signor Dragone; Ferrando, Signor Kinni; Manrico, Signor Mario.

This was announced as an unprecedented cast, but the only remarkable feature was the Azucena of Alboni, whose singing was, of course, magnificent; but as a dramatic representation, it was far inferior to many others witnessed on previous occasions.

Wednesday, 23rd. "Norma." Norma, Mdme. Grisi; Adalgisa, Mdme. Gassier; Clotilda, Mdme. Baillon; Oroveso, Signor Deriviz; Flavio, Gabussi; Pollio, Benedetti.

Thursday, 24th. "Lucrezia Borgia." Lucrezia, Grisi; Maffeo Orsini, Alboni; Alfonso, Signor Deriviz; Astolfo, Mattoni; Gubetta, Kinni; Gazella, Signor Baillon; Rustighello, Signor Annoni; Liverotto, Signor Gabussi; Petrucci, Signor Chiesi; Gennaro, Mario.

Friday, 25th. "Sonnambula." Amina, Mdme. Gassier; Lisa, Mdme. Gramaglia; Teresa, Mdme. Baillon; Rodolfo, Signor Baillon; Allessio, Signor Mattoni; Elvino, Signor Benedetti.

This performance of "Sonnambula" was only remarkable for the wonderful vocal efforts of Mdme. Gassier, who, in the *finale*, reached the extraordinary vocal height of A in alt, the highest note ever attempted on the Dublin stage.

Saturday, 26th. "Trovatore" repeated.

Monday, 28th. "Semiramide." Semiramide, Grisi; Arsace, Alboni; Idreno, Mr. Tennant; Assur, Signor

Deriviz; Oroe, Signor Baillon; L'Ombra di Nino, Signor Kinni.

Old Opera-goers will remember the grand performance of the duet by Grisi and Alboni, more particularly "Giorno d' orrore."

Tuesday, 29th. "Traviata" repeated; after which "Ah, non giunge" by Madame Gassier.

Wednesday. "Don Giovanni." Donna Anna, Grisi; Zerlina, Alboni; Donna Elvira, Mdme. Gassier; Don Giovanni, Signor Dragone; Leporello, Signor Deriviz; Commendatore, Signor Kinni; Masetto, Signor Baillon; Don Ottavio, Signor Benedetti.

The enormous size of Alboni rendered the appearance of Zerlina peculiar. The transposition of the song, "Batti, batti," a full tone below the original, considerably marred the effect, as the violoncello obligato is thereby spoiled. However, the change becomes necessary with contralto vocalists. The appeal to Masetto during the song was, on this occasion, rather forcible; he was in person the reverse of muscular or powerful; and the sudden concussion with such an immense body of animated matter as Zerlina presented was well-nigh causing a curious scene, for if one "gave way" the other would have followed. However, by a little artistic management on Zerlina's part, matters righted themselves, and a little sensation in the pit was the only result.

Thursday, "Les Huguenots." Valentine, Grisi; Marguerite, Mdme. Gassier; Urbano, Mdme. Gramaglia; Raoul, Signor Benedetti; Marcello, Signor Deriviz; San Bris, Signor Baillon; Nevers, Signor Kinni; Tavannes,

Signor Annoni; Cosse, Signor Gabussi; Meru, Signor Mattoni; Retz, Signor Talamo.

With the exception of Grisi's great impersonation of Valentine, there was nothing worthy of much notice in this performance.

Friday, October 2nd. Repetition of " Don Giovanni." Saturday, 3rd. " Les Huguenots." Last night.

First appearance of Giuglini.

On Monday, October 12th, 1857, the following Italian Opera engagement commenced :—Mdlle. Spezia (first appearance), Mdlle. Poma, Mdlle. Ortolani, Signor Giuglini (his first appearance), Signor Aldighieri, Signor Vialetti, Signor Rossi, Signor Belletti. Conductor, Signor Arditi; Leader, Mr. Levey.

Monday. " Il Trovatore." Leonora, Mdlle. Spezia; Azucena, Mdlle. Poma; Il Conte di Luna, Aldighieri; Ferrando, Vialetti; Ruiz, Signor Mercuriali; Manrico, Signor Giuglini.

Tuesday. " La Figlia del Reggimento." Marie, Mdlle. Piccolomini; La Marchesa, Mdlle. Poma; Tonio, Signor Luchesi; Pesano, Signor Mercuriali; Sergeant Sulpizio, Signor Belletti.

Wednesday. " La Traviata." Violetta, Piccolomini; Florio Bervois, Mdlle. Poma; Alfredo, Signor Giuglini; Gastone, Signor Mercuriale; Dottore, Signor Rossi; Germont, Signor Belletti.

Thursday, October 15th. " La Sonnambula." Amina, Mdlle. Ortolani (her first appearance); Lisa, Mdlle. Poma; Elvino, Signor Giuglini; Rodolpho, Belletti.

Saturday. " Lucia di Lammermoor." Lucia, Piccolomini; Enrico, Belletti; Bidebent, Signor Vialetti; Arturo, Signor Mercuriale; Edgardo, Giuglini.

Monday, October 19th. "La Traviata," as before.

Tuesday. "Don Pasquale." Norina, Piccolomini; Ernesto, Signor Luchesi; Malatesta, Belletti; Don Pasquale, Rossi. Also, the Third Act of "La Favorita." Leonora, Mdlle. Spezia; Baldassare, Signor Vialetti, Fernando, Signor Giuglini; Walter, Signor Mercuriale; Riccardo, Signor Belletti.

Wednesday, October 21st. "I Puritani." Elvira, Mdlle. Ortolani; Enrichetta, Mdlle. Poma; Arturo, Giuglini; Georgio, Signor Vialetti.

Thursday. "La Figlia," as before; and last Act of "Lucia."

Friday. Benefit of Giuglini, "I Puritani," as before.

Saturday. Last night, "Don Giovanni."

This formed the fourth Italian Opera engagement during the year 1857, an unprecedented occurrence in the annals of "the Royal," and which has never since been repeated; the *prima-donnas* being Grisi, Catherine Hayes, Mdme. Bosio, and Piccolomini. The last of the four engagements was, indeed, remarkable for the first appearance of Giuglini. Report had combined all the qualities of Mario and Rubini in this wonderful tenor, and facts fully verified the report. The style was not so florid as that of Rubini; Mario had, perhaps, some superior qualities, and was a better actor; but "take him for all in all," so satisfying a tenor as Giuglini never appeared. The most enchanting "timbre" of voice, the highest possible finish in style—every single note producing the impression of severe study—the effect on the audience was, indeed, electrifying. London was naturally raised to the highest pitch of enthusiasm by the appearance of this new and unexpected star in the lyric firmament, and in each successive part his reputation seemed, if possible, to increase. The Dublin audience did not fail to appreciate Giuglini, and fiat to the fullest extent the opinion of London on this occasion—which is not always the case; as some tenors have since appeared with the London stamp, whose efforts have not been so highly appreciated in Dublin—perhaps from the fact that the London criticisms were much overwrought—a great mistake, most unfair and injurious to the artist criticized. It is sad to relate the end of poor Giuglini. He died in an asylum in London, in a state bordering on idiocy. Although given to simple, boyish ways in private life, such as kite-flying, &c., there was nothing to indicate so fearful a breakdown in intellect. His extreme care at rehearsals was most remarkable; and his suggestions with reference to the orchestral accompaniment were most artistic, when he wished for a *pianissimo* or *crescendo* at any particular point. As before remarked, every individual note seemed to him of the greatest importance; and the most minute error, orchestral or choral, would not escape him. He was always much pleased by the applause of the members of the orchestra, which, at rehearsals, was, with Giuglini, more constant and hearty than with any other artist. He always sang in the morning as if before the audience at night (an example which might well be followed by many dramatic artists in their particular line). On one occa sion, at a rehearsal of "La Favorita," Giuglini seemed actually inspired, singing so divinely as to enchant every member of the company present. The repeated bursts of applause pleased him so much, that he exerted his voice almost to exhaustion, against the advice of the leader; and consequently in the evening the wondrous voice manifested signs of fatigue. All who remember this rehearsal still look back, with a "longing, lingering" wish that the day might "come again." Giuglini enjoyed a game of pool, in which he joined at the billiard table attached to the Theatre, and at which only a few chosen friends of the outside world were privileged to partake. The great tenor seemed to appreciate the small coin of sixpence, earned for a "life" taken by him, much more than the large premium of £50, or perhaps £60, paid for each night's professional services. A revenue exceeding that of an English Lord Chancellor, nay, that of a Prime Minister, awaits a legitimate and real successor to Giuglini.

During this last engagement, Signor Arditi made his first appearance in Dublin as conductor of the Italian Opera. He at once established himself a favourite with the audience, who fully appreciated his masterly capabilities for his high position. He has up to the present (1878) continued, with few interruptions, to visit us, and still meets with the strongest possible demonstrations of almost affectionate favour, which will doubtless continue as long as he fulfils the same office in Dublin.

In July, 1858, Mdme. Gassier appeared in a series of concerts given by Mr. Harris (in connection with the firm of Cramer, Beale & Co.) at the Rotundo Gardens; the "venue" being changed, after a few nights, to the Portobello Gardens, as it was found that the music and fireworks could be enjoyed at the Rotundo quite as well, if not better, outside the railings of the gardens as inside—"distance lending enchantment" to sound as well as view. The public did not fail to take advantage of this poetic fact, and the enormous crowds of non-paying outsiders presented a strong contrast to the simple-minded few who paid to become insiders—the former increasing, the latter decreasing nightly. Some amusing episodes resulted. On the third evening a rather long delay occurred, and the band (the Garde Nationale of Paris) were half-an-hour late in attendance. During this "wait," the outside public manifested strong signs of impatience, while the paying few inside enjoyed their promenade without the slightest signs of disapproval. Mr. Levey, not being musically engaged, was assisting in the business department (giving tickets, checks, &c.) at the gate attached to the railings in Rutland-square. His duties in "money-taking" were not heavy, but he had to bear several severe rebukes from those who were anxiously awaiting their gratuitous musical and pyrotechnic treat. "What's the delay, Lavey?"—"Are you goin' to keep us standin' out here all night?" and such searching inquiries were directed on the poor temporary official. At last, his patience being exhausted, one indignant "member" raised himself on the curb-stone, looked over the palisading, and called out: "Look here, Lavey, tell Harris if you don't begin soon, we'll all go home!"

We adjourned the next evening to the Portobello Gardens, where to enjoy the sound and sight the money should be forthcoming. The name of Mdme. Gassier, as connected with the Italian Opera, will be our excuse for this digression.

Wednesday, August 11th, 1858, the following Italian Opera Company commenced :—Mdlle. Piccolomini (her farewell engagement previous to her departure for America), Mdme. Viardot Garcia, Mdme. Ghioni, Signor Giuglini, Signor Vialetti, Signor Aldighieri, Signor Castelli, Signor Mercuriale, Signor Rossi, Signor Belart. Conductor, Signor Arditi; Leader, Mr. Levey.

Wednesday, August 11th, 1858. "La Figlia." Maria, Piccolomini; Marchese, Mdme. Ghioni; Sulpizio, Signor Vialetti; Hortensio, Signor Castelli; Notaro, Signor Mercuriale; Tonio, Signor Belart (his first appearance in Dublin).

Thursday. "Il Trovatore." Leonora, Piccolomini; Azucena, Viardot Garcia; Inez, Mdme. Ghioni; Conte di Luna, Signor Aldighieri; Ferrando, Signor Vialetti; Ruiz, Signor Mercuriale; Zingaro, Signor Castelli; Manrico, Giuglini.

Saturday, August 14th. "La Traviata." Violetta, Piccolomini; Flora, Mdme. Ghioni; Germont, Aldighieri; Dottore, Castelli; Marchese, Mercuriale; Barone, Rossi; Alfredo, Giuglini.

Monday, August 16th. First time of "La Zingara," the Italian version of Balfe's "Bohemian Girl," as performed at Her Majesty's Theatre with unprecedented success. Zerlina, Mdlle. Piccolomini; Yelva (Queen of the Gipsies), Mdme. Viardot Garcia; Il Conte Abano, Signor Aldighieri; Frederico, Signor Mercuriali; Un Officiale, Signor Castelli; Falco, Signor Vialetti; Gualtiero, Signor Giuglini.

Tuesday, 17th. "Don Giovanni." Donna Anna, Viardot Garcia; Zerlina, Mdlle. Piccolomini; Elvira, Mdme. Ghioni; Don Giovanni, Signor Aldighieri; Leporello, Rossi; Commendatore, Vialetti; Masetto, Signor Castelli; Don Ottavio, Giuglini.

Wednesday, 18th. "Il Trovatore," repeated.

Thursday, 19th. "Il Barbiere." Ronna, Viardot Garcia; Berta, Mdme. Ghioni; Figaro, Signor Aldighieri; Bartolo, Signor Rossi; Basilio, Signor Vialetti; Officiale, Castelli; Notario, Mercuriale; Conte Almaviva, Signor Belart.

Saturday, 21st. "Lucia di Lammermoor." Lucia, Mdlle. Piccolomini: Ashton, Aldighieri; Arturo, Signor Mercuriale; Bidebent, Vialetti; Edgardo, Giuglini.

Monday, 23rd. "La Traviata," repeated.

Tuesday, 24th. "La Figlia," as before.

Wednesday, 25th. "La Sonnambula." Amina (her first appearance in that character in Dublin), Mdlle. Piccolomini; Lisa, Mdme. Ghioni; Notario, Signor Mercuriale; Allessio, Signor Castelli; Count Rodolfo, Signor Vialetti; Elvino, Giuglini.

Thursday, 26th. "Lucia," as before; with a Scena and Duo from "I Martiri" (first time in Dublin), by Mdlle. Piccolomini and Signor Giuglini.

Saturday, August 28th. Farewell benefit of Mdlle. Piccolomini, and last night of the engagement. Last Act of "La Zingara," as before; followed by the first and last Acts of "La Traviata;" after which the Scena and Duo from "I Martiri," concluding with a Farewell Cantata, composed expressly for the occasion, and sung by the entire Company, aided by the chorus and military band. Music by Signor Giuglini; Poetry by Signor Aldighieri; Instrumentation by Signor Arditi.

GLI ITALIANI AGLI IRLANDESI ADDIO.

Coro.

Viva l'Irlanda, libera è grande!
Viva il tuo ciels, viva il tuo suol!
Dovunque il raggio del sol se spande,
  Dovunque il vento agita il vol,
Assisa in grembo della tempesta,
  Come guerriera, pionta a pugnar;
Chini gentila, la bella testa,
  Come fanciulla ch'esce dal mar.

Terzetto—Signori Giuglini, Aldighieri è Vialetti.

Addio redente, piaggia Irlandese,
  Addio fratelli, figlia del mar.
Sea benedetto, l'uom che n'appresse
  La vostra sponda a salutar.
Ultima giaci lontan lontano;
  Come un perduto solingo fior,
Ma benché figlia dell' oceano,
  Nutri potenit vita ad amor.

Solo—Mdlle. Piccolomini.

Triste, si triste, è l'abbandono;
  Come un accento nol puo ridir.

Partir ci è forza v'offriamo in dono,
   Un mesto vale, ed un sospir.
Ma allor che lunge sa questa care
   Terra il piensiero ritornera,
Una segreta lagrima amara,
   Sul mesto ciglio ci spuntera.
Il mesto labbro dira' un addio ;
   L'eco per l'aere, lo ridera ;
Come una prece rivolta a Dio,
   L'onda dei pelaghi vel portera.

(Translation.)
THE FAREWELL OF THE ITALIANS TO IRELAND.

Hail to thee, Erin, ever great and free !
   Hail to thy changeful skies, thy fertile land !
Far as the sun extends his generous heat,
   Far as the winds their rapid wings expand.
Set 'mid the stormy seas that gird thee round,
   A warrior maid thou seem'st, secure and free ;
Or liftest up thy fair head, ocean-crowned,
   Rising in beauty from thy parent sea.

Trio—Signori Giuglini, Aldighieri and Vialetti.

Kind friends, farewell; adieu, each friendly spot ;
   Farewell your beauteous mountains, shores and bays.
Happy the hour, and ne'er may be forgot,
   When these first broke upon our wond'ring gaze.
Thee from our Italy far realms remove ;
   Thou seem'st to us some lovely flow'r on earth,
Radiant with life, and warmth, and love,
   Albeit the cold waves may have given thee birth.

Solo—Mdlle. Piccolomini.

Glad, oh, how glad, is still the hour we meet ;
   Sad, oh, how sad, the hour we needs must part.

The fond farewell I fain would oft repeat,
　The word is lost 'mid sighs that rend my heart.
And oft when distant seas between us roll,
　Back to thy loved land will my thoughts return,
Regretful memory fill my longing soul,
　And on my eyelids the mute teardrops burn.
My lips, when far, will falter forth, "Farewell!"
　Back by the breeze its echo will be given;
The waves that part us back my thoughts will tell,
　As angels waft the unspoke prayer to Heaven.

The production of "La Zingara," a very good Italian version of Balfe's "Bohemian Girl," formed the chief event on this occasion. It had been well received in London and on the Continent. The singing of Giuglini was surpassingly beautiful. It may with justice be said that "When other lips" never had such a rendering, either before or since. Indeed, he bestowed especial pains on the study of the part in detail, as well from his high artistic feeling as with the intent of pleasing the fellow-citizens of the composer. The profound silence which prevailed during his singing of the ballad, and the repeated bursts of applause at the end, gave evident signs of his great success. In "When the fair land of Poland," he betrayed most extraordinary power of voice and dramatic force, which seemed to be treasured up for the occasion. Indeed, the Italian Company seemed all "on their mettle;" for, leaving aside their professional anxiety, Balfe was an especial and personal favourite with all Continental artistes, and each member of the present Company bestowed all possible pains and attention to their several parts. Piccolomini—not a great vocalist in the true sense—seemed to "come out" better as a vocalist in this than in any other Opera. The soprano music, although showy, is not difficult. The first song, "I dreamt that I dwelt," suited her peculiar style, and created at once a good impression; and the duet with Giuglini, which follows, "The secret of my birth," was a wonderful success—the great tenor adding to the effect by, now and then, a judicious "new reading," without marring the intention of the composer, but, as was ever the case, prompted by careful and conscientious study. Signor Aldighieri, an accomplished artiste, made the most of the Count; and certainly the Gipsy Queen never had such a representative as Viardot Garcia. It will be inferred that Balfe's work had on this occasion a "good chance," and, indeed, it was a performance which never can be forgotten by those who were present.

A large pecuniary success was the result of this engagement; the Morning Concert, on August 20th, producing nearly £600.

It would be unjust to pass over the appearance in this troupe of a charming little tenor of the florid school, Mons. Belart—a Frenchman—whose singing, more especially as the Count Almaviva in "Il Barbiere," gave great satisfaction, and caused a universal wish that he might be again heard in Dublin. The school was, of course, quite French, and highly elaborated. The difficult passages in the second movement of "Ecco ridenti" were, perhaps, never given with more precision, and no instrument could have given the scales with greater perfection.

The next Italian engagement commenced on Monday,

March 28th, 1859 :—Mdme. Grisi, Mdme. Viardot Garcia, Mdlle. Zedlatzek, Mdme. Bellosio, Mdlle. Colberti. Signor Mario, Signor Corsi, Signor Armoni, Signor Lanzoni, Signor Graziani, Signor Kinni, Signor Vairot. Conductor, Signor Stanzieri; Leader, Mr. Levey.

On Monday, March 28th, 1859, "Il Trovatore." Leonora, Grisi; Azucena, Viardot Garcia; Inez, Mdlle. Bellosio; Manrico, Mario; Conte di Luna, Graziani; Fernando, Lanzoni; Ruiz, Annoni.

Tuesday, 29th. "Norma." Norma, Grisi; Pollio, Mario.

Wednesday, 30th. Verdi's Opera, "Macbeth" (first time). Lady Macbeth, Viardot Garcia; Dama, Mdlle. Sedlatzek; Macbeth, Signor Graziani; Banco, Signor Lanzoni; Macduff, Signor Corsi; Malcolm, Signor Annoni; Medico, Signor Vairot; Silvario, Signor Kinni.

Thursday, 31st. "Lucrezia Borgia." Lucrezia, Grisi; Maffeo, Sedlatzek; Gennaro, Mario; Alphonso, Lanzoni; Rustighello, Annoni; Guibetta, Vairot; Gazella, Kinni.

Saturday, April 2nd. "Trovatore," as before.

Monday, April 4th. "Don Giovanni." Donna Anna, Grisi; Zerlina, Viardot Garcia; Elvira, Mdlle. Zedlatzek; Ottavio, Mario; Don Giovanni, Graziani; Leporello, Lanzoni; Masetto, Kinni; Commendatore, Kinni.

Tuesday, 5th. "Lucrezia," repeated. Maffeo, on this occasion, Viardot Garcia.

Wednesday, 6th. "Macbeth," repeated.

Thursday, 7th. "Norma," repeated.

Saturday, 9th. First performance in Dublin of "Marta." Tristram, Lanzoni; Lionello, Mario; Plunketto, Graziani; Sheriffo, Kinni; Lady Henrietta, Grisi; Nancy, Viardot Garcia.

Monday, 11th. "Marta," repeated.
Tuesday, 12th. "Trovatore."
Wednesday, 13th. "Macbeth."
Thursday, 14th. "Marta."
Saturday, 16th. "Marta," repeated. Grisi's benefit, and last night of the engagement.

The first performance of "Macbeth" formed a special feature during this engagement. This work contains some of Verdi's best writing and scoring, but the absence of a soprano part has prevented the Opera from becoming as popular as others by the same eminent composer. Lady Macbeth is a mezzo-soprano—indeed, almost a contralto part—and the interpretation was such as might be expected from the musical and dramatic powers of a Viardot. Her "make-up" was evidently formed on that of Mrs. Siddons; and in the bedroom scene the likeness to the received portraits of the latter great actress was very striking; and some very old playgoers, who had seen the sister of the great Kemble act the part in Crow-street Theatre, gave evidence to this effect, and were much struck with Viardot's magnificent performance, which was, indeed, a high Shakesperean study, well worthy of witnessing, even if deprived of the beautiful music. Graziani, also, added much to his already great reputation as a vocalist by his excellent reading, and, in some parts, powerful efforts to do justice, in a histrionic point of view, to the grand part of the great English poet, as far as the crippled medium of a rather weak translation set to music would permit. The witches' choruses in this Opera, although of rather light character for the ponderous subject, are dramatic and effective, and, as before remarked, the instrumentation excellent, and not over *brassed*.

Another important event in our operatic annals was the first performance in Dublin of "Marta," destined to become a most popular and established favourite up to the present, and perhaps for years to come. The cast on this occasion was well calculated to lead to this result, for never since has there been one more complete and effective. It is unnecessary to remind Dublin opera-goers of Guila Grisi's Enrichetta, Mario's Lionello, or Graziani's Plunketto; but we may refer to this the only occasion on which Viardot held forth as Nancy. Those who had seen her "heavy tragedy" the night before, and now beheld her on the "light fantastic," dancing like a sylph (for in everything she was perfect), could hardly believe it was the same person. The effect of "The Last Rose," as given by Grisi now for the first time, may well be conceived; and the enthusiasm which followed on the repetition (at the *encore*), with the English words, made so interesting by the slightly broken Italian-English, which is much softer than from the lips of a native of France or Germany.

From some indescribable cause, the "Spinning Wheel" quartet has never "gone" with such enthusiasm as with Grisi, Viardot, Mario, and Graziani.

First appearance of Titiens.

August, 6th, 1859, the following Company was announced:—Mdlle. Titiens, Mdlle. Guarducci, Mdlle. Vaneri, Mdlle. Dell'Anese, Signor Badiali, Signor Vialetti, Signor Corsi, Signor Castelli, Signor Mercuriali, Signor Rossi, Signor Borchardt, and Signor Giuglini. Conductor, Signor Arditi; Leader, Mr. Levey.

On Saturday, August 6th, 1859, " Les Huguenots." San Bris, Badiali; Conte de Nevers, Signor Borchardt; Tavannes, Signor Mercuriali; De Retz, Signor Rossi; Raoul, Signor Giuglini; Marcello, Signor Vialetti; Marguarita, Mdlle. Vaneri,; Urbano, Mdlle. Guarducci; Dame d'Onore, Mdlle. Dell'Anese; Valentina, Mdlle. Titiens.

On Monday, August 8th, " Norma." Pollio, Giuglini; Flavio, Mercuriale; Oroveso, Signor Vialetti; Adalgisa, Mdlle. Vanere; Clotilda, Mdlle. Dell'Anese; Norma, Titiens.

On Tuesday, 9th, " La Favorita," Leonora, Guarducci; Alfonso, Signor Borchardt; Baldassore, Signor Vialetti; Gasparo, Signor Corsi; Inez, Mdlle. Dell'Anese; Fernando, Giuglini.

On Wednesday, 10th, " Trovatore." Manrico, Giuglini; Il Conte di Luna, Badiali; Azucena, Mdlle. Guarducci; Leonora, Mdlle. Titiens.

On Friday, 12th, " Il Barbiere." Figaro, Badiali; Don Bartolo, Signor Castelli; Basilio, Vialetti; Fiorello, Signor Mercuriali; Conte Almaviva, Corsi; Berta, Mdlle. Dell'Anese; Rosina, Mdlle. Guarducci.

Saturday. " Les Huguenots," repeated.

On Monday, " Trovatore," repeated.

On Tuesday, August 16th, " Lucrezia Borgia." Gennaro,

Giuglini; Alfonso, Badiale; Rustighello, Mercuriale; Astolfo, Borchardt; Gubetta, Vialetti; Gazella, Signor Castelli; Liverotto, Signor Corsi; Maffio Orsini, Guarducci; Lucrezia Borgia, Titiens.

On Wednesday, 17th, "Norma," and selections from "Il Barbiere."

On Thursday, 18th, "Il Trovatore." Giuglini's benefit.

On] Saturday, August 20th, 1859, " Don Giovanni." Benefit of Titiens, and last night of engagement. Donna Anna, Titiens; Elvira, Mdlle. Vaneri; Zerlina, Mdlle. Guarducci; Ottavio, Giuglini; Leporello, Vialetti; Commendatore, Borchardt; Maretto, Castelli; Don Giovanni, Badiali.

A worthy successor to the great Grisi (now on the "wane") seemed a distant probability, when almost suddenly the immortal Titiens made her appearance, and startled the musical world by fulfilling worthily the now almost vacant place. For the lighter works, such as " Don Pasquale," " L'Elisire," &c., in which Grisi was so great, younger artistes were springing up, but the question arose, where is the coming " Norma," " Lucrezia Borgia," " Semiramide," " Medea," &c. ? Jenny Lind and others had essayed without success; when now comes one whom the Dublin Press named most aptly the " Queen of Song;" and now commences an historic, and indeed an affectionate relationship between the Dublin audience and the wonderful Titiens, which continued for 14 or 15 years, and was only terminated by her most lamented death. Titiens was indeed great in every particular. Queenly in person and stature, gigantic in talent, and possessing a heart (well described by a Dublin "Boy") as big as herself. By her voice and purse she constantly contributed to increase the funds of many charitable institutions, and the extreme kindness with which she tendered her great services, doubly enhanced the favours bestowed. Long years will indeed elapse before the public of Dublin can forget Titiens! Mdlle. Guarducci was married during this engagement at the Cathedral in Marlborough-street, by the Rev. Canon Murphy (now P.P. of St. Kevin's), on which occasion, at the conclusion of the ceremony, he gave a beautiful address in "very choice Italian."

On Saturday, October 1st, 1859, a short engagement. Mdlle. Piccolomini, Mdlle Dell'Anese, Signor Belart, Signor Corsi, Signor Aldighieri, Signor Mercuriali, Signor Rossi, Signor Castelli, Signor Badi ; Conductor, Signor Biletta ; Leader, Mr. Levey.

On Saturday, 1st, "La Figlia." Tonio, Belart; Salpizio, Aldighieri ; Ortensio, Castelli ; Caporale, Rossi ; Palrano, Mercuriali ; Maria, Piccolomini.

On Monday, October 3rd, "La Traviata." Germont, Signor Aldighieri ; Duphol, Signor Rossi ; Gastone, Signor Mercuriale ; Medico, Signor Castelli ; Commissionaro, Signor Badi ; Alfredo, Signor Belart ; Flora, Mdlle. Dell'Anese ; Violetta, Mdlle. Piccolomini.

On Tuesday, 4th, "Lucia." Ashton, Aldighieri ; Bedebent, Castelli ; Arturo, Corsi ; Raimondo, Mercuriali ; Edgardo, Belart ; Alice, Mdlle. Dell'Anese ; Lucia, Piccolomini.

On Wednesday, "La Figlia" repeated ; and on Saturday, repeat of "La Traviata," for the benefit of Mdlle. Piccolomini, and last night.

On the Saturday following, viz.:—October 8th, 1859, Mdlle. Titiens, Mdlle. Dell'Anese, Mdlle. Borchardt, Signor Giuglini, Signor Badiali, Signor Vialetti, Signor Mercuriali. Commenced with "Il Trovatore." Manrico, Giuglini; Il Conte di Luna, Badiali; Fernando, Vialetti; Ruiz, Mercuriali; Azucena, Mdlle. Borchardt; Inez, Mdlle. Dell'Anese; Leonora, Titiens.

On Monday, "Don Giovanni;" with (as announced), "the following powerful cast"—Don Ottavio, Giuglini; Don Giovanni, Badiali; Leporello, Vialetti; Commendatore, Castelli; Mazetto, Aldighieri; Donna Anna, Titiens; Elvira, Mdlle. Vaneri; Zerlina, Mdlle. Piccolomini (expressly engaged).

On Tuesday, October 11th, 1859, "Il Trovatore." Leonora, Titiens; Inez, Mdlle. Dell'Anese; Azucena, Borchardt; Ruiz, Signor Mercuriali; Fernando, Signor Vialetti; Conte di Luna, Badiali; Manrico, Giuglini.

On Thursday, 13th, "Marta." Tristano, Signor Castelli; Lionelli, Giuglini; Plunkett, Signor Vialetti; Sheriffo, Rossi; Nancy, Mdlle. Borchardt; Marta, Titiens;

And on Saturday, for the joint benefit of Mdlle. Titiens and Signor Giuglini, a repeat of "Marta." Conductor, Signor Arditi.

NOTE:—On the 27th of this month Madame Jenny Lind Goldsmid visited Dublin, for the purpose of singing at a Concert given for the joint benefit of "Mercer's Hospital" and the "Irish Musical Fund Society," the profits of which exceeded £900, equally divided between the two institutions. Madame Lind not only gave her gratuitous services, but refused her railway fare.

Mr. Harris, in conjunction with Mr. Willert Beale, announced a short series of Italian Operas, to commence on Monday, February 27th, 1860, supported by Mdlle. Piccolomini, Mdme. Borchardt, Mdme. Gramaglia, Mdme. Rudersdorff, Signor Belart, Signor Mercuriali, Signor Attavilla, Signor Aldighieri, Signor Castelli, Signor Allara, Mr. Patey (Primo Basso del Tetro Reggio Torino). Conductor, Signor Arditi.

On Monday, February 27th, "La Traviata." Violetta, Piccolomini; Alfredo, Belart; Germont, Aldighieri; Flora, Mdme. Gramaglia; Barone, Signor Allara; Gaston, Signor Mercuriali.

On Tuesday, 28th, "Lucrezia Borgia." Lucrezia, Mdme. Rudersdorff; Gennaro, Signor Attavilla; Duca, Mr. Patey; Orsini, Madame Borchardt; Vitellozo, Signor Allara; Gubetta, Signor Castelli; Rustighello, Signor Mercuriali.

On Wednesday, 29th, "La Figlia." Maria, Piccolomini; Marchesa, Madame Gramaglia; Salpizio, Signor Castelli; Ortensio, Signor Allara; Caporale, Signor Mercuriale; Tonio, Signor Belart. "Il Bacio;" concluding with a "Valtz Brilliant," sung by Mdlle. Piccolomini, composed expressly for her by Signor Arditi.

NOTE:—This was the first appearance of this Valtz, which has attained great popularity, and still continues by an enormous sale a profit to composer and publisher.

On Thursday, March 1st, "Lucrezia" (repeat).

On Friday, 2nd March, "La Traviata" (repeat).
On Saturday, March 3rd, "I Puritani." Elvira, Mdlle. Piccolomini ; Arturo, Signor Belart ; Giorgio, Mr. Patey ; Riccardo, Signor Aldighieri ; Regina, Mdme. Gramaglia.

On Monday, March 5th, "Trovatore." Leonora, Madame Rudersdorff; Azucena, Madame Borchardt; Manrico, Signor Attavilla; Di Luna, Aldighieri; Ferrando, Castelli.

On Tuesday, repeat of "Puritani."

On Wednesday, "La Figlia," "Il Bacio" and the fourth Act of "La Favorita ;" with Piccolomini, Belart, and Patey.

On Thursday (first time in Dublin), Mozart's "Nozze de Figaro" (in Italian.) Susanna, Mdlle. Piccolomini ; Contessa, Mdme. Rudersdorff; Cherubino, Mdme. Borchardt ; Barbara, Mdme. Gramaglia ; Conte Almaviva, Signor Aldighieri; Basilio, Attavilla ; Bartolo, Signor Castelli; Figaro, Mr. Patey ; Giardiniere, Signor Allara. The following note appeared in the bills of this evening— " Mozart is said to have chosen this subject when ordered to compose an Opera for the stage of Vienna, about four years after the appearance of his "Ent fuhring aus den Serail." Its success was not decided, even at rehearsal, when, according to the account left us by Michael Kelly, the enthusiasm both of singers and of the orchestra rose to a pitch that must seem quite incredible to those accustomed to a colder mode of expressing satisfaction. Nor did the result disappoint the expectations of the Viennese artistes ; so great was the delight of the audience on its first representation, that scarcely a single piece of music was allowed to pass without an encore, in consequence of which the Opera was so extravagantly prolonged, that the Emperor thought himself obliged to interfere, and commanded that nothing for the future should be called for a second time in the course of the same evening." Oh! for such an Emperor at the present time!

On Saturday, March 10th, repeat of "Lucrezia; and first time in Dublin, a "Farsa Musicale" by Fioravante, entitled, " La Serva Padrona." Serpina, Mdlle. Piccolomini; Oberto, Signor Castelli; Tempesta, Signor Casalioni.

Monday, March 12th, repeat of "Le Nozze."

On Tuesday, 13th, "La Figlia."

Wednesday, "Trovatore" and "Serva Padrona."

On Thursday, 15th, "Marta." Enrichetta, Piccolomini; Nancy, Mdme. Rudersdorff (in consequence of Mdme. Borchardt's accident); Lionello, Signor Belart; Plunkett, Signor Aldighieri; Tristani, Signor Castelli; Podesta, Signor Mercuriali.

On Friday, March 16th, a Concert in Rotundo.

On Saturday, March 17th," Marta." Benefit of Mdlle. Piccolomini, and last night.

The first performance in Italian of " Le Nozze" marked this engagement, and was decidely the best performed work during the short season. Mdme. Rudersdorff's version of the Countess was marked by the thorough musicianlike qualities which attended every classical *role* attempted by the same artiste. As before stated, she was daughter of Monsieur Rudersdorff, an excellent violinist; (a resident in Dublin some years since), who, in connection with Mr. Pigott, the eminent violoncellist, and Mr. John

Wilkinson, gave a most successful series of Promenade Concerts at the Rotundo. Mr. Patey, a young Englishman, who had pursued his studies in Italy, was an excellent Figaro; Aldighieri, a capital Count; and with the minor parts well filled, Mozart's (by some considered) best work was rendered every justice. It has ever since justly increased in public estimation. The accident alluded to, and which caused Mdme. Rudersdorff to undertake the Nancy in " Marta," occurred to Mdme. Borchardt while singing at the window as " Le Nozze " she fell, and hurt severely the cap of her knee; this, unfortunately, laid her up for the remainder of the engagement, and she was delayed six weeks after at the Gresham Hotel under surgical care.

The Company performed for two additional nights, viz. :—On Thursday, March 22nd, " Lucia" (benefit of Mdme. Rudersdorff). Lucia, Mdme. Rudersdorff; Edgardo, Signor Belart;

And on Saturday, March 24th, 1860, it was announced, " Mdlle. Piccolomini will most positively make her last appearance, and take a formal farewell of the Dublin public in the Opera of ' La Traviata;'" which was performed with the same cast; concluding with "La Serva Padrona" and " Il Bacio."

The next troupe consisted of Mdme. Grisi, Mdme. Viardot Garcia, Mdme. Orvil, Mdlle. Sedlatzek, Mdme. Rita, Madame Gassier, Signor Mario, Signor Angelo Luise, Signor Graziana, Signor Fallar, Signor Kinni, Signor Cherricci, Signor Forsi, and Signor Ciampi. Conductor, Signor Viannese.

On Monday, September 10th, 1860, "Il Trovatore." Leonora, Madame Grisi; Azucena, Viardot Garcia; Inez, Madame Cherricci; Manrico, Mario; Conte di Luna, Signor Graziani; Ferrando, Signor Ciampi; Ruiz, Signor Kinni; Zingaro, Signor Cherricci.

On Tuesday, "Macbeth." Lady Macbeth, Viardot Garcia; Dame, Mdme. Cherricci; Macbeth, Signor Graziani; Banquo, Signor Ciampi; Macduff, Signor Luise; Medico, Signor Kinni.

On Wednesday, 12th, "Norma." Norma, Grisi; Adalgisa, Madame Orvil; Clotilde, Madame Cherricci; Pollio, Signor Luise; Oroveso, Signor Ciampi; Flavio, Kinni.

On Thursday, 13th, "Rigoletto." Gilda, Madame Gassier; Madalena, Madame Viardot; Giovanni, Mdme. Cherricci; Duca, Signor Mario; Rigoletto, Signor Graziani; Sparafucili, Signor Ciampi.

On Friday, 14th, "Marta." Lionelli, Mario; Plunkett, Graziani; Tristano, Signor Ciampi; Sheriffo, Kinni; Enrichetta, Grisi; Nancy, Viardot.

On Saturday, 15th, "Lucrezia Borgia." Lucrezia, Grisi; Orsini, Viardot; Gennaro, Mario; Alfonso, Graziani; Gubetta, Signor Fallar; Rustighello, Signor Cherricci; Vitellozo, Kinni.

On Monday, September 17th, "Don Giovanni." Giovanni, Graziani; Donna Anna, Grisi; Ottavio, Mario; Commendatore, Fallar; Donna Elvira, Madame Gassier; Leporello, Signor Ciampi; Masetto, Signor Kinni; Zerlina, Madame Viardot Garcia.

On Tuesday, 18th, "Norma," as before.

On Wednesday, 19th, "Rigoletta," as before.

On Thursday, 20th, "Marta."

On Friday, September 21st (first time in Dublin), Gluck's Opera, "Orfeo and Euridice." (The version performed at the Theatre Lyrique, Paris.) Orfeo, Mdme. Viardot Garcia; L'Amore, Madame Gassier; Euridice, Madame Orvil; after which "Don Bucefalo." Bucefalo (a composer at his first rehearsal), Signor Ciampi; concluding with last Scene of "Somnambula." Amina, Madame Gassier.

On Saturday, 22nd, "Trovatore" (repeat).

On Monday, 24th, "Il Barbiere." Rosina, Madame Gassier; Berta, Mdlle. Cherricci; Count Almaviva, Signor Mario; Figaro, Signor Graziani; Bartolo, Signor Ciampi; Basilio, Signor Fallar; Officiale, Signor Cherricci.

On Tuesday, 25th, "Norma."

Wednesday, 26th, "La Favorita." Leonora, Madame Grisi; Luis, Madame Cherricci; Fernando, Signor Mario; Alfonso, Graziani; Gaspare, Signor Cherricci.

On Thursday, 27th, "Orfeo and Euridice" (repeat).

On Friday, 28th, "Don Giovanni."

On Saturday, "Lucrezia Borgia," as before—last night.

The Opera of "Macbeth" proved more attractive during this engagement than when first presented, the Lady Macbeth of Viardot having produced a deep impression; however, it may here be remarked that, as a rule, new works are not generally attractive in Dublin; it is when the music becomes familiar that the audience increases in numbers. Several instances of this truth might be quoted, but that the fact is universally acknowledged—there may be a few exceptions, but the rule still holds. The production of Gluck's "Orfeo and Euridice" was the feature of the season, Viardot adding another laurel wreath to her already overcrowded brow by her extraordinary performance of "Orfeo," which, indeed, realized all the classical ideas that could possibly be formed of the heart-broken god of the lyric art. It was, indeed, a highly, deeply-wrought study, most delightful to witness from the first scene to the last; in fact it would require a volume to enter into a just criticism of this effort of genius, either with reference to the rendering of the music of the great composer, who first formed the classic French school, or as a histrionic embodiment of the part which it is said Gluck set his heart on. The impression produced by the "Che faro senza Eurydice" can never be forgotten; its exquisite tenderness caused tears to flow, and the contrast between the death-like silence during the song, and the "thunders of applause" at the end, was indeed striking. If any proof were wanted of the extraordinary versatility of this great artiste-musicienne, it only required to see her Lady Macbeth one evening, then Orfeo, and then Zerlina in "Don Giovanni," all equally excellent, and fully proving that she had "gone through each mode of the lyre, and was mistress of all."

September, 1861.—Italian Opera Company.—Mdlle. Titiens, Madame Lemaire, Madame Bellini, Mdlle. Anna Whitty, Signor Giuglini, Signor Della Sedie, Signor Fallar, Signor Ciampi, Signor Bossi, Signor Bellini, Signor Casaboni, and Mr. Swift. Conductor, Signor Arditi.

Monday, September 16th, 1861, "Il Trovatore." Leonora, Titiens; Azucena, Mdme. Lemaire; Inez, Madame

Bellini; Conte di Luna, Signor Della Sedie; Fernando, Signor Bossi; Ruiz, Casaboni; Manrico, Giuglini.

Tuesday, 17th, " I Puritani." Elvira, Miss Anna Whitty; Georgio, Signor Ciampi; Ricardo, Signor Della Sedie; Arturo, Signor Giuglini.

On Wednesday, 18th, " Norma." Norma, Titiens; Adalgisa, Mdlle. Anna Whitty; Oroveso, Signor Ciampi; Clotilde, Madame Bellini; Pollio, Mr. Swift.

Thursday, 19th, " Marta." Lady Enrichetta, Titiens; Nancy, Madame Lemaire; Lionello, Giuglini; Plunketto, Signor Della Sedie; Tristano, Signor Ciampi; Sheriffo, Signor Casaboni.

Friday, 20th, " Il Barbiere." Rosini, Anna Whitty; Figaro, Signor Della Sedie; Bartolo, Ciampi; Basilio, Signor Fallar; Conte Almaviva, Mr. Swift.

On Saturday, 21st, " Lucrezia Borgia." Lucrezia, Titiens; Orsini, Madame Lemaire; Alfonso, Signor Ciampi; Gubetta, Signor Bossi; Gazella, Signor Fallar; Vitellozo, Signor Casaboni; Liverotto, Signor Bellini; Gennaro, Giuglini.

On Monday, 22nd, " Don Giovanni." Donna Anna, Titiens; Zerlina, Madame Lemaire; Elvira, Mdlle. Anna Whitty; Don Giovanni, Signor Della Sedie; Leporello, Signor Ciampi; Mazetto, Signor Casaboni; Commendatore, Signor Bossi; Don Ottavio, Signor Giuglini.

On Wednesday, September 25th, 1861, for the first time in Dublin, Verdi's Grand Opera, " Il Ballo in Maschera." Amelia, Mdlle. Titiens; Renato, Signor Della Sedie; Oscar, Mdlle. A. Whitty; Ulrica, Madame Lemaire; Samuele, Signor Bossi; Tomaso, Signor Ciampi; Silvano,

Signor Fallar; Un Guidice, Signor Casaboni; Servo, Signor Lavini; Ricardo, Signor Giuglini. The Band of the 11th Hussars performed in the Masquerade Scene, conducted by Signor Operti.

On Thursday, 26th, "Norma," as before.
On Friday, 27th, "Marta."
Saturday, 28th, "Ballo in Maschera."
Monday, 30th, "Trovatore."
Tuesday, October 1st, "Don Giovanni."
Wednesday, 2nd, "Un Ballo."
Thursday, 3rd, "Marta." Benefit of Titiens and Giuglini.
Friday, 4th, "Il Barbiere," as before.
Saturday, 5th, "Un Ballo." Last night.

Miss Anna Whitty, who created a favourable impression as a soprano during this engagement, was a daughter of Mr. Whitty, proprietor of one of the principal daily journals of Liverpool. She had a good and well-cultivated voice, having studied under the best masters in Italy. After a short and successful career on the stage, she accepted a good matrimonial offer of engagement, and retired from public, to delight her friends in social life by her musical abilities. The first production of Verdi's charming Opera, "Un Ballo in Maschera," formed the chief feature, and was a great event in our operatic annals. The work created an immediate impression, as well from the attractive nature of the music, as from the very efficient "cast." Titiens was of course, as usual, at home; Mdlle. Whitty, an excellent "Seconda Donna;" but the palm seemed to lie with Giuglini and Della Sedie; the singing of "Eri tu" by the latter great artiste created quite a startling sensation, and most deservedly, for a more finished piece of vocalism has seldom, if ever, been heard. Although nearly 30 years have elapsed, there are many who preserve a lively recollection of this "Eri tu" of Della Sedie. The same remarks will apply to Giuglini, whose singing in this work almost excelled any former effort. The first eight bars of "E Scherzo" was given with such marvellous point and beauty, that a double encore was the result every night, thus delaying the "ensemble," which follows, for a considerable time. Madame Lemaire, Signor Ciampi, Signor Bossi (a capital *basso profondo*), and Casaboni, the most useful of "utility men," contributed much to the general effect of the very beautiful concerted pieces. The Band of the 11th Hussars bore an important "hand" in the Masquerade Scene, led by Signor Operti, the efficient master, who first visited Dublin in the capacity of "Suggeritore" with former companies. A great financial success attended this engagement, much enhanced by the production of "Un Ballo."

Later in October, 1861, the following announcement appeared:—"Mr. Harris has very great pleasure in announcing that, in compliance with the generally-expressed wish to hear Mdlle. Adelina Patti, he has, at an enormous expense, succeeded in making arrangements for that celebrated artiste to sing once in each of those Operas in which she achieved such unparalleled success at the Royal Italian Opera, Covent Garden, during the past season." Accordingly, on Tuesday, October 29th, 1861, was given,

"La Sonnambula." Amina, Mdlle. Patti; Ina, Mdlle. Sedlatzek; Elvino, Signor Galvani; Rodolfo, Signor Manfredi; Alessio, Signor Kinni; Notaro, Signor Annoni.

On Thursday, October 31st, "La Traviata." Violetta, Mdlle. Patti; Flora, Mdlle. Sedlatzek; Georgio Germont, Signor Cima; Gaston, Signor Annoni; Baron Duphol, Signor Galli; Dottore, Signor Kinni; Alfred Germont, Signor Galvani.

On Saturday, November 2nd, "Lucia." Lucia, Mdlle. Patti; Aston, Signor Cima; Raimondo, Signor Manfredi; Arturo, Signor Annoni; Normanno, Signor Kinni; Edgardo, Signor Galvani.

On Monday, 4th, "Il Barbiere." Rosina, Mdlle. Patti; Berta, Mdlle. Sedlatzek; Figaro, Signor Cima; Bartolo, Signor Manfredi; Basilio, Signor Kinni; Fiorello, Signor Annoni; Almaviva, Signor Galvani.

On Wednesday, repeat of "Sonnambula."

On Saturday, 9th, "Marta." Lady Enrichetta, Mdlle. Patti; Nancy, Mdlle. Sedlatzek; Plunketto, Signor Cima; Lionello, Signor Galvani; Sheriffo, Signor Kinni; Tristano, Signor Manfredi. In the course of the evening Patti sang "Home, Sweet Home," and "'Twas within a Mile of Edinbro' Town." Last night, for Patti's benefit.

The prices on this occasion were—Dress Circle, 10s.; Second Circle, 6s.; Pit, 3s. 6d; Lower Gallery, 2s. 6d.; Upper Gallery, 1s. 6d.

Since the engagement of Jenny Lind the prices had not been so high, and many signs of disapproval were manifested, as, with the exception of the great *prima-*

donna, the Company was not " of the strongest." It was on the first night, during the progress of the song, "Vi Raviso," by Rodolfo, when, from nervousness or otherwise, the singer "broke down" on an important note, a "member" of the upper gallery exclaimed, in a rather subdued tone, but with a melancholy whine, "Oh! Blood-an-'ouns, my eighteenpence!" An enormous success of course attended the engagement, proving fully the profitable results to managers of the starring system. Patti, if not the greatest, certainly as great a genius as ever appeared in the musical world, deserved all the "kudos" that could possibly be bestowed. It is quite unnecessary to descant on her transcendant merits, as she still reigns supreme, and, if possible, increases year after year in public favour, commanding the largest terms ever bestowed on any other vocalist, except Jenny Lind—terms, it is to be feared, which may prevent the possibility of Patti's re-appearance in the Dublin Theatre. Happily, however, the facility of travelling now offers the opportunity of hearing her in London; and all are hereby advised to witness her Catarina in "L'Etoile du Nord," and her Americaine, &c., &c., and, if occasion should offer, she should also be heard in "Oratorio," in which she "shines resplendent." At the last Triennial Handel Festival, she positively eclipsed all her compeers.

Farewell Engagement of Mdme. Grisi. On Tuesday, December 3rd, 1861, the above-announced appeared. The Company thus:—Madame Grisi, Madame Lemaire, Mdlle. Bossi, Mdlle. Dario, Miss Ellen Conran (her first appearance); Signor Galvani, Mr. Swift, Signor

Aspa, Signor Cresci, Signor Fallar, Signor Bellini, Signor Ciampi. Conductor, Signor Vianesi; Leader, Mr. Levey.

On Tuesday, December 3rd, "Lucrezia Borgia." Lucrezia, Mdme. Grisi; Maffeo Orsini, Mdme. Lemaire; Don Alfonso, Signor Cresci; Vitellozo, Signor Fallar; Liverotto, Signor Aspa; Gubetta, Signor Bellini; Gennaro, Signor Galvani.

On Wednesday, 4th, "Rigoletto." Gilda, Mdlle. Dario; Madelina, Mdme. Lemaire; Contessa, Mdlle. Bossi; Rigoletto, Signor Cresci; Sparafucele, Signor Ciampi; Marcello, Signor Fallar; Monteroni, Signor Ceni; Il Duca, Signor Galvani.

On Thursday, "Norma." Norma, Madame Grisi; Adalgaisa, Miss Ellen Conran (her first appearance); Pollio, Mr. Swift; Flavio, Signor Aspa; Oroveso, Signor Ciampi.

On Saturday, "Trovatore." Leonora, Mdme. Grisi; Azucena, Mdme. Lemaire; Inez, Mdlle. Bossi; Conte di Luna, Cresci; Ferrando, Signor Ciampi; Un Zingara, Signor Bellini; Manrico, Signor Galvani.

On Monday, December 9th, "Don Giovanni." Donna Anna, Grisi; Donna Elvira, Mdlle. Dario; Zerlina, Miss Ellen Conran; Ottavio, Signor Galvani; Leporello, Ciampi; Masetto, Bossi; Commendatore, Fallar; Don Giovanni, Signor Cresci.

On Tuesday, December 10th, "Un Ballo in Maschera." Amelia, Miss Ellen Conran; Ulrica, Mdme. Lemaire; Oscar, Mdlle. Dario; Renato, Signor Cresci; Tomaso, Signor Fallar; Samuele, Signor Ciampi; Silvano, Signor Bellini; Riccardo, Signor Galvani.

On Wednesday, repeat of " Lucrezia."
On Thursday, " Trovatore."
On Friday, " La Traviata." Violetta, Mdlle. Dario; Flora, Mdme. Bossi ; Germont, Signor Cresci ; Il Barone, Signor Fallar ; Alfredo, Signor Galvani. Second Act of " Un Ballo" and First Act of " Il Barbiere." Rosina, Miss E. Conran ; Figaro, Signor Cresci ; Almaviva, Signor Galvani.

On Saturday—last night—(benefit of Miss Conran) "Marta." Enrichetta, Grisi; Nancy, Miss E. Conran; Plunketto, Signor Ciampi; Tristano, Signor Fallar; Sheriffo, Signor Bellini; Lionelli, Signor Galvani.

The Company proceeded to Cork and Limerick, and, on the return, " Norma" was given for the benefit of Mdme. Grisi, announced as " positively her last appearance on any stage in the United Kingdom." Miss Ellen Conran was the daughter of William Sarsfield Conran, an eminent pianist of Dublin, and great public favourite. She made a most successful *debut;* Mdme. Grisi taking the greatest interest in her welfare, and bestowing much pains in imparting to Miss Conran at rehearsals the most careful lessons in stage business ; teaching her also, with the greatest care, the different passages and cadenzas which occur in the duets which occur between Adalgisa and Norma, " De Conte," &c. It is hardly necessary to say that Grisi did not require rehearsal for music which she had so repeatedly sung. She, however, went over every note with this young artiste, so that no hitch might possibly occur; of course it was of the last importance to Norma that all should be smooth ; and the uninitiated are not aware of the extreme pains exercised, and the perfect understanding which must exist between two even of the most finished artistes, to ensure the precision which is indispensable for public performance. Grisi, was, however, on this occasion prompted more by kindness for the young Dublin Adalgisa than from any selfish motives, and displayed a nervous anxiety which gave strong evidence of a kindness of heart worthy of a great artiste.

This Engagement was not a marked success.

On Tuesday, October 7th, 1862, the following Company:—Mdlle. Titiens, Mdme. Louise Michal, Mdlle. Florio, Mdme. Lemaire, Mdme. Pauline Castro, Signor Badiali, Herr Formes, Signor Casaboni, Signor Soldi, Signor Bossi, Signor Giuglini. Conductor, Signor Arditi.

On Tuesday, "Il Trovatore;" with Titiens, Louisa Michal, Badiali, Formes and Giuglina.

On Wednesday, "Lucia;" with Mdlle. Pauline Castro, Signor Badiale, Herr Formes, Giuglini.

On Friday, "Puritani." Titiens, Giuglini, Badiali, Formes.

On Saturday, 11th, "Marta." Titiens, Pauline Castro, Giuglini, Badiali, Formes.

Monday, 13th, " Lucrezia Borgia." Lucrezia, Titiens; Orsino, Mdme. Lemaire; Gennaro, Giuglini; Il Duca, Badiali.

Tuesday, 14th, "Don Giovanni." Donna Anna, Titiens; Elvira, Louise Michal; Zerlina, Pauline Castro; Leporello, Herr Formes; Giovanni, Badiali; Masetto, Bossi; Commendatore, Casaboni; Ottavio, Giuglini.

On Wednesday, 15th, "Norma." Norma, Titiens; Adalgisa, Louise Michal; Oroveso, Bossi; Pollio, Signor Palmiera (his first appearance).

On Friday, 17th, "Lucrezia Borgia." Cast as before.

Saturday, 18th, benefit of Titiens, and last night. "Puritani" and Third Act of "Robert le Diable." Bertram, Formes; Rambaldo, Signor Ubalde; Robert, Signor Palmieri; Alice, Mdlle. Titiens. (No remarkable event.)

Mdlle. Titiens, Mdme. Volpini (her first appearance), Mdlle. Giraldoni, Mdlle. Trebelli (her first appearance), Signor Volpini (his first appearance); Signor Bettini (his first appearance), Signor Soldi, Mr. Sims Reeves (his first appearance these nine years), Mr. Santley (his first appearance), Signor Bossi, Signor Casaboni. Suggeritore, Signor Fontana; Regisseur, Signor Grua; Conductor, Signor Arditi; Leader, Mr. Levey.

Saturday, September 26th, 1863, "Lucia." Edgardo, Mr. Sims Reeves; Arturo, Signor Soldi; Normanno, Signor Casaboni; Ashton, Mr. Santley; Raimondo, Signor Bossi; Alice, Mdlle. Giraldoni; Lucia, Mdlle. Volpini (in consequence of Mdlle. Titiens having missed the train).

On Monday, September 28th, "Marta." Lionello, Signor Bettini; Tristano, Signor Casaboni; Plunketto, Signor Bossi; Sheriffo, Signor Pretti; Nancy, Mdlle. Trebelli; Marta, Mdlle. Volpini.

Tuesday, September 29th. The following announcement appeared—" Postponement of the production of 'Faust' until Thursday next, when it will positively be performed.

In consequence of the amount of preparation necessary for the representation of a work of such importance and magnitude, and which has created such a remarkable sensation throughout the whole of the principal Theatres of Europe, it has been deemed necessary, in order to attain that *ensemble* so indispensable to this celebrated work, to postpone the first performance until Thursday next, October 1st, when will be presented for the first time Gounod's celebrated Opera of ' Faust.' "

On Tuesday evening, September 29th, " Il Trovatore." Manrico, Signor Volpini ; Conte di Luna, Mr. Santley ; Ferrando, Signor Bossi ; Ruiz, Signor Vercellini ; Un Zingara, Signor Casaboni ; Azucena, Mdlle. Trebelli ; Inez, Mdlle. Giraldoni ; Leonora, Mdlle. Titiens.

On Wednesday, 30th, " Un Ballo in Maschera." Ricardo, Volpini ; Renato, Mr. Santley ; Samuele, Vercellini ; Tomaso, Signor Bossi ; Ulrica, Mdlle. Trebelli ; Oscar, Mdlle. Volpini ; Amelia, Mdlle. Titiens.

On Thursday evening, October 1st, 1863, Gounod's Opera, "Faust." Faust, Mr. Sims Reeves ; Valentino, Mr. Santley ; Wagner, Signor Casaboni ; Mephistophele, Signor Bossi ; Siebel, Mdlle. Trebelli ; Marta, Mdlle. Giraldoni ; Margherita, Mdlle. Titiens. (The Band of the 86th Regiment.)

Friday, October 2nd, "La Traviata." Alfredo, Signor Bettini ; Germont, Mr. Santley ; Gastone, Mdlle. Trebelli (" who has kindly undertaken the part, in which she will introduce ' No, no, no,' from ' Les Huguenots.' ") Obigny, Signor Vercellini ; Medico, Signor Bossi ; Anina, Mdlle. Giraldoni ; Violetta, Mdlle. Volpini.

On Saturday, October 3rd (in consequence of the immense success), "Faust," as before.

On Monday, "Norma." Norma, Mdlle. Titiens; Adalgisa, Mdlle. Volpini; Clotilda, Mdlle. Giraldoni Oroveso, Signor Bossi; Flavio, Signor Casaboni; Pollio, Signor Volpini.

On Tuesday, 6th October, "Faust," as before.

On Wednesday, "Marta" (repeat).

On Thursday, 8th, "Oberon" (first time in Italian). Sir Huon, Sims Reeves: Sherasmin, Mr. Santley; Oberon, Signor Bettini; Babakin, Signor Bossi; Califo, Signor Casaboni; Puck, Mdlle. Volpini; Fatima, Mdlle. Trebelli; Reiza, Mdlle. Titiens.

On Friday, "Traviata" (repeat).

On Saturday (last night), " in consequence of the immense success," repeat of "Oberon."

This engagement is, indeed, memorable for the first production of "Faust" and of "Oberon;" also for the numerous "first appearances" of so many artistes destined to become immense favourites—Trebelli, Santley, Signor Bettini, &c. Signor Volpini made his mark as a genuine, substantial, manly tenor, most satisfactory in every part he undertook. The Dublin audience may be considered very fastidious with reference to tenors, still, coming after all the great ones, Volpini held his ground well, and became a great favourite. Mdlle. Volpini was fortunate in meeting an opportunity the very first night of the engagement. In consequence of the accidental absence of Titiens, by missing a train, the young soprana, at a short notice, sustained the part of "Lucia."

Audiences in general are, on all such occasions, indulgent to a rising artiste who can on an emergency undertake an important *role*—when successful, the applause will be greater than if announced as " Prima-Donna" beforehand. Mdlle. Volpini took the public quite by surprise by her admirable singing and acting, and established herself so firmly, that the announcement appeared the next day that, " In consequence of Mdlle. Volpini's great success, she will appear on Friday in ' La Traviata.' " Several similar instances have occurred, which have made the fortune of " Remplaçantes." Miss Rainsforth (in English Opera) is one instance. She undertook the part of " Norma " at a moment's notice, when Miss Adelaide Kemble was taken ill, and thus elevated herself to the position of *prima-donna*, which she enjoyed for several years on the English Stage.

It is unnecessary to allude to the almost unprecedented success of Trebelli, who up to the present moment enjoys a world-wide reputation, which in every city in Europe seems to increase, and which must still increase, as long as purity of style and finished taste—indeed, art, in its highest lyric form—continue to be appreciated. Then Santley, the greatest baritone England has yet produced—indeed, unsurpassed by any foreign artist in voice or high-toned musical education. An instrumentalist in his younger days (having played the violin at the Liverpool Philharmonic), he enjoyed the advantage of a most perfectly formed " ear," which those may lack who have not studied a stringed instrument. As Mr. Santley is still in the enjoyment of all his great powers, and continues periodically to visit Dublin, more welcome each time, it is unnecessary to enlarge more on his merits. Signor Bettini, though last, not least, must not be forgotten. This tenor only required a little more power of voice to have placed him amongst those who have arrived at the top of the ladder. The wonderfully artistic manner in which he managed the rather limited organ which nature placed at his disposal, was most remarkable. Although wanting force, the voice was exquisitely sweet, and in music requiring flexibility, such as Rossini's Count Almaviva, &c., he was perfection, varying his passages on the repetition of a phrase with great judgment—a proceeding very often admissible in florid composers, but sometimes abused. It is related that Rossini, after hearing a song of his own performed by a great Parisian soprano, was asked: "Well, Maestro, what do you think of that?" "Magnificent," replied Rossini; "but who is the composer?" Bettini did not go so far, but "used all gently." His singing in "Oberon" was something charming.

The first performance of the now familiar "Faust" was a success, but a *succès d'estime*. It must be admitted that the audience were a little puzzled, and varied were the critical remarks. The journals were for the most part favourable, but the pit-goers, in particular, were doubtful. All admitted the "grandeur" of the work, the fulness of the orchestra, &c.; but it was asked, "Where is the melody? Why, the only tune is 'The Soldiers' Chorus,'" &c., &c. (Valentine's first song, "Dio possente," was not then introduced.) The cavillers were answered by "What do you say to Trebelli's song, 'Le parlati d'amor?'" the reply to which was, "Ah, it's very short." "Well, but 'The Jewel Song?'" one enthusiast asked seriously. "Now, who could whistle any of that song?" Altogether, "Faust" at first left the impression of a great work of high art—some thought rather too high—and this is not to be wondered at after so many years of the "Lucias," "Sonnambulas," "Puritanis," &c., &c., where the attention of the listener must be concentrated on the star on the stage singing, doubtless, a very pretty tune, with the orchestra, "vilely subservient," giving a tickling arpeggio accompaniment. Happily this state of things is passing away; and although the old melodious works will, doubtless, still hold ground for some time, the public taste is fast improving, and the constant hearing of "Faust," with the works of Meyerbeer, Thomas, Wagner, &c., must surely educate us up to the more classical school, where luxuriant orchestration and more unity of "form" exist.

Weber's "Oberon," in Italian guise, came on us now also for the first time. This work (written by Weber for Miss Paton, afterwards Mrs. Wood) had lain dormant for some years, partly, it was stated, because it was hopeless to find a vocalist who could declaim the great scena, "Ocean, thou mighty Monster," equal to the eminent English soprano, whose "reading" of this wonderfully descriptive composition was, indeed, an extraordinary effort of genius. However, Mr. Mapleson, with his accustomed foresight, knew he had an artiste equal to the occasion; and, indeed, Titiens even excelled the great original in this piece. By the addition of a recitative by Sir Julius Benedict, and some additions from other Operas of his old master, Weber, Sir Julius elevated a rather patchy musical drama, with certainly some exquisite songs, duets, quartets, &c., to an Italian Opera, or as near as possible thereto. When shall we again hear "Over the dark blue Waters," as given by Titiens, Trebelli, Sims Reeves, and Santley? What could equal the duet, "Let us be Merry," with Trebelli and Santley; the songs, "A lonely Arab Maid" and "Oh! Araby" of Trebelli? The "Mermaid's Song" by Mdlle. Volpini must not be forgotten; and then, as already noticed, the "Ocean, thou mighty Monster" of Titiens. By-the-way, a slight inconsistency occurred on the last occasion but one of the performance of "Oberon." It was for the benefit of Titiens. At the forcible request—indeed, the continued and boisterous command—of the members of the upper gallery, immediately following "Ocean, thou mighty Monster," a pianoforte had to be carried on the stage (the waters of said ocean supposed to be running thereon), that poor Titiens should sing "The Last Rose of Summer!" This she did with her (on this occasion) too yielding kindness and good-nature, notwithstanding her dishevelled hair and sea-like appearance. The pianoforte, on being rolled off the stage, unfortunately rolled over, creating shouts of laughter. "Oberon" has well held its ground, but its repetition, it is to be feared, is a distant event.

NOTE.—Thalberg's farewell Concerts took place this season, commencing on the 16th November.

Sothern made his first appearance at the Royal, November 9th, 1863, as Lord Dundreary.

Opera Company—Mdlle. Titiens, Mdlle. Grossi, Mdlle. Giraldini, and Mdlle. Sinico (her first appearance); Signor Gardoni, Mr. Santley, Signor Bossi, Signor Marini, Signor Vercellini, Signor Casaboni, and Mr. Swift. Conductor, Signor Arditi.

On Saturday, September 24th, 1864, "Lucrezia Borgia." Gennaro, Signor Gardoni; Alfonso, Santley; Rustighello, Marini; Liverotto, Vercellini; Astolfo, Casaboni; Gubetta, Bossi; Orsini, Mdlle. Grossi; Lucrezia, Titiens.

On Monday, "Faust." Faust, Gardoni; Valentino, Santley; Mephistophele, Bossi; Wagner, Casaboni; Siebel, Mdlle. Grossi; Marta, Mdlle. Giraldini; Margherita, Titiens.

On Tuesday, 27th, "La Traviata." Alfredo, Gardoni; Germont, Santley; Gaston, Marini; Barone, Vercellini; Marchese, Casaboni; Medico, Bossi; Flora, Mdlle. Giraldini; Violetta, Mdlle. Sinico.

On Wednesday, 28th, "Norma." Pollio, Swift; Oroveso, Bossi; Flavio, Marini; Clotilda, Mdlle. Giraldini; Adalgisa, Mdlle. Sinico; Norma, Titiens.

On Thursday, September 29th, 1864, first time in Dublin, Gounod's Grand Opera, "Mirella." Vincenzo, Signor Gardoni; Orvias, Mr. Santley; Ramon, Signor Bossi; Ambrozio, Signor Casaboni; Vincenzina, Mdlle. Sinico; Tavena, Mdlle. Grossi; Mirella, Mdlle. Titiens.

On Friday, 30th, "Trovatore." Conte di Luna, Santley; Ferrando, Bossi; Manrico, Mr. Swift; Azucena; Mdlle. Grossi; Leonora, Mdlle. Sinico.

On Saturday, October 1st, "Oberon." Huon, Gardoni; Oberon, Mr. Swift; Sultano, Signor Bossi; Scherasmin, Santley; Fatima, Mdlle. Grossi; Puck, Mdlle. Sinico; Reiza, Mdlle. Titiens.

On Monday, 3rd, "Faust." Faust, Gardoni; Valentini, Santley; Mephistophele, Bossi; Wagner, Casaboni; Siebel, Mdlle. Grossi; Martha, Mdlle. Giraldini; Margherita, Mdlle. Titiens.

On Tuesday, 4th, "Fidelio." Ferdinando, Gardoni; Pizzaro, Mr. Santley; Rocco, Signor Bossi; Jacquino, Mr. Swift; Ministro, Signor Casaboni; Marcellina, Mdlle. Sinico; Leonora, Mdlle. Titiens.

On Wednesday, 5th, "Trovatore."

On Thursday, 6th, "Norma."

On Friday, 7th, "Marta." Lionello, Gardoni; Plunketto, Santley; Sheriffo, Marini; Enrichetta, Mdlle. Sinico; Nancy, Mdlle. Grossi.

On Saturday, 8th, "Fidelio." Last night; benefit of Titiens.

Gounod's charming pastoral "Tone Poem," "Mirella," was not a great success, and has never since been repeated. This result is unaccountable; the work is quite worthy of its great author, full of charming melody and rich scoring. Poor Titiens was much disappointed, having set her heart on its success in Dublin. Indeed, she was under the impression that her grand scena in "Mirella" would have produced even greater effect than her "Jewel Song" in "Faust." She was, however, mistaken, and was, in consequence, much depressed. She expressed her opinion, in which she is joined by many eminent musicians, that "Mirella" is still destined to force its way in the lyric world.

Italian Opera Company.—Mdlle. Titiens, Mdlle. Veralli, Mdlle. Taccani, Mdlle. Zandrina (her first appearance), Mdlle. Sinico, Signor Giuglini, Mr. Santley, Signor Garcia, Signor Celli, Signor Bossi, Signor Marini, Signor Vercellini, Signor Casaboni, Mr. Swift and Mons. Joulain (his first appearance). Conductor, Signor Arditi. Leader, Mr. Levey.

On Monday, March 6th, 1865, "Lucrezia Borgia." Gennaro, Mr. Swift; Alfonso, Signor Garcia; Rustighello, Signor Marini; Liverotto, Signor Casaboni; Astolfo, Signor Celli; Gubetta, Signor Bossi; Orsini, Mdlle. Veralli; Lucrezia, Mdlle. Titiens.

On Tuesday, 7th, "Il Trovatore." Manrico, Mons. Joulain; Conte di Luna, Santley; Ferrando, Bossi; Ruiz, Marini; Zingaro, Casaboni; Azucena, Mdlle. Veralli; Leonora, Titiens.

On Thursday, 9th, "Faust." Faust, Mons. Joulain; Valentino, Santley; Mephistophele, Bossi; Siebel, Mdlle. Veralli; Margherita, Titiens.

On Saturday, 11th, "Lucia." Edgardo, Mons. Joulain; Ashton, Santley; Raimondo, Bossi; Lucia, Titiens.

On Monday, 13th, "Faust," cast as before, except Siebel, Mdlle. Zandrina (first appearance).

Tuesday, "Norma." Pollio, Signor Sinico (in consequence of Mr. Swift's illness). Oroveso, Signor Bossi; Adalgisa, Mdme. Sinico; Norma, Titiens.

On Wednesday, 15th, "Rigoletto." Il Duca, Mons. Joulain; Rigoletto, Santley; Sparafucile, Bossi; Monte-

roni, Garcia; Paggio, Mdlle. Zandrina; Contessa, Mdlle.
Taccani; Madalena, Mdlle. Veralli; Gilda, Madame
Sinico.

Thursday, 16th, "Trovatore" (repeat).

Saturday, 18th, "Ernani." Ernani, Mons. Joulain;
Don Carlo, Santley; Riva, Bossi; Elvira, Titiens.

Monday, 20th, "Lucia, as before.

Tuesday, "Faust."

Thursday, "Ernani."

Saturday, March 25th, first Act of "Fidelio," the
Garden Scene from "Faust," and the fourth Act of
"Trovatore"—last night.

It will be perceived that Giuglini was announced to
appear in this Company, but the following appeared on
the first night's announcements :—" Signor Giuglini
having been delayed by indisposition on his return
from St. Petersburgh, the part of Gennaro will be undertaken by Mr. Swift, to prevent disappointment by change
of Opera." Poor Giuglini never appeared again in
Dublin; he died soon after, under the melancholy circumstances before recorded. When shall we hear such
a tenor? The remarks of Charles Lamb with reference
to John Kemble may well (with a little alteration) be
applied to Giuglini—" He made his defects a grace; his
exact declamatory manner, as he managed it (in vocalism),
only served to convey his points with more precision.
It seemed to head the shafts, to carry them deeper; not
one of his sparkling effects was lost. We remember how
minutely he delivered each in succession, and cannot by
any effort imagine how any of them could be altered for

the better." It required the united efforts of Mr. Swift (a thorough good musician-like English tenor), Mons. Joulain, a very charming French artiste, and (on an extraordinary occasion), Signor Sinico, to fill up the place of the "great departed." Signor Sinico only appeared the one night, on which occasion, relieving the management from a great emergency, he proved himself a thorough good and experienced musician, and one who, in his younger days, and in freshness of voice, must have enjoyed a well-earned reputation. Joulain made a marked impression, more particularly in the last scene of "Lucia," by his singing of the "Fra poco," the last movement being encored doubly, and the audience remaining long after the falling of the curtain to call "Joulain out !" Mdlle. Zandrina was a niece of Titiens, with fair promise; she soon retired from the stage. It was reported that a matrimonial engagement existed between herself and and Signor Vizzani, which report has not as yet been verified.

Italian Company, commencing September 18th, 1865. Mdlle. Titiens, Mdme. Sinico, Mdlle. Sarolta (her first appearance), Mdlle. Redi (first appearance), Mdme. De Meric Lablache (her first appearance in Dublin), Signor Mario, Signor Filippi, Signor Stagno (his first appearance), Signor Foli (his first appearance), Signor Bossi, Signor Casaboni, Signor Vercellini, and Mr. Santley. Conductor, Signor Arditi.

On Monday, September 18th, "Faust." Faust, Mario; Valentino, Santley; Mephistophele, Bossi; Siebel, Mdlle. Sarolta ; Monta, Mdlle. Redi; Margherita, Titiens.

On Tuesday, "Norma." Norma, Titiens; Adalgisa, Sinico; Oroveso, Foli; Pollio, Stagno.

On Wednesday, "Rigoletto." Il Duca, Mario; Rigoletto, Santley; Sparafucile, Bossi; Madelina, Madame De Meric Lablache; Gilda, Madame Sarolta.

On Thursday, 21st, "Don Giovanni." Donna Anna, Titiens; Elvira, Mdme. Sinico; Zerlina, Mdlle. Sarolta; Giovanni, Santley; Leporello, Bossi; Ottavio, Mario.

On Friday, 22nd, "La Traviata." Alfredo, Signor Stagno; Germont, Santley;, Barone, Casaboni; Marchese, Filippi; Medico, Bossi; Violetta, Mdme. Sarolta.

On Saturday, 23rd, "Trovatore." Manrico, Mario; Conte di Luna, Santley; Ferrando, Bossi; Azucena, Mdme. De Meric Lablache; Leonora, Titiens.

On Monday, "Faust" (repeat).

Tuesday, 26th, "Fidelio." Pizarro, Santley; Rocco, Bossi; Il Ministri, Foli; Fernando, Swift; Marcellina Mdme. Sinico; Leonora, Titiens.

On Wednesday, 27th, "Marta." Lionello, Mario; Plunketto, Bossi; Nancy, Mdme. De Meric Lablache; Lady Enrichetta, Mdme. Sinico.

Thursday, "Lucrezia Borgia." Alfonso, Santley; Gennaro, Stagno; Gubetta, Bossi; Rustighello, Filippi; Orsini, De Meric Lablache; Lucrezia, Titiens.

Friday, 29th, "Un Ballo in Maschera," Ricardo, Mario: Renato, Santley; Tomaso, Bossi; Samuele, Foli; Falvio, Casaboni; Ulrica, Mdme. De Meric Lablache; Oscar, Mdlle. Sarolta; Amelia, Mdme. Sinico.

On Saturday, 30th, "Don Giovanni" (repeat.)

Monday, October 2nd, "Trovatore."

Tuesday, October 3rd, "Marta."

Wednesday, 4th October, "Der Freischutz." Casparo, Santley; Rodolfo, Stagno; Kuno, Bossi; Hermit, Foli; Killiano, Casaboni; Ottakar, Filippi; Annetta, Madame Sinico; Agata, Mdlle. Titiens.

On Thursday, 5th, "Faust," as before.

On Friday, 6th, "Der Freischutz"—last night.

The first appearance of Foli rendered this engagement special. Fourteen years (who would suppose it?) have passed, still his grand voice seems better on each successive visit. His fine manly person, and easy bearing on the stage, will ever be welcome to the Dublin audience, who live in hope to welcome their favourite and eminent basso for years to come.

Madame De Meric Lablache also "came out" during this engagement, and a more substantial, universally-accomplished lady could hardly be found, with a voice (mezzo-soprano) almost contralto in quality and in general fulfilling parts of this class. Mdme. De Meric Lablache is "under studied" in almost every part in the Operatic Calendar, and therefore, in cases of illness or disappointment, from whatever cause, this most useful of "members" is ready at a moment's notice to become the *prima* or *seconda donna*, and has often, by so doing, relieved the management of much embarrassment.

Mdme. Sarolta was also a successful *debutante*.

1866—The following Italian Company :—Mdme. Grisi, Mdlle. Enequist, Mdme. De Meric Lablache, Mdlle. Edi, and Mdme. Sinico; Signor Amodio, Signor Caravoglio, Signor Bossi, Signor Capello, Signor Casaboni,

Signor Foli, Signor Stagno, Signor Mario. Conductor, Signor Arditi.

On Monday, March 12th, 1866, " Faust." Faust, Mario ; Mephistophele, Bossi ; Valentino, Signor Amodio (first appearance) ; Siebel, Mdme. De Meric Lablache ; Margherita, Mdme. Sinico.

Tuesday, 13th, " Lucrezia Borgia." Gennaro, Stagno ; Alfonso, Foli ; Gubetta, Bossi ; Maffio Orsini, De Meric Lablache ; Lucrezia, Grisi.

Wednesday, 14th, " Marta." Lionello, Mario ; Plunketto, Bossi ; Nancy, De Meric Lablache ; Henrietta, Mdme. Sinico.

Thursday, 15th, " Norma." Pollio, Stagno ; Oroveso, Foli ; Adalgisa, Enequist ; Norma, Grisi.

On Friday, 16th, " Trovatore." Manrico, Mario ; Il Conte, Amodio ; Ferrando, Bossi ; Azucena, De Meric Lablache ; Leonora, Mdme. Sinico.

On Saturday, 17th, " Don Giovanni." Donna Anna, Grisi ; Elvira, Enequist ; Zerlina, De Meric Lablache ; Leporello, Bossi ; Masetto, Casaboni ; Commendatore, Foli ; Don Giovanni, Signor Caravoglio ; Ottavio, Mario.

On Monday, 19th, " Faust," repeated.

On Tuesday, 20th, " Norma."

On Wednesday, 21st, " La Traviata." Alfredo, Signor Stagno ; Germont, Amodio ; Dottore, Bossi ; Violetta, Sinico.

Thursday, 22nd, "Trovatore," repeated, except Manrico, played by Stagno.

Friday, 23rd, " Don Giovanni " repeated.

Saturday, 24th, " Don Giovanni " repeated. Last night.

This was really the third and last "last appearance" of Grisi. Even after the enormous sums of money received during a long professional career, circumstances obliged her to remain too long before the public. Like other great artistes, she would not believe in the decline of her powers. The public were naturally surprised at each announcement of her appearance after her last farewell; the manifest change was too apparent, and, of course, the houses "fell off;" and on this occasion, more particularly, the result was not profitable. It was also the season of Lent, which did not improve matters. When some musical Agnes Strickland shall chronicle "The Lives of the Queens of Song," Grisi and Titiens will hold first places.

On Monday, September 17th, 1866, Italian Opera commenced, as follows :—Mdme. Titiens, Mdlle. Baumeister (first appearance), Mdlle. Zandrina, Mdme. De Meric Lablache, Mdme. Sinico; Signor Mario, Signor Morini (first appearance), Signor Gassier, Signor Capello, Signor Foli, Signor Bossi, Signor Casaboni, Mr. Santley. Conductor, Signor Arditi.

Monday, 17th, "Faust." Faust, Mario; Valentino, Santley; Mephistophele, Gassier; Wagner, Bossi; Siebel, Mdlle. Zandrina; Marta, Mdme. Baumeister; Margherita, Titiens.

Tuesday, 18th, "Lucia." Lucia, Sinico; Alisa, Baumeister; Ashton, Gassier; Raimondo, Bossi; Normanno, Casaboni; Arturo, Capello; Edgardo, Morini.

Wednesday, 19th, "Marta." Lionello, Mario; Plunketto, Santley; Tristano, Bossi; Nancy, De Meric Lablache; Henrietta, Titiens.

Thursday, 20th, "Lucrezia Borgia." Gennaro, Morini; Alfonso, Gassier; Gubetta, Bossi; Maffeo, De Meric Lablache; Lucrezia, Titiens.

Friday, 21st, "Traviata." Alfredo, Morini; Germont, Santley; Marchese, Capello; Medico, Bossi; Annina, Mdlle. Baumeister; Violetta, Sinico.

On Saturday, 22nd, "Trovatore." Manrico, Mario; Conte di Luna, Santley; Ferrando, Bossi; Ruiz, Capello; Azucena, De Meric Lablache; Leonora, Titiens.

On Monday, 24th, "Semiramide." Assur, Gassier; Oroe, Bossi; Idreno, Morini; L'Ombra, Casaboni; Arsace, De Meric Lablache; Semiramide, Titiens.

On Tuesday, 25th, "Les Huguenots." Raoul, Mario; St. Bris, Gassier; Nevers, Santley; Marcello, Foli; Meru, Bossi; Tavannes, Capello; Maurevert, Casaboni; De Retz, Balesca; De Cosse, Bolli; Marguerite, Sinico; Dame d'Onore, Mdlle. Baumeister; Urbano, Mdlle. Zandrina; Valentina, Titiens.

On Wednesday, 26th, "Der Freischutz." Rodolfo, Morini; Caspar, Santley; Killiano, Gassier; Kuno, Bossi; Eremita, Foli; Ottaker, Capello; Annetta, Mdme. Sinico; Agata, Titiens.

On Thursday. "Rigoletto." Il Duca, Mario; Rigoletto, Santley; Sparafucile, Bossi; Monteferone, Foli; Il Paggio, Mdlle. Zandrina; Giovanna, Mdlle. Baumeister; Madelina, Mdlle. De Meric Lablache; Gilda, Mdlle. Sinico.

On Friday 28th. "Don Giovanni." Ottavio, Mario; Don Giovanni, Gassier; Commendatore, Foli; Leporello,

Bossi; Masetto, Casaboni; Elvira, Mdlle. Sinico; Zerlina, Mdlle. Zandrina; Donna, Titiens.

On Saturday. "Faust" (repeat).

Monday, October 1st. "Huguenots" (repeat).

Tuesday, 2nd. "Le Nozze di Figaro." Figaro, Gassier; Il Conte, Santley; Don Bartolo, Bossi; Basilio, Morini; Antonio, Casaboni; Susanna, Sinico; Cherubino, Zandrina; La Contessa, Titiens.

On Wednesday, October 3rd. "Il Puritani." Arturo, Mr. Tom Hohler (first appearance in Dublin); Ricardo, Gassier; Georgio, Foli; Bruno, Bossi; Enrichetta, Mdlle. Baumeister; Elvira, Mdlle. Sinico.

Thursday. "Trovatore" (repeat).

On Friday, October 5th. Benefit of Titiens and last night. First and second Acts of "Norma." Pollio, Morini; Oroveso, Foli; Adalgisa, Sinico; Norma, Titiens. Second and third Acts of "Faust," and third Act of "Puritani," as before.

It would be unjust to pass over the first appearance of Mdlle. Baumeister, one of the most useful and universal of Operatic artistes, who is ever ready to "rush into the breach" on any emergency; having studied almost every part in the lyric catalogue, acquitting herself on all occasions as an excellent and finished vocalist, as well as a ready and accomplished "musicienne." Gassier's high finish has been already noticed, his scale-singing during this engagement, more particularly in the first scene of "Semiramide," was delightful. "Tom Hohler" made a good impression.

The Company thus: Mdlle. Titiens, Mdlle. Clara Doria

(her first appearance), Mdlle. De Meric Lablache, Mdlle. Baumeister, Mdlle. Sinico, Signor Tombesi (first appearance), Mr. Hohler, Signor Bolli, Signor Agretti, Signor Balesca, Signor Casaboni, Mr. Lyall, Signor Gassier, Signor Foli, Signor Zoboli (her first appearance), Mr. Santley. Conductor, Signor Bevignani.

On Monday, September 16th, 1867. "Le Nozze di Figaro." Il Conte, Santley; Figaro, Gassier; Bartolo, Foli; Basilio, Mr. Lyall; Antonio, Casaboni; Cherubino, De Meric Lablache; Marcellini, Mdlle. Baumeister; Susanna, Madame Sinico; La Contessa, Titiens.

On Tuesday, "Norma." Pollio, Tombesi; Oroveso, Foli; Clotilda, Baumeister; Adalgisa, Sinico; Norma, Titiens,

On Wednesday, "Marta." Lionello, Mr. T. Hohler; Plunketto, Santley; Sheriffo, Mr. Lyall; Nancy, De Meric Lablache; Marta, Sinico.

Thursday. "Trovatore." Manrico, Tombesi; Conte di Luna, Santley; Ferrando, Foli; Azucena, De Meric Lablache; Leonora, Titiens.

On Friday, 20th, "Sonnambula." Elvino, T. Hohler; Conte Rodolfo, Gassier; Lisa, Mdlle. Baumeister; Amina, Mdlle. Clara Doria (first appearance).

N.B.—The names of Mdlle. Trebelli Bettini and Signor Bettini (first appearance for four years) were now added to the list.

On Saturday, Sept. 21st, "Les Huguenots." Raoul, Signor Bettini; Conte di San Bris, Gassier; Conte di Nevers, Santley; De Cosse, Mr. Lyall; Tavannes, Agretti; Bois Rose, Bolli; De Retz, Casaboni; Marcello, Foli;

Margherita, Madame Sinico; Urbano, Madame Trebelli Bettini; Dame d'Onore, Baumeister; Valentino, Titiens.

On Monday, 23rd, "Faust." Faust, Signor Bettini; Valentino, Santley; Mephistophele, Gassier; Siebel, Madame Trebelli Bettini; Marta, Mdlle. Baumeister; Margherita, Titiens.

First production of Nicolai's "Falstaff."

On Tuesday, September 24th, was given, for the first time in Dublin, Nicolai's favourite Opera of "Falstaff." Mrs. Ford, Titiens; Mrs. Page, Mdlle. De Meric Lablache; Anne Page, Madame Sinico; Mr. Ford, Mr. Santley; Mr. Page, Signor Gassier; Fenton, Mr. Hohler; Dr. Caius, Signor Zoboli; Slender, Mr. Lyall; Sir John Falstaff, Signor Foli.

On Wednesday, "Il Barbiere." Il Conte Almaviva, Bettini; Figaro, Gassier; Dr. Bartolo, Zoboli; Basilio, Foli; Berta, Mdlle. Baumeister; Rosina, Mdme. Trebelli Bettini.

On Thursday, "Don Giovanni." Donna Anna, Titiens; Zerlina, Trebelli Bettini; Elvina, Sinico; Ottavio, Hohler; Leporello, Boboli; Commendatore, Foli; Masetto, Casaboni; Don Giovanni, Gassier.

On Friday, 27th, "Lucia." Edgardo, Tombesi; Ashton, Santley; Arturo, Agretti; Raimondo, Foli; Alice, Baumeister; Lucia, Mdlle. Clara Doria.

On Saturday, 28th, "Oberon." Reiza, Titiens; Fatima, Madame Trebelli Bettini; Puck, De Meric Lablache; Mermaid, Baumeister; Scherasman, Santley; Babekan, Gassier; L'Emiro, Boboli; Astrakan, Agretti; Sir Huon, Tombesi; Oberon, Signor Bettini.

Monday, 30th. "Lucrezia Borgia." Gennaro, Signor Bettini; Alfonso, Gassier; Gubetta, Foli; Rustighello, Agretti; Liverotto; Zoboli; Petrucci, Lyall; Maffeo Orsini; Madame Trebelli Bettini; Lucrezia, Titiens.

Tuesday, Oct. 1st. "La Traviata." Alfredo, Hohler; Germont, Santley; Medico, Foli; Gaston, Agretti; Il Barone, Zoboli; Marchese, Casaboni; Guiseppe, Lyall; Amina, Baumeister; Violetto, Madame Sinico.

On Wednesday, 2nd, "Semiramide." Idreno, Signor Bettini; Assur, Gassier; Oroe, Foli; L'Ombra, Casaboni; Arsace, Madame Trebelli Bettini; Semiramide, Titiens.

On Thursday, 3rd, "Faust" (as before).

On Friday, 4th, "Trovatore" (as before).

Saturday, 5th. "Oberon." Titiens' benefit, and last night.

The additions of Signor Bettini and his wife tended to "pull up" this engagement, which was "flagging." The event was the first performance of Nicolai's "Falstaff," a charming work, replete with sparkling ideas, well worked out; but it failed to make a great impression—in fact, as is very often the case in Dublin with new works, the public did not come to judge; the house being about half filled, if so much; the risk of repetition was not attempted, Trovatore, Lucia, or any of the oft-repeated Operas proving much more profitable.

We must not pass over an amateur performance of "Il Trovatore," which took place on Tuesday, March 31st, 1868, with the following cast:—Leonora, Miss Annie Doyle; Azucena, Mrs. E. L. Shaw; Inez, Miss Levey; Conte di Luna, Mr. J. J. Marlow; Fernando, Mr. P. Hayes;

Ruiz, Mr. Montgomery; Manrico, Mr. C. Cummins. Conductor, Mr. George G. Lee. A capital performance of the Opera, alike creditable to the Conductor and all the amateurs concerned in it.

1868.—(First appearance of Mongini).—September. Italian Opera Company. Mdlle. Titiens, Mdme. Sinico, Mdme. De Meric Lablache, Mdlle. Baumeister, Mdlle. Hersee, Mdlle, Zandrina, Mdme. Trebelli Bettini, Signor Mongini (first appearance), Signor Bettini, Signor Bulterini (first appearance), Signor Bolli, Signor Campi (first time), Signor Crosti (first time), Signor Foli, Signor Zoboli, Mr. Santley, Herr Formes and Mr. Lyall. Conductor, Signor Bevignani; Leader, Mr. Levey.

Monday, 14th September, 1868, " Trovatore." Manrico, Mongini; Conte di Luna, Santley; Ferrando, Foli; Azucena, De Meric Lablache; Inez, Baumeister; Leonora, Titiens.

Tuesday, " Der Freischutz." Rudolph, Mongini; Caspar, Santley; Eremita, Foli; Killano, Casaboni; Kuno, Zoboli; Annetta, Madame Sinico; Agata, Titiens.

Wednesday, 16th, "Lucia." Edgardo, Signor Bulterini; Ashton, Crosti; Raimondo, Foli; Arturo, Agretti; Alice, Baumeister; Lucia, Mdme. Sinico.

Thursday, "Lucrezia Borgia." Gennaro, Mongini; Alfonsi, Crosti; Gubetta, Foli; Rustighello, Agretti; Astolfo, Campi; Petrucci, Mr. Lyall; Orsini, Mdlle. Zandrina; Lucrezia, Titiens.

Friday, 18th, " Rigoletto." Il Duca, Bulterini, Rigoletto, Santley; Sparafucile, Foli; Paggio, Mdlle.

Baumeister ; Madelina, Zandrina, Giovanni, Hersee; Gilda, Mdme. Sinico.

Saturday, 19th, "Faust." Faust, Bulterini ; Valentino, Santley ; Mephistophele, Crosti ; Siebel, Sandrina ; Marta, Baumeister ; Margharita, Titiens.

Monday, 21st, "Norma." Pollio, Mongini ; Oroveso, Foli ; Adalgisa, Sinico ; Coltilda, Baumeister; Norma, Titiens.

Tuesday, 22nd, "Le Nozze." Il Conte, Santley; Figaro, Herr Formes ; Don Basilio, Lyall ; Don Curzio, Agretti ; Susanna, Sinico ; Marcellina, Baumeister; Cherubino, Sandrina ; La Contessa, Titiens.

Wednesday, 23rd, "Marta." Lionello, Mongini ; Plunketto, Santley ; Tristram, Zoboli ; Guiseppa, Lyall ; Nancy, Trebelli ; Marta, Sinico.

Thursday, 24th, "Don Giovanni." Ottavio, Bettini ; Don Giovanni, Santley ; Leporéllo, Formes ; Commendatore, Foli ; Mazetto, Zoboli ; Zerlina, Trebelli Bettini ; Elvira, Sinico ; Donna Anna, Titiens.

Friday, 25th, "Il Barbiere." Il Conte, Bettini ; Figaro, Tagliafico ; Don Bartolo, Zoboli ; Fiorello, Casaboni ; Basilio, Foli ; Marcellina, Baumeister ; Rosina, Trebelli Bettini.

Saturday, 26th, "Fidelio." Florestan, Bulterini ; Pizzaro, Santley ; Rocco, Foli ; Ministro, Tagliafico ; Jaqueno, Lyall ; Marcellina, Sinico ; Leonora, Titiens.

Monday, 28th, "Les Huguenots." Raoul, Mongini ; San Bris, Santley ; Nevers, Tagliafico ; De Corsi, Lyall ; Tavannes, Agretto ; Bois Rose, Bollio ; De Retz, Casaboni ; Mera, Belasco ; Marcello, Foli ; Margharita, Sinico

Urbano, Trebelli Bettini ; Dama D'Onore, Baumeister; Valentina, Titiens.

Tuesday, September 29th, 1868. First production in Dublin of "Il Flauto Magico." Tamino, Bettini; Papageno, Santley; Sarastro, Foli ; Monastos, Lyall ; Due Uomini, Agretti and Campi ; Due Sacerdoti, Bolli and Tagliafico ; Tre Geni, Hersee, Zandrina and Mdlle. Giacomina ; Tre Damigelli, Miss Cruise, Miss Baily and Miss Eiffe ; Regina della Notte, Baumeister ; Papagena, Sinico ; Pamina, Titiens.

Wednesday, 30th, "La Sonnambula." Elvino, Mongini ; Rodolfo, Tagliafico ; Alessio, Zoboli ; Lisa, Baumeister ; Teresa, Miss Cruise ; Amina, Sinico.

Thursday, October 1st, "Semiramide." Idreno, Bettini ; Assur, Foli ; Oroe, Tagliafico ; Arsace, Trebelli Bettini ; Semiramide, Titiens.

Friday, "Il Flauto Magico" (repeat).

Saturday, 3rd, "Oberon." (Benefit of Titiens.) Huon, Mongini ; Oberon, Bettini ; Scherasmin, Santley ; Fatima, Trebelli Bettini ; Mermaid, Baumeister ; Reiza, Titiens.

Three first appearances this engagement, viz. :—Bulterini (tenor), Campi (baritone), Mongini (tenor). Signor Mongini had made a great "stir" in London—a most powerful *tenore robusto*—he produced some great effects, but wanted the finish of many who preceded him ; he was the first who gave the *ut de poitrine* in the " Di quella pira" (Trovatore), and the night he introduced this change in Drury Lane, the pit audience rose *en masse* and cheered heartily ; it was also duly applauded in Dublin. In the "Huguenots," during a *melee*, Mongini was stabbed with a wooden dagger, from which he was laid up for some days. The immortal "Flauto Magico" also now made its first appearance, and with as complete a cast as could well be obtained to interpret this charming work. The tenor music might have been written for Bettini, whose singing was perfection. Santley (Papageno) " goes without saying." " Charley " Lyall (artist in everything,) the best of Monastos. Nothing could exceed the amusement created in the " frightened " duet between Papageno and Monastos. Everybody will remember Foli's " Qui S'degno;" also the "Pa, Pa," duet with Santley and Sinico, never equalled by others. The concerted trios of the Geni and Damigelli were remarkably well sung. The Opera was therefore naturally a great success, and has continued to be a great "draw " when well performed.

First appearance of Ilma di Murska.

Italian Company.—Mdlle. Titiens, Madame Sinico, Mdlle. Scalchi (first appearance), Mdlle. Baumeister, Mdlle. Corsi, Mdlle. Ilma di Murska (first appearance), Signor Gardoni, Signor Della Rocca (first appearance), Signor Marino (first appearance), Mr. Lyall, Signor Mongini, Signor Gassier, Signor Baggagiolo (first appearance, Signor Zoboli, Signor Campi, Herr Formes and Mr. Santley. Conductors, Signor Arditi and Signor Bevignani; Principal Danseuse, Mdlle. Rosalia; Maitre de Ballet, Mons. De Places.

Monday, 13th September, 1869, "Les Huguenots" (with the whole strength).

Tuesday, " Dinorah" (with the whole strength).

Wednesday, 15th, "Trovatore." Manrico, Mongini;

Il Conte, Santley: Ferrando, Baggagiolo; Azucena, Scalchi; Leonora, Titiens.

Thursday, 16th, "Lucia." Edgardo, Mongini; Arturo, Marino; Raimondo, Baggagiolo; Lucia, Ilma di Murska.

Friday, 17th, "Don Giovanni." Donna Anna, Titiens; Zerlina, Sinico; Elvira, Baumeister; Don Giovanni, Santley; Leporello, Zoboli; De Ottavio, Gardoni.

Saturday 18th, "Il Flauto Magico." Tamino, Gordini; Papageno, Santley; Sarastro, Baggagiolo; Oratore, Campi; Monastatos, Lyall; Astrifiammanti, Ilma di Murska; Papagena, Sinico; Tre Geni, Mdlles. Baumeister, Schofield, Clinton; Tre Damigelli, Mdlles. Cruise, Corsi, and Scalchi; Pamina, Titiens.

Monday, 20th, "Faust." Siebel, Scalchi; Marta, Mdme. Corsi; Mephistophele, Gassier; Valentino, Santley; Faust, Gardoni.

Tuesday, 21st, "Sonnambula." Elvino, Mongini; Conte Rodolfo, Gassier; Terese, Corsi; Lisa, Baumeister; Amina, Ilma di Murska.

Wednesday, 22nd, "Lucrezia Borgia." Gennaro, Mongini (in which he introduced "Deserto in Terra"); Alfonso, Gassier; Gazella, Lyall; Maffio Orsini, Scalchi; Lucrezia, Titiens.

Thursday, 23rd, "Il Flauto," as before.

Friday, 24th, "La Traviata." Germont, Santley; Gaston, Marino; Baron, Zoboli; Dottore, Campi; Alfredo, Della Rocca (first appearance); Violetta, Sinico.

Saturday, 25th, "Robert le Diable." Roberto, Gardoni; Bertram, Baggagiolo; Rambalda, Della Rocca; Alberto,

Campi; First Cavaliere, Marino; Second Cavaliere, Lyall; Third Cavalier, Casaboni; Eraldo, Marino; Isabella, Ilma di Murska; Helena, Mdlle. Ricois; Alice, Titiens.

Monday, 27th, " Linda di Chamouni." Carlo, Gardoni; Antonio, Santley; Prefetto, Baggagiolo; Pierotto, Scalchi; Linda, Ilma di Murska.

Tuesday, 28th, " Norma." Pollio, Mongini; Oroveso, Baggagiolo; Adalgisa, Sinico; Norma, Titiens.

Wednesday, 29th, " Lucia " (repeat).

Thursday, 30th, " Faust " (repeat).

Friday, October 1st, " Marta." Lionello, Mongini; Plunketto, Gassier; Nancy, Scalchi; Marta, Ilma di Murska.

Saturday, 2nd, " Il Flauto."

Monday, 4th, " Robert le Diable."

Tuesday, 5th, " Der Freischutz." Rodolfo, Mongini; Caspar, Santley; Killiano, Gassier; Annetta, Sinico; Agata, Titiens.

Wednesday, 6th, " Sonnambula " (repeat).

Thursday, 7th, " Fidelio." Florestano, Gardoni; Pizzaro, Santley; Rocco, Herr Formes; Jacqueno, Lyall; Marcellina, Sinico; Leonora, Titiens.

- Friday, 8th, " Marta " (second Act), as before; first Act of " Traviata ;" concluding with the fourth Act of " Hamlet," containing the celebrated mad scene. Ophelia, Ilma di Murska.

Saturday, 9th, " Il Trovatore "—last night.

" The cry was still they come !"—More first appearances, viz:—Ilma di Murska, Mdlle. Scalchi, Signor Marino, Signor Baggagiolo, the Danseuse Rosalia, and the celebrated Maitre de Ballet, Mons. Des Places. This Company was remarkably strong in quantity and quality. Di Murska sang the "Queen of Night's" song (Il Flauto) in Mozart's original key (F), taking the audience quite by surprise from her extraordinary and distinct execution of the different *staccato* passages incidental to the work. Two encores every night. Mdlle. Di Murska also proved herself an accomplished artiste by her performance of Ophelia in the last act of Ambrose Thomas's "Hamlet," which she sang for the first time, and at a short notice, very beautifully. Mdlle. Scalchi at once established herself; and rapidly advancing in her profession, has elevated herself to the position of first contralto in Covent Garden. Signor Baggagiolo was a good basso; indeed all the "first appearances" found favour.

First appearances of Fancelli, Vizzani, Ciampi, Caravoglia.

Italian Company—Mdlle. Titiens, Mdlle. Scalchi, Mdlle. Baumeister, Mdlle. Madigan (first appearance), Mdlle. Leon Duval (first appearance), Mdlle. Sinico, Madame Trebelli Bettini, Mdlle. Ilma di Murska, Signor Vizzani (first appearance), Signor Bettini, Signor Rinaldini (first appearance), Signor Fancelli (first appearance), Signor Ciampi (first appearance), Signor Caravoglia (first appearance), Signor Tagliafico, Signor Casaboni, Mr. Morgan, Signor Antonucci (first appearance), Signor Cotogni (first appearance). Conductor, Signor Bevignani.

On Monday, September 12th, 1870, "Lucrezia Borgia." Gennaro, Signor Fancelli; Alfonso, Antonucci; Rustighello, Signor Rinaldini; Liverotto, Mr. Morgan; Gubetta, Tagliafico; Maffeo Orsini, Mdlle. Scalchi; Lucrezia, Titiens.

Tuesday, 13th. "Puritani." Arturo, Vizzani; Ricardo, Cotogni; Georgio, Antonucci; Bruno, Rinaldini; Walton, Tagliafico; Enrichetta, Baumeister; Elvira, Sinico.

Wednesday, 14th. "Trovatore." Manrico, Fancelli; Conte, Cotogni; Inez, Baumeister; Leonora, Titiens.

Thursday, 15th. "Il Barbiere." Almaviva, Bettini; Figaro, Cotogni; Bartolo, Ciampi; Basilio, Tagliafico; Rosina, Mdlle. Leon Duval. And second and third Acts of "Massaniello." Massaniello, Mr. Morgan (in consequence of Signor Fancelli's illness).

Friday, 16th. "Norma." Oroveso, Antonucci; Flavio, Mr. Morgan; Adalgisa, Sinico; Norma, Titiens.

Saturday, 17th. "Don Giovanni." Don Giovanni, Cotogni; Leporello, Ciampi; Zerlina, Trebelli Bettini; Elvira, Sinico; Donna Anna, Titiens.

Monday, 19th. "Le Nozze." Figaro, Cotogni; Conte, Caravoglia; Bartolo, Ciampi; Cherubino, Trebelli Bettini; Contessa, Titiens.

Tuesday, 20th. "Faust." Faust, Bettini; Mephistophele, Antonucci; Valentino, Cotogni; Siebel, Trebelli Bettini; Margherita, Mdlle. Leon Duval.

Wednesday, 21st. "Trovatore" (repeat).

Thursday, 22nd. "Sonnambula." Elvino, Fancelli; Rodolpho, Tagliafico; Amina, Ilma di Murska.

Friday, 23rd. "Semiramide." Idreno, Bettini; Assur, Antonucci; Arsace, Trebelli Bettini; Semiramide, Titiens.

Saturday, 24th. "Il Flauto." Tamino, Bettini; Papageno, Cotogni; Sarastro, Antonucci; Queen of Night, Di Murska; Papagena, Sinico; Pamina, Titiens.

Monday, 26th. "Les Huguenots." Raoul, Bettini; San Bris, Caravoglia; Nevers, Cotogni; Marcello, Antonucci; Margherita, Sinico; Valentino, Titiens.

Tuesday, 27th. "Lucia." Edgardo, Fancelli; Enrico, Caravoglia; Lucia, Ilma di Murska.

Wednesday, 28th. "Don Giovanni" (as before).

Thursday, 29th. "Il Flauto" (repeat):

Friday, 30th. "Marta." Lionello, Vizzani; Plunketto, Ciampi; Tristano, Tagliafico; Nancy, Scalchi; Marta, Ilma di Murska.

Saturday, 31st. "Oberon." Huon, Fancelli; Oberon, Bettini; Scherasmin, Cotogni; Fatima, Trebelli; Reiza, Titiens. Last night.

Fancelli came amongst us now for the first time. His fame had of course preceded him through the Press, and, unlike others, he did not disappoint; if not quite up to the standard of the great ones heard before, he may certainly be placed as a first-class tenor, perhaps the best, or certainly the equal of any present aspirant. His voice is a pure and powerful tenor, and he improves in style each season. Signor Vizzani was also a success, and displayed most promising powers as a tenor, possessing an organ not very robust but of exquisite quality. He gave the "A te o Cara" with much effect, and all through the very trying music of "Puritani" he displayed much taste, using his voice skilfully and artistically. Signor Rinaldini, a most useful, indeed indispensable member of the Company, also made good way. Caravoglia and Ciampi, both most efficient baritones, received full appreciation; and Mr. Wilton Morgan proved his well-known efficiency by "rushing" into "Massaniello" in place of Fancelli, and coming off with honours.

First appearances of Mdlle. Marimon, Agnesi, Men-

NOTE.

Thursday, 29th. "Il Flauto" (repeat). Madame Trebelli and Mdlle. Scalchi took parts in the "Tre Damigelli," an almost unprecedented musical event.

(first appearance), Signor Mendiorez (first time), Signor Caravoglia, Signor Zoboli, Signor Casaboni, Signor Stefano, Signor Foli, Mr. Morgan. Conductor, Signor Li Calsi.

Monday, September 11th, 1871. "Trovatore." Manrico, Prudenza; Conte di Luna, Mendiorez; Ferrando, Foli; Ruiz, Rinaldini; Azucena, Trebelli; Leonora, Titiens,

Tuesday, 12th. "La Figlia." Tonio, Vizzani; Sulpizio, Agnesi; Marchesa, Baumeister; Maria, Marimon.

Wednesday, 13th. "Anna Bolena." Henry VIII., Agnesi; Percy, Prudenza; Rochford, Caravoglia; Smeaton, Fernandez; Jane Seymour, Columbo; Anne Boleyn, Titiens.

Thursday, 14th. "Sonnambula." Elvino, Vizzani; Rodolfo, Foli; Lisa, Baumeister; Teresa, Miss Cruise; Amina, Marimon.

Friday, 15th. "Semiramide." Assur, Agnesi; Idreno,

Saturday, 24th. "Il Flauto." Tamino, Bettini; Papageno, Cotogni; Sarastro, Antonucci; Queen of Night, Di Murska; Papagena, Sinico; Pamina, Titiens.

Monday, 26th. "Les Huguenots." Raoul, Bettini; San Bris, Caravoglia; Nevers, Cotogni; Marcello, Antonucci; Margherita, Sinico; Valentino, Titiens.

Ilma di Murska.

Saturday, 31st. "Oberon." Huon, Fancelli; Oberon, Bettini; Scherasmin, Cotogni; Fatima, Trebelli; Reiza, Titiens. Last night.

Fancelli came amongst us now for the first time. His fame had of course preceded him through the Press, and, unlike others, he did not disappoint; if not quite up to the standard of the great ones heard before, he may certainly be placed as a first-class tenor, perhaps the best, or certainly the equal of any present aspirant. His voice is a pure and powerful tenor, and he improves in style each season. Signor Vizzani was also a success, and displayed most promising powers as a tenor, possessing an organ not very robust but of exquisite quality. He gave the "A te o Cara" with much effect, and all through the very trying music of "Puritani" he displayed much taste, using his voice skilfully and artistically. Signor Rinaldini, a most useful, indeed indispensable member of the Company, also made good way. Caravoglia and Ciampi, both most efficient baritones, received full appreciation; and Mr. Wilton Morgan proved his well-known efficiency by "rushing" into "Massaniello" in place of Fancelli, and coming off with honours.

First appearances of Mdlle. Marimon, Agnesi, Mendiorez.

Troupe: Mdlle. Titiens, Mdlle. Columbo, Mdlle. Baumeister, Mdlle. Maria Marimon, Madame Trebelli Bettini, Mdlle. Fernandez (first appearance), Mdlle. di Murska, Signor Vizzani, Signor Tesseman, Signor Rinaldini, Signor Prudenza (first appearance), Signor Agnesi (first appearance), Signor Mendiorez (first time), Signor Caravoglia, Signor Zoboli, Signor Casaboni, Signor Stefano, Signor Foli, Mr. Morgan. Conductor, Signor Li Calsi.

Monday, September 11th, 1871. "Trovatore." Manrico, Prudenza; Conte di Luna, Mendiorez; Ferrando, Foli; Ruiz, Rinaldini; Azucena, Trebelli; Leonora, Titiens.

Tuesday, 12th. "La Figlia." Tonio, Vizzani; Sulpizio, Agnesi; Marchesa, Baumeister; Maria, Marimon.

Wednesday, 13th. "Anna Bolena." Henry VIII., Agnesi; Percy, Prudenza; Rochford, Caravoglia; Smeaton, Fernandez; Jane Seymour, Columbo; Anne Boleyn, Titiens.

Thursday, 14th. "Sonnambula." Elvino, Vizzani; Rodolfo, Foli; Lisa, Baumeister; Teresa, Miss Cruise; Amina, Marimon.

Friday, 15th. "Semiramide." Assur, Agnesi; Idreno,

Rinaldini; Oroe, Foli; Arsace, Trebelli; Semiramide, Titiens.

Saturday, 16th. "La Figlia" (repeat).

Monday, 18th. "Don Giovanni." Donna Anna, Titiens; Elvira, Columbo; Zerlina, Trebelli; Don Giovanni, Mendiorez; Leporello, Agnesi; Mazetto, Zoboli; Commendatore, Foli; Ottavio, Vizzani.

Tuesday, 19th. "Sonnambula" (as before).

Wednesday, 20th. "Anna Bolena."

Thursday, 21st. "Il Barbiere." Almaviva, Vizzani; Bartolo, Zoboli; Figaro, Mendiorez; Basilio, Foli; Rosina, Marimon.

Friday, 22nd. "Lucrezia." Gennaro, Prudenza; Alfonso, Agnesi; Gubetta, Stefano; Orsini, Trebelli; Lucrezia, Titiens.

Saturday, 23rd. "Lucia." Edgardo, Prudenza; Ashton, Mendiorez; Raimondo, Foli; Lucia, Di Murska.

Monday, 25th. "Il Flauto." Tamino, Vizzani; Papageno, Mendiorez; Sarastro, Foli; Astrifiammenti, Di Murska; Papagena, Columba; Tre Damegelli, Miss Cruise, Miss Grosvenor, Mdme. Trebelli Bettini; Pamina, Titiens.

Tuesday, 26th. "Il Barbiere" (repeat).

Wednesday, 27th. "Roberto il Diavolo." Roberto, Prudenza; Bertramo, Foli; Un Prete, Agnesi; Isabella, Di Murska; Alisa, Titiens.

Thursday, 28th. Morning performance of "Marta." Lionello, Vizzani; Plunketto, Agnesi; Nancy, Trebelli; Lady Enrichetta, Di Murska.

Thursday, 28th (evening). "Sonnambula" (repeat).

Friday, 29th. "Trovatore" (repeat).
Saturday, 30th. "Oberon." Sir Huon, Vizzani; Oberon, Tesseman; Scherasmin, Caravoglia; Fatima, Trebelli; Reiza, Titiens. Last night.

The first hearing of two great artistes occurred during this series—Mdlle. Marimon and Signor Agnesi. The recollection of the former is so fresh that comment is al- almost unnecessary, the same impression produced here as in London and all the Continental cities, viz. an extraordinary soprano of the very highest education and finish. The very same remarks (in a baritone sense) may be applied to Agnesi, who to a grand voice combined a style the most masterly, bringing strongly to mind the great Tamburini, whose wonderful flexibility and high education Agnesi seemed almost to improve on. The Lyric Drama lost too soon this much-esteemed vocalist, who died about 1874 or 1875. He fulfilled during the latter period of his life the position of "Maitre de Chant" in the Paris Conservatoire. Signor Mendiorez also worthily filled the position of a first baritone, passing through the trying ordeal of "The Conte di Luna" with the exacting "Il Balen" (after so many), with marked success.

First appearance of Campanini. Titiens, Baumeister, Marimon, Trebelli, Filomena, Di Murska, Signor Bettini, W. Morgan, Rinaldini, Signor Campanini (first appearance), Agnesi, Mendiorez, Borella, Arnoldi, Casaboni, Campobello, Foli. Conductor, Li Calsi.

Monday, September 30th, 1872. "Lucrezia Borgia." Gennaro, Signor Campanini; Alfonso, Agnesi; Astolfo, Campobello; Maffeo Orsini, Trebelli; Lucrezia, Titiens.

Tuesday, October 1st. "Sonnambula." Elvino, Bettini; Roldolfo, Agnesi; Lisa, Baumeister; Amina, Marimon.

Wednesday, 2nd. "Il Flauto Magico." Tamino, Bettini; Papageno, Mendiorez; Sarastro, Foli; Sacradoti, Campbello; Astrifiammenti, Di Murska; Tre Damigelli, Mdlles. Mara, Grosvenor, and Trebelli.

Thursday, 3rd. "Il Trovatore." Manrico, Campanini; Conte di Luna, Mendiorez; Fernando, Foli; Azucena, Trebelli; Leonora, Titiens.

Friday. "La Figlia." Tonio, Bettini; Sulpizio, Agnesi; Marchesa, Baumeister; Maria, Marimon.

Saturday, 5th. "Lucia." Edgardo, Campanini; Aston, Mendiorez; Raimondo, Foli; Lucia, Di Murska.

Monday, October, 7th. "Don Pasquale" (first time for 17 years). Ernesta, Signor Bettini; Malatesta, Mendiorez; Pasquale, Borella; Norina, Marimon.

Tuesday, 8th. "Don Giovanni." Ottavio, Bettini; Giovanni, Mendiorez; Leporello, Borella; Commendatore, Foli; Masetto, Zoboli; Zerlina, Trebelli; Elvira, Di Murska; Donna Anna, Titiens.

Wednesday, 9th. "Marta." Lionello, Campanini; Plunketto, Agnesi; Tristano, Borella; Nancy, Trebelli; Marta, Marimon.

Thursday, 10th. "Faust." Faust, Campanini (first appearance); Valentino, Mendiorez; Mephistophele, Foli; Siebel, Trebelli; Margherita, Titiens.

Friday. "Il Barbiere." Almaviva, Bettini; Bartolo, Borella; Figaro, Mendiorez; Basilio, Agnesi; Rosiña, Marimon.

Saturday, 12th. "Il Flauto" (repeat).

Monday, 14th, "Les Huguenots." Raoûl, Campanini; San Bris, Agnesi; Nevers, Mendiorez; Marcello, Foli; Maurevert, Campobello; Urbano, Trebelli; Margherita, Di Murska; Valentina, Titiens.

Tuesday, 15th. "Sonnambula" (repeat).

Wednesday, 16th. "Semiramide." Assur, Agnesi; Oroe, Foli; Arsace, Trebelli; Semiramide, Titiens.

Thursday, 17th. "Rigoletto." Duca, Campanini; Rigoletto, Mendiorez; Sparafucile, Foli; Monterone, Campobello; Maddalena, Trebelli; Gilda, Di Murska.

Friday, 18th. "Faust" (as before).

Saturday. Repeat of "Don Giovanni." Last night.

The injury occurring to an artist from extreme over criticisms beforehand was evident in the case of Campanini. With his glorious voice and dramatic qualities it was quite unnecessary, his merits were and are quite sufficient; but the public were led to believe they were about to hear "the greatest tenor that ever appeared, none excepted." Campanini is a great artist: himself and Fancelli now hold the first places. Comparisons in art are particularly odious, both fully deserve the positions they have attained, and can "well hold their own" on their merits. It will be observed that Trebelli on this, as on a former occasion, with that self-sacrifice always attached to a true artiste, joined the "Tre Damigelli," adding thereby wonderful effect to the beautiful concerted music.

The next Italian Opera took place at the Gaiety Theatre, viz. :—Mdlle. Marimon, Mdlle. Ida Corani, Mdlle. Baronetti, Madame Elena Corani, Miss Sinclair, Mdlle. Arnoldi, Madame De Meric Lablache, Signor Mottino,

Signor Toppai, Signor Bettini, Signor Celli, Signor Tagliafico, Signor Arnoldi, Signor Riccobuono, Signor Foli, Signor Enrico Serazzi. Conductor, Mons. Maton.

Monday, August 25th, 1873. "La Sonnambula." Amina, Marimon; Lisa, Mdlle. Arnoldi; Conte, Celli; Elvino, Bettini.

Tuesday, 26th. "Lucrezia." Elena Corani; Orsini, De Meric Lablache; Gennaro, Serazzi.

Wednesday, 27th. "Il Barbiere." Rosina, Marimon; Figaro, Mottino; Almaviva, Bettini.

Thursday, 28th. "Trovatore." Leonora, Corani; Azucena, Lablache; Di Luna, Mattino; Manrico, Bettini.

Friday, 29th. "Lucrezia Borgia." Lucrezia, Corani; Orsini, De Meric Lablache; Duca, Celli; Gennaro, Serazzi.

Saturday, 30th. "Faust." Margherita, Marimon; Siebel, Lablache; Mephistophele, Foli; Valentino, Mattino; Faust, Serazzi.

Monday, Sept. 1st. "Norma." Norma, E. Corani; Adalgisa, Sinclair; Oroveso, Foli; Pollio, Serazzi.

Tuesday, 2nd. "Marta." Marta, Marimon; Nancy, Lablache; Plunketto, Mattino; Lionello, Bettini.

Wednesday, 3rd. "Un Ballo in Maschera." Amelia, E. Corani; Ulrica, Lablache; Oscar, Ida Corani; Renato, Mattino; Samuele, Foli; Ricardo, Serazzi.

Thursday, 4th. Repeat of "Faust."

Friday, 5th. "Don Giovanni." Donna Anna, Corani; Elvira, Arnoldi; Zerlina, Sinclair; Giovanni, Celli; Commendatore, Foli; Leporello, Toppai; Masetto, Tagliafico; Ottavio, Bettini.

Saturday, 6th. "Il Flauto." Astrifiammenti, Mdlle. Marimon; Papagena, Sinclair; Pamina, E. Corani; Sarastro, Foli; Papageno, Celli; Tamino, Bettini. Last night.

Elena Corani is the identical Miss Ellen Conran who came out some time before at the Royal under the kind auspices of Grisi, and who made sufficient progress in her profession to become *prima-donna*, and fulfil many of the characters of her great friend (to whom she bore some resemblance), with every success. Miss Ida Corani was a younger sister, and fully sustained the musical reputation of their father, the great Dublin pianist, William Sarsfield Conran. We return to the "Royal."

First appearance of Marie Roze and Alwina Valleria. Company: Titiens, Sinico, Mdlle. Marie Roze (first time), Trebelli, Mdlle. Justia MacVitz (first time), Baumeister, Mdlle. Alwina Valleria (first time), Signor Camero (first time), Signor Urio (first time), Signor Cantoni (first time), Fabbrini (first time), Rinaldini, Marchetti, Aramburro (first time), Agnesi, Catalani (first time), Mendiorez, Campobello, Signor Pro, Zoboli, Casaboni, Guilio Perkins (first appearance), Castlemary (first time). Conductor, Signor Li Calsi.

Monday, September 15th, 1873. "La Favorita. Fernando, Aramburro; Alfonso, Sterbini; Baldassore Perkins; Leonora, Titiens.

Tuesday, 16th. "Marta." Lionello, Urio; Tristani, Borella; Plunketto, Agnesi; Nancy, Trebelli; Marta, Sinico.

Wednesday, 17th. "Il Trovatore." Manrico, Aramburro; Conte di Luna, Sterbini; Ferrando, Campobello; Azucena, Trebelli; Leonora, Sinico.

Thursday, 18th. "Norma." Pollio, Aramburro; Oroveso, Agnesi; Adalgisa, Sinico; Norma, Titiens.

Friday, 19th. "Faust." Faust, Camero; Mephistophele, Perkins; Valentino, Campobello; Siebel, MacVitz; Marta, Baumeister; Margherita, Marie Roze.

Saturday, 20th. "Oberon." Sir Huon, Urio; Oberon, Cantoni; Scherasmina, Agnesi; Puck, MacVitz; Fatima, Trebelli; Reiza, Titiens.

Monday, 22nd. "Semiramide." Assur, Agnesi; Oroe, Campobello; Arsace, Trebelli; Idreno, Rinaldini; Semiramide, Titiens.

Tuesday. "Rigoletto." Duca, Aramburro; Rigoletto, Catalani; Sparafucile, Pro; Monterone, Campobello; Maddalena, MacVitz; Gilda, Alwina Valleria.

Wednesday, 24th. "Don Giovanni." Ottavio, Cantoni; Giovanni, Sterbini; Leporello, Borella; Commendatore, Perkins; Zerlina, Trebelli; Donna Anna, Titiens.

Thursday, 25th. Repeat of "La Favorita."

Friday, 26th, "Il Barbiere." Almaviva, Camero; Bartolo, Borella; Figaro, Sterbini; Basilio, Agnesi; Rosina, Trebelli.

Saturday, 27th. "Il Flauto Magico." Tamino, Cantoni; Papageno, Catalani; Sarastro, Perkins; Sacradoti, Campobello; Astrifiammenti, Valleria; Papagena, Sinico; Pamina, Titiens. Trebelli again joined the "Tre Damigelli," with Marie Roze and Baumeister.

Monday, 29th. "Lucrezia Borgia." Gennaro, Aramburro; Alfonso, Agnesi; Maffeo Orsini, Trebelli; Lucrezia, Titiens.

Tuesday, 30th. "Le Nozze di Figaro." Cherubini, Trebelli; Sigaro, Agnesi; Il Conte, Campobello; Bartolo, Borella; Basilio, Rinaldini; Susanna, Sinico; La Contessa, Titiens.

Wednesday, October 1st. Repeat of "Faust."
Thursday, 2nd. Repeat of "Don Giovanni."
Friday, 3rd. "Lucia." Edgardo, Aramburro; Ashton, Catalani; Raimondo, Campobello; Lucia, Alwina Valleria.

Saturday, 4th. "Il Trovatore," as before, except Leonora, Titiens, being her benefit and last night.

Marie Roze, who was Madame Perkins, and has since married Mr. H. Mapleson (son of the great *impresario*), made a "decided hit" in Margherita. Admirably suited to the part in personal appearance, and imparting to her music a well-studied and classic "reading," she won "golden opinions." She also displayed her respect for Mozart by becoming one of the "Tre Damigelli" in "Il Flauto." The name of Alwina Valleria added much strength to this troupe, her performance of "Lucia" and "Gilda" placing her high in the soprano list. The early death of Giulo Perkins left a blank in the list of useful bassi. Noble appearance, fine features, grand voice of great extent, he walked the stage "like a man" (to use a pit expression regarding him), and gave out the low E in "Qui S'degno" with grand effect. This was indeed a strong troupe.

- First appearance of Brignoli and Mdlle. Singelli, and first performance of "Il Talismano."

Theatre Royal. Italian Company :—Titiens, Alwina Valleria, Mdlle. Risarelli (first time), Marie Roze, Trebelli, De Meric Lablache, Mdlle. Baumeister, Mdlle. Louise Singelli (first time), Signor Campanini, Mr. Bentham, Rinaldini, Grazzi, Paladini (first time), Signor Brignoli (first appearance), Signor Agnesi, Signor Di Reschi (first time), Gallassi (first time), Campobello, Casta, Casaboni, Guilio Perkins, and Herr Conrad Behrens. Conductor, Signor Li Calsi.

Monday, September 21st, 1874. "Lucrezia Borgia." Gennaro, Campanini; Alfonso, Agnesi; Maffeo Orsini, Trebelli; Lucrezia, Titiens.

Tuesday, 22nd. "Marta." Lionello, Brignoli; Tristani, Zoboli; Plunketto, Behrens; Nancy, Trebelli; Marta, Louise Singelli.

Wednesday, 23rd. "Il Talismano" (first time in Dublin). Sir Kenneth, Campanini; Richard Cœur de Lion, De Reschi; Nectabanas, Catalani; L'Emiro, Campobello; Il Re de France, Costa; Duca, Casaboni; Berengana, Marie Roze; Edith Plantagenet, Titiens.

Thursday, 24th. "Il Flauto." Astrifiammenti, Singelli; Tamino, Mr. Bentham; Papageno, Catalani; Sarastro, Perkins; Sacradoti, Campobello; Papagena, Alwina Valleria; Pamina, Titiens.

Friday, 25th. "Lucia." Edgardo, Campanini; Ashton, Galassi; Raimondo, Campobello; Lucia, Alwina Valleria.

Saturday, 26th. "Les Huguenots." Raoul, Campanini; St. Bris, Agnesi; Nevers, Galassi; Marcello, Behrens; Urbano, Trebelli; Margherita, Singelli; Valentina, Titiens.

Monday, 28th. Repeat of "Il Talismano."

Tuesday, 29th. "Le Nozze." Cherubini, Trebelli; Figaro; Agnesi; Il Conte, Campobello; Bartolo, Zoboli; Susanna, Marie Roze; La Contessa, Titiens.

Wednesday, 30th. "Faust." Faust, Campanini; Mephistophele, Perkins; Valentino, De Reschi; Siebel, Trebelli; Margherita, Marie Roze.

Thursday, October 1st. "Il Trovatore." Manrico, Brignoli; Conte di Luna, Galassi; Ferrando, Campobello; Azucena, Trebelli; Leonora, Titiens.

Friday, 2nd. "Catarina le Donna Novi." Don Enrico, Bentham; Il Conte, Campobello; Mayer, Agnesi; Rebolledo, Costa; La Catarina, Louise Singelli.

Saturday, 3rd. Repeat of "Il Talismano."

Monday, 5th. "Semiramide." Assur, Agnesi; Oroe, Campobello; Arsace, Trebelli; Semiramide, Titiens.

Tuesday, 4th. Repeat of "Faust."

Wednesday, 5th. "Don Giovanni." Ottavio, Brignoli; Giovanni, De Reschi; Leporello, Behrens; Zerlina, Trebelli; Elvira, Risarelli; Donna Anna, Titiens.

Thursday, 8th. Repeat of "Trovatore."

Friday, 9th. "Sonnambula." Elvino, Campanini; Rodolfo, Agnesi; Amina, Mdlle. Singelli.

Saturday, 10th. "Norma." Pollio, Campanini; Oroveso, Costa; Adalgisa, Baumeister; Norma, Titiens. Last night.

Colonel Mapleson's capacity for discovering talent was strongly developed in the case of Brignoli, who made his first appearance now, a tenor of vast experience; he must in youth have been well worth hearing, indeed at present many of the "younger branch" might study him with advantage: Brignoli and Badiali bear close comparison. The tenor, not quite so advanced in life as the grand old baritone, still shows somewhat more lack of freshness of voice, which quality Badiali retained to the last; the singing for itself of each was perfect, both equally inspired with dramatic feeling, which found its way into every movement on the stage, or every note given forth. The parallel might be extended if space permitted; some young baritones such as Badiali had been, and a few juvenile tenors with the qualities of Brignoli, would be very desirable. Mdlle. Louise Singelli is a young and talented Belgian student, daughter of the late well-known and highly-respected Concert conductor of Brussels, Mons. Singelli, whose violin arrangements are much valued, and have a large sale all over Europe. Mdlle. Singelli has doubtless a bright future before her, having in "Amina" and in "Marta" made a most favourable impression.

First appearance of Mdlle. Albani and Mdlle. Zara Thalberg.

1875. The Italian Opera this season was from Covent Garden, and under the direction of Sir Julius Benedict; thus—Soprani: Mdlle. Albani, Mdlle. Bianchi, Mdlle. Estelle, Mdlle. Cruise, Mdlle. Stewart, Mdlle. Paoli, and Mdlle. Zara Thalberg; Contralti: Mdlle. Phillipini D'Edelsburgh, and Mdlle. Ghiotto; Tenori: Mons. Naudin, Signor Pavani, and Mons. De Vèllier; Baritoni: Mons. Maurel and Signor Medica; Bassi: Signor Scolari, Signor Tagliafico, Signor Bolli, and Signor Pronti; Leader, Mr. Levey; Organist, Mr. Pitman; Conductor, Signor Vianesi.

Monday, October 4th, 1875. "Don Giovanni." Donna Anna, Mdlle. Paoli; Zerlina, Zara Thalberg; Elvira, Mdlle. Ghiotti; Ottavio, Mr. Richard Sydney (MacNevin);*

* From the *Freeman's Journal*, Tuesday, October 5th, 1875:—
"The extraordinary interest in Italian Opera which prevails in Dublin at this time of year was manifested last night with all its wonted intensity. The stir and bustle about the exterior of the Theatre were quite as troublesome as usual; and although notices had been duly published that programmes and books of the opera would be sold inside the house, the yelling and importunity outside were not a whit abated. Up to the very last moment the arrivals were fast, and in many cases furious. We say furious, for as a rule a late-comer is in an ill-temper, and disturbs everybody by special privilege. Last night there were many late-comers, and the overture was frequently marred in effect by persons whose exterior would have suggested better manners. This observation is made not indeed with a view of wounding anybody in Dublin, experience has dissolved all such views, and converted suffering into a sort of expectation. So far as the orchestra was heard in the overture it appeared to be adequate, finished, and thoroughly under the command of Signor Vianesi. The stringed instruments, without which Mozart is impossible, were tolerably full; and if the effect was not startling, it was satisfactory. A notice to the effect that Signor Pavani being ill Mr. Richard Sydney (MacNevin) would assume the character of Don Ottavio was posted about the house in quite a wonderful manner; and there was a nervous anxiety lest something should happen to spoil the evening's entertainment. Nothing really did happen, for, notwithstanding Mr. Sydney's disquiet, he succeeded very well, and, under the circumstances, he must have surpassed expectation. The sort of dilemma caused by the sudden illness of an artiste is just of that order in which rapidity of judgment is most essential. Mr. Gunn decided on having a Dublin amateur, and the result proved that Mr. Gunn was right, and that Dublin was rich in talent of a high and educated order. In how many cities in the empire could there be found a private gentleman competent and willing to sing at a few hours' notice the music of Mario and Guiglini in *Don Giovanni?* The answer must suggest something in favour of Dublin, in which the feat has been accomplished, and well accomplished."

Leporello, Signor Scolari; Masetto, Signor Tagliafico; Commendatore, Signor Pronti; Don Giovanni, Signor Maurel.

Tuesday, 5th. "Trovatore." Leonora, Mdlle. Paoli; Azucena, Mdlle. D'Edelsburgh; Manrico, Mons. De Vèllier; Conte di Luna, Signor Medica.

Wednesday, 6th. "Fra Diavolo." Zerlina, Zara Thalberg; Lady Coburg, Mdlle. Ghiotti; Lord Coburg, Signor Scolari; Lorenzo, Signor Filli; Beppo, Tagliafico; Giacomo, Signor Pronti; Matteo, Bolli; Fra Diavolo, Signor Naudin.

Thursday, 7th. "La Sonnambula." Amina, Albani (first appearance in Dublin); Rodolfo, Medica; Elvino, Naudin.

Friday, 8th. "La Figlia." Maria, Mdlle. Bianchi; Marchesa, Mdlle. Ghiotti; Sulpizio, Scolari; Tonio, Pavani.

Saturday, 9th. "Lucia." Lucia, Albani; Enrico, Medico; Raimondo, Pronti; Edgardo, Pavani.

Monday, 11th. "Lohengrinn" (first time). Eliza, Mdlle. Albani; Artuso, Mdlle. D'Edelsburgh; Frederic, Maurel; L'Araldo del Re, Pronti; Enrio, Scolari; Lohengrinn, Naudin.

Tuesday, October 12th. "Dinorah." Dinorah, Zara Thalberg; Un Caprara, Estelle; Un Capraro, Ghiotti; Un Cassiatore, Tagliafico; Corentini, Pavani; Hoel, Maurel.

Wednesday, 13th. "Rigoletto." Gilda, Albani; Madalena, Ghiotti; Giovanna, Mdlle. Estelle; Il Duca, Mons. De Vèllier; Sparafucile, Tagliafico; Rigoletto, Signor Medica.

Thursday, 14th. "Don Giovanni" (as before, except Ottavio, Naudin).

Friday, 15th. "Un Ballo." Amelia, Mdlle. Paoli; Oscar, Bianchi; Ricardo, Pavani; Renato, Signor Medica.

Saturday, 16th. "Faust." Margherita, Albani; Siebel, Mdlle. Ghiotti; Marta, Mdlle. Estelle; Mephistophele, Scolari; Wagner, Tagliafico; Faust, Pavani; Valentino, Maurel.

Monday, 18th. "Dinorah" (cast as before).

Tuesday, 19th. "La Figlia," repeat.

Wednesday, 20th. "Puritani." Elvira, Albani; Enrichetta, Ghiotti; Georgio, Maurel; Ricardo, Pronti; Arturo, Naudin.

Thursday, 21st. "La Favorita." Leonora, Mdlle. D'Edelsburgh; Alfonso, Signor Medica; Baldassare, Pronti; Ferrando, Naudin.

Friday, 22nd. First and second Acts of "Fra Diavolo." The shadow-scene from "Dinorah" (benefit of Zara Thalberg).

Saturday, 23rd. "La Sonnambula" (as before). Last night.

The recollection of Albani is still fresh in our memory—a more perfect representation of Margherita cannot well be imagined; indeed, the same applies to every part this great artiste undertakes. Beautiful in appearance, and highly accomplished in art, she, as a matter of course, found her due appreciation in Dublin. She has since accepted an engagement for life with Mr. Ernest Gye, proprietor of Covent Garden, and the public are (now, 1879) anxiously waiting for her re-appearance, after the interesting event.

Mdlle. Zara Thalberg, daughter of the late great pianist, had made a sensation in London, and (youth and inexperience considered) showed remarkable promise, since realized, of a coming "star :" her "Zerlina" was specially successful. Wagner's "Lohengrinn" had not a fair chance, Signor Vianesi did everything possible with the means at his disposal; but it is hardly necessary to say that a work which would require about 300 choristers of the very best, 100 picked instrumentalists, and nearly three months' rehearsals, could not possibly with, say two rehearsals and limited numbers, receive a worthy interpretation. Albani's "Elsa di Brabante" will not, however, soon be forgotten.

Italian Company : Mdlle, Titiens (first appearance for two years), Mdme. Trebelli, Mdme. Marie Roze, Mdme. Alwina Valleria, Mdlle. Baumeister, Mdlle. Elena Varesi, Mdlle. Selina Bignarini, Miss Emma Abbott (first appearance), Signor Gillandi, Signor Dorini, Signor Rinaldini, Signor Grazzi, Signor Faustu Bellotti, Signor Galassi, Signor Del Puente, Signor Rocca, Signor Costa, Signor Broccolini, Herr Behrens. Conductor, Signor Li Calsi.

Monday, Sept. 25th, 1876. "Semiramide." Arsace, Trebelli; Assur, Del Puente; Oroe, Broccolini; Idreno, Rinaldini; Semiramide, Titiens.

Tuesday, 26th. "Lucia." Edgardo, Gillandi; Enrico, Galassi : Arturo, Rinaldini; Raimondo, Behrens; Alice, Mdlle. Baumeister; Lucia, Mdlle. Alwina Valleria.

Wednesday, 27th. "Trovatore." Manrico, Gillandi; Conte di Luna, Galassi; Azucena, Trebelli; Leonora, Titiens.

The following important engagement was omitted in first issue:—

Italian Opera Company, commencing, for six nights only, November 15th, 1875. Principal artistes—Madame Christine Nilsson (her first appearance on the stage in Dublin), Madame Trebelli-Bettini, Madame Marie Roze, Madame Demeric-Lablache, Madame Bauermeister, and Mdlle. Elena Varesi (her first appearance in Dublin), Signor Gillandi (his first appearance in Dublin), Signor Campanini, Signor Palladini, Signor Rinaldini, Signor Grazzi, Signor Brignoli, Signor Galassi, Signor Del Puente, Signor Costa, Signor Zoboli, Signor Casaboni, Signor Castelmary (his first appearance in Dublin), and Herr Behrens. Musical Director and Conductor, Signor Li Calsi.

Monday, November 15th. Gounod's Opera of " Faust." Faust, Signor Gillandi (his first appearance in Dublin); Mephistopheles, Signor Castelmary (first appearance in Dublin); Valentino, Signor Galassi; Wagner, Signor Costa; Siebel, Madame Trebelli; Marta, Madame Demeric-Lablache; and Margherita, Madame Nilsson (first appearance).

Tuesday 16th. Donizetti's Opera, " Lucia di Lammermoor." Edgardo, Signor Gillandi; Ashton, Signor Galassi; Raimondo, Herr Behrens; Arturo, Signor Rinaldini; Normano, Signor Zoboli; Alice, Madame Bauermeister; Lucia, Mdlle. Elena Varesi (first appearance in Dublin).

Wednesday, 17th. Flotow's Opera, " Marta." Lionello,

Signor Brignoli; Plunketto, Herr Behrens; Lord Tristano, Signor Zoboli; Sheriffo, Signor Casaboni; Nancy, Madame Trebelli; Lady Henrietta (Marta), Madame Christine Nilsson.

Thursday, 18th. Verdi's Opera, "Rigoletto." Il Duca, Signor Gillandi; Rigoletto, Signor Del Puente; Sparafucile, Signor Castelmary; Monterone, Signor Costa; Borsa, Signor Rinaldini; Marcello, Signor Zoboli; Madalena, Madame Trebelli; Giovanni, Madame Bauermeister; Gilda, Mdlle. Elena Varesi.

Friday, 19th. Benefit of Madame Christine Nilsson. Verdi's Opera, "Il Trovatore." Manrico, Signor Brignoli; Il Conte di Luna, Signor Galassi; Ferrando, Signor Costa; Ruiz, Signor Rinaldini; Azucena, Madame Trebelli; Inez, Madame Bauermeister; Leonora, Madame Christine Nilsson.

Last night of the Italian Opera Company. Benefit of Mdlle. Elena Varesi.

Saturday, 20th. "La Sonnambula." Elvino, Signor Brignoli; Il Count Rodolfo, Signor Del Puente; Alessio, Signor Casaboni; Il Notario, Signor Rinaldini; Liza, Madame Bauermeister; Teresa, Madame Lablache; Amina, Mdlle. Elena Varesi (her third appearance in Dublin).

Thursday, 28th. "Le Nozze di Figaro." Cherubini, Trebelli; Conte, Del Puente; Figaro, Galassi; Bartolo, Galazzi; Basilio, Rinaldini; Susanna, Marie Roze; Contessa, Titiens.

Friday, 29th. "Il Barbiere." Conte Almaviva, Signor Dorini (first appearance); Bartolo, Zoboli; Basilio, Rocca; Rosina, Trebelli.

Saturday, 30th. "Norma." Pollio, Bellotti; Oroveso, Broccolini; Adalgisa, Alwina Valleria; Norma, Titiens.

Monday, October 2nd. "Les Huguenots." Raoul, Gillandi; Count di Nevers, Del Puente; St. Bris, Galassi; Marcello, Behrens; Margherita de Valois, Alwina Valleria; Urbano, Trebelli; Valentino, Titiens.

Tuesday, 3rd, "Faust." Faust, Dorini; Mephistophele, Del Puente; Valentino, Galassi; Siebel, Mdlle. Bignarini (first appearance); Marta, Baumeister; Margherita, Miss Emma Abbott (first appearance).

Wednesday, 4th. "Don Giovanni." Ottavio, Gillandi; Giovanni, Del Puente; Leporello, Behrens; Zerlina, Trebelli; Elvira, Marie Roze; Donna Anna, Titiens.

Thursday, 5th. "Lucrezia Borgia." Gennaro, Gillandi; Alfonso, Behrens; Orsini, Trebelli; Lucrezia, Titiens.

Friday, 6th. "Rigoletto." Il Duca, Dorini; Rigoletto, Del Puerte; Madalena, Trebelli; Gilda, Alwina Valleria.

Saturday, October 7th. "Trovatore" (repeat). Last night.

This was the last appearance of the ever-to-be-lamented Titiens—she is gone from amongst us ! Let us "passionate our tenfold grief with folded arms," and be consoled with the fact that she was "worthy to inlay Heaven with stars."

Engagement for three weeks only of Mr. Mapleson's Italian Opera Company. Director of Music and Conductor, Signor Li Calsi.

Monday, October, 1st, 1877. "Un Ballo in Maschera." Ricardo, Signor Runcia (his first appearance these eight years); Renato, Signor Galassi; Samuelo, M. Gounet; Tomasso, Signor Franceschi; Il Giudice, Signor Rinaldini; Silvano, Signor Fallar; Oscar, Mdlle. Mila Rodani (her first appearance in Ireland); Ulrica, Madame Lablache; Amelia, Mdlle. Caroline Sala (her first appearance in Ireland).

Tuesday, October 2nd. "Il Barbiere di Siviglia." Il Conte Almaviva, Signor Bettini; Figaro, Signor Del Puente; Fiorello, Signor Rinaldini; Il Dottore Bartolo, Signor Zoboli; Don Basilio, Signor Broccolini; Officiali, Signor Grazzi; Berta, Mdlle. Baumeister; Rosina, Mdlle. Anna de Belocca (her first appearance in Ireland).

Wednesday, October 3rd. "Il Trovatore." Manrico, Signor Fancelli (his first appearance for eight years); Il Conte di Luna, Signor Galassi; Ferrando, Signor Broccolini; Ruiz, Signor Rinaldini; Un Zingaro, Signor Fallar; Azucena, Madame Lablache; Inez, Mdlle. Filomena; Leonora, Mdlle. Marie Roze.

Thursday, October 4th. "Le Nozze di Figaro." Cherubino, Mdlle. Anna de Belocca; Il Conte, Signor Del Puente; Figaro, Signor Galassi; Bartolo, Signor Zoboli; Basilio, Signor Rinaldini; Don Curzio, Signor

Grazzi; Antonio, Signor Franceschi; Susanna, Mdlle. Marie Roze; La Contessa, Mdlle. Caroline Sala.

Friday, Oct. 5th. "La Figlia del Reggimento." Tonio, Signor Bettini; Sergente Sulpizio, Signor Del Puente; Un Paesano, Signor Rinaldini; Ortenzio, Signor Fallar; Caporale, M. Gounet; La Marchesa, Madame Lablache; Maria, Mdlle. Mila Rodani.

Saturday, October 6th. "Faust." Under the Patronage and presence of Her Grace the Duchess of Marlborough. Faust, Signor Fancelli; Mephistophele, Signor Del Puente, Valentino, Signor Galassi; Wagner, Franceschi; Siebel, Mdlle. Anna de Belocca; Martha, Madame Lablache; Margherita, Mdlle. Alwina Valleria.

Monday, October 8th. "Robert le Diable." Roberto, Signor Fancelli; Bertramo, Signor Foli; Rambaldo, Signor Rinaldini; Alberti, M. Gounet; Araldo, Signor Grazzi; Un Preto, Signor Broccolini; Elena, Madame Katti Lanner (her first appearance in Dublin); Isabella, Mdlle. Alwina Valleria; Alice, Mdlle. Marie Roze.

Tuesday, October 9th. "Martha." Lionello, Mr. Talbo* Brennan (his first appearance on the stage in this his native city); Lord Tristano, Signor Zoboli; Plunketto, Signor Del Puente; Un Sheriffo, Signor Fallar; Un Servitore, Signor Grazzi; Nancy, Mdlle. Anna de Belocca; Martha, Mdlle. Alwina Valleria.

Wednesday, October 10th. "Les Huguenots." Raoul, Signor Fancelli; Il Conte de Nevers, Signor Del Puente; Il Conte di San Bris, Signor Galassi; Tavannes, Signor

---

* It required but little change to render Talbot Talbo (Lionello).

Rinaldini; De Retz, M. Gounet; De Cosse, Signor Grazzi; Meru, Signor Fallar; Maurevert, Signor Zoboli; Marcello, Signor Foli; Margherita di Valois, Mdlle. Mila Rodani; Urbano, Mdlle. Anna de Belocca; Dama d'Onore, Mdlle. Robiati; Valentina, Mdlle. Caroline Sala.

Thursday, October 11th, "Il Flauto Magico." Tamino, Signor Bettini; Papageno, Signor Del Puente; Sarastro, Signor Foli; Monastatos, Signor Rinaldini; Un Oratore, Signor Broccolini; Due Uomini Armati, Signor Grazzi, and Signor Franceschi; I Tre Geni, Mdlle. Robiati, Mdlle. Clinton and Mdme. Lablache; La Tre Damigelli della Regina, Mdlle. Baumeister, Mdlle. Parodi, and Mdlle. Risiani; Astrifiammanti, Mdlle. Alwina Valleria; Papagena, Mdlle. Mila Rodina; Pamina, Mdme. Marie Roze.

Friday, Oct. 12th, "Rigoletto." Il Duca, Signor Talbo (his second appearance in Opera in this, his native city); Rigoletto, Signor Galassi; Sparafucile, Signor Broccolini; Monterone, M. Gounet; Marallo, Signor Zoboli; Borsa, Signor Rinaldini; Caprano, Signor Fallar; Usciere, Signor Grazzi; La Contessa, Mdlle. Robiate; Madalena, Mdlle. Lisa Perdi (her first appearance); Giovanni, Mdlle. Baumeister; Gilda, Mdlle. Alwina Valleria.

Saturday, October 13th, "Il Don Giovanni." Don Ottavio, Signor Bettini; Don Giovanni, Signor Del Puente; Leporello, Signor Zoboli; Masetto, Signor Fallar; Il Commendatore, Signor Broccolini; Zerlina, Mdlle. Anna de Belocca; Donna Elvira, Mdlle. Alwina Valleria; Donna Anna, Mdme. Marie Roze.

Monday, October 15th, "Der Freischutz." Rodolfo, Signor Fancelli; Caspar, Signor Foli; Killiano, Signor Franceschi; Kuno, M. Gounet; Ottocar, Signor Rinaldini; Hermit, Signor Broccolini; Annetta, Mdlle. Baumeister; Agata, Mdme. Marie Roze.

Tuesday, October 16th, "Faust." Faust, Signor Runcia; Mephistophele, Signor Del Puente; Valentino, Signor Galassi; Wagner, Signor Franceschi; Siebel, Mdlle. Anna De Belocca; Martha, Madame Lablache; Margherita, Mdlle. Caroline Sala.

Wednesday, October 17th, "Robert Le Diable." Roberto, Signor Fancelli; Bertramo, Signor Foli; Rambaldo, Signor Rinaldini; Alberti, M. Gounet; Araldo, Signor Grazzi; Un Preto, Signor Broccolini; Elena, Mdme. Katti Lanner; Isabella, Mdlle. Alwina Valleria; Alice, Mdlle. Marie Roze.

Thursday, October 18th, "Lucia di Lammermoor." Edgardo, Signor Fancelli; Enrico Ashton, Signor Galassi; Arturo, Signor Rinaldini; Raimondo, Signor Broccolini; Normanno, Signor Fallar; Alice, Mdlle. Baumeister; Lucia, Mdlle. Alwina Valleria.

Friday, October 19th, "Il Flauto Magico." Tamino, Signor Bettini; Papageno, Signor Del Puente; Sarastro, Signor Foli; Monastatos, Signor Rinaldini; Un Oratore, Signor Broccolini; Due Uomini Amati, Signor Grazzi and Signor Franceschi; I Tre Geni, Mdlle. Robiati, Mdlle. Clinton and Mdme. Lablache; Le Tre Damigelli della Regina, Mdlle. Baumeister, Mdlle. Parodi, and Mdlle. Risiani; Papagena, Mdlle. Mila Rodani; Astrifiammanti, Mdlle. Alwina Valleria; Pamina, Mdme. Marie Roze.

Saturday, October 20th, "Il Trovatore." Manrico, Signor Fancelli; Il Conte di Luna; Signor Galassi; Ferrando, Signor Broccolini; Ruiz, Signor Rinaldini; Un Zingaro, Signor Fallar; Azucena, Mdme. Lablache; Inez, Mdlle. Filomena; Leonora, Mdlle. Caroline Sala.

On Monday, April 2nd, 1877, the Imperial Italian Company commenced an engagement of 12 nights, with the following artistes :—Mdme. Ernestina Robiati, Mdlle. Emma Howson, Mdme. De Meric Lablache, Mdlle. Hughes, Signor Vizzani, Signor Bolli, Signor Campobello, Signor Rollo, Signor Garda, Signor Campi, Signor Montini. The *troupe* was under the management of Signor Frank Rialp, who also acted as Director of Music and Conductor. The Operas performed were " Le Nozze di Figaro," "Maritana,"* "Guiglielmo Tell," "La Traviata," "Il Trovatore," " " Rigoletto," and " Faust," in which Mr. Snazelle (who has since joined Carl Rosa) performed Mephistophele. This engagement concluded on Saturday, April 14th.

Engagement for 12 nights only of Mr. Mapleson's Italian Opera Company. Director of Music and Conductor, Signor Arditi.

Monday, September 2nd, 1878, "La Sonnambula." Elvino, Signor Frapolli; Il Conte Rodolfo, Signor Del Puente; Alessio, Signor Grazzi; Un Notaro, Signor Bolli; Liza, Mdlle. Robiati; Teresa, Mdme. Lablache; Amina, Mdme. Etelka Gerster (her first appearance in Ireland). The perfect vocalism of Mdme. Gerster was fully appreciated in Dublin.

* First time in Italian.

Tuesday, September 3rd, "Le Nozze di Figaro." Cherubino, Mdme. Trebelli; Il Conte Almaviva, Signor Del Puente; Figaro, Signor Galassi; Il Dottore Bartolo, Signor Zoboli; Basilio, Signor Rinaldini; Don Curzio, Signor Grazzi; Antonio, Signor Franceschi; La Contessa, Mdlle. Parodi; Marcellina, Mdme. Lablache; Susanna, Mdme. Helene Crosmond.

Wednesday, September 4th, "Lucia di Lammermoor." Edgardo, Signor Gillandi; Enrico Ashton, Signor Galassi; Raimondo, Signor Franceschi; Arturo, Signor Bolli; Normanno, Signor Grazzi; Alisa, Mdlle. Robiati; Lucia, Madame Etelka Gerster (her second appearance in Ireland).

Thursday, September 5th, "La Traviata." Alfredo, Signor Frapolli; Germont, Signor Galassi; Gastone, Madame Trebelli, who, on this occasion, will introduce the Brindisi, "Il Segreto;" Medico, Signor Franceschi; Il Marchese, Signor Grazzi; Il Barone, Signor Zoboli; Amina, Mdlle. Robiati; Flora, Mdlle. Filomena; Violetta Valèry, Mdlle. Minnie Hawk (her first appearance in Ireland). The incidental *divertissement* will be supported by Mdlle. Malvina Cavalazzi and the *Corps de Ballet*.

Friday, September 6th, "Faust." Faust, Signor Gillandi; Mephistophele, Signor Franceschi; Valentino, Signor Del Puente; Siebel, Mdme. Trebelli; Martha, Mdme. Lablache; Margherita, Mdlle. Alwina Valeria.

Saturday, September 7th, "Il Flauto Magico." Tamino, Signor Frapoli; Papageno, Signor Del Puente; Sarastro, Herr Behrens; Sacerdote, Signor Pyatt; Due

Uomini Amati, Signor Franceschi and Signor Bolli; Monostatos, Signor Rinaldini; Il Due Oratori, Signor Grazzi and Signor Zoboli; I Tre Geni, Mdlle. Martini, Mdlle. Lido and Mdme. Lablache; I Tre Damigelli della Regina, Mdlle. Robiati, Mdlle. Parodi, Mdme. Trebelli; Papagena, Mdlle. Alwina Valleria; Pamina, Mdlle. Parodi; Astrifiammanti, Madame Etelka Gerster.

Monday, September 9th, "Carmen" (first time in Ireland). Don Jose, Signor Runcio; Escamillo (Toreado), Signor Del Puente; Il Dancairo, Signor Rinaldini; Il Remendado, Signor Grazzi; Zuniga, Signor Franceschi; Morales, Signor Bolli; Michaela, Mdlle. Alwina Valleria; Paquita, Mdlle. Robiati; Mercedes, Mdme. Lablache; Carmen (a gipsy), Mdlle. Minnie Hawk. "Carmen" has become an established favourite in Dublin—in English as well as Italian.

Tuesday, September 10th, "Rigoletto." Il Duca, Signor Gillandi; Rigoletto, Signor Galassi; Sparafucile, Signor Franceschi; Monterone, Signor Gandini; Marcello, Signor Zoboli; Borsa, Signor Grassi; Perano, Signor Bolli; La Contessa, Mdlle. Filomena; Madalena, Mdme. Trebelli; Giovanni, Mdlle. Robiati; Gilda, Mdme. Etelka Gerster.

Wednesday, 11th, "Don Giovanni." Don Ottavio, Signor Gillandi; Don Giovanni, Signor Del Puente; Leporello, Herr Behrens; Masetto, Signor Zoboli; Il Commendatore, Signor Pyatt; Donna Anna, Mdlle. Crosmond; Don Elvira, Mdlle. Alwina Valleria; Zerlina, Mdme. Trebelli.

Thursday, September 12th, "Carmen"—cast as before.

Friday, September 13th, "Il Trovatore." Manrico, Signor Gillandi; Il Conte di Luna, Signor Galassi; Ferrando, Signor Franceschi; Ruiz, Signor Rinaldini; Inez, Mdlle. Robiati; Leonora, Mdme. Sinico (her first appearance this season); Azucena, Mdme. Trebelli.

Saturday, September 14th, "Faust." Faust, Signor Gillandi; Mephistophele, Signor Del Puente; Valentino, Signor Galassi; Wagner, Signor Franceschi; Siebel, Mdme. Trebelli; Martha, Mdme. Lablache; Margherita, Mdme. Etelka Gerster.

The last Italian engagement in the "Old Royal."